William Shakespeare
AN INTRODUCTION TO HIS LIFE, TIMES, AND THEATRE

A BLAISDELL BOOK
IN THE HUMANITIES

AN INTRODUCTION TO HIS

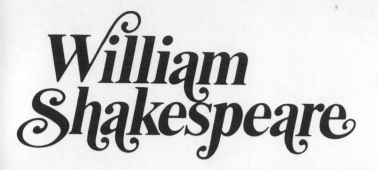

William Shakespeare

LIFE, TIMES, AND THEATRE

IRVING RIBNER
STATE UNIVERSITY OF NEW YORK AT STONY BROOK

BLAISDELL PUBLISHING COMPANY

A Division of Ginn and Company

WALTHAM, MASSACHUSETTS · TORONTO · LONDON

FOR ROSLYN

Preface

◇◇◇◇◇
◇◇◇◇
◇◇◇◇   The last century of Shakespeare scholarship has been so
phenomenal in its productivity that the serious student
and the general reader of today have, at once, more to work with
than ever before and more reason to be confused. The following
pages are not designed to increase the already formidable store of
either historical fact or critical insight. They are intended to provide in one convenient place some of the essential information
which a reader of today needs to approach the plays of Shakespeare
in a meaningful manner, to indicate the bases of the various editions
among which he is constantly being asked to choose, and to provide
him with a guide to the vast body of critical commentary which has
made Shakespeare probably the most written about poet of all time.
These ends themselves are vast ones, and this slight volume can make
no claim to completeness. Every reader will find subjects that have
not been treated adequately, if at all; these subjects will vary from
one reader to the next. All that can be offered to the unsatisfied is a
bibliography which may point the way to further study.

To name all of the books upon which I have drawn is virtually
impossible, although some are mentioned in the body of the text,
and I have attempted to include as many as possible in the bibliography. Other debts are easier to acknowledge. Peter B. Murray of
Macalester College, Franklin B. Newman of the University of Dela-
ware, and Brooks McNamara of New York University have been
of special assistance to me. All have read parts of the manuscript
and have offered suggestions for improvement which I have rarely
failed to follow. Brooks McNamara has helped further with the
illustrations. My graduate assistant, Harry B. Shramm, has performed many useful tasks. Donald K. Moore has prepared the

index. Evelyn Smith and Monique Boucher have provided valuable secretarial assistance. The sharp eye of Barbara Martin, in typing as in proofreading, has saved me from many an error. To all, my thanks.

IRVING RIBNER

Stony Brook, L.I.
New York

Contents

1

Shakespeare and the English Renaissance

◇◇◇◇◇
◇◇◇◇◇ It is a commonplace but true observation that Shakespeare
◇◇◇◇◇ was a poet whose work exceeded the limitations of the age
in which he lived. Although he wrote at the end of the sixteenth
and the beginning of the seventeenth centuries, the large issues which
he probed are as meaningful to our own time as they were to his,
and as they have been to every intervening period of history. As
a dramatist he may, in like manner, be said to have exceeded the
limitations of his own stage. The universals implicit in the dramatic
illusion he created could never exhaustively be expressed by the
theatrical techniques of his own day. Indeed, there are levels of
meaning in his dramatic dialogue to which even the most skillful
of today's theatre producers, with all of modern technology at
their disposal, may find it impossible to give expression. We can
never hope to lay bare every facet of meaning in his work, in spite
of the endless efforts of commentators. It is this very elusive
density of his art which makes his plays a perpetual source of
fascination. The director in his theatre and the literary critic in his
study may reveal different dimensions of meaning, beyond the
reach of each other. In every generation these two kinds of critical
examination must begin afresh, for with every passing era mankind,
through its own experience, becomes more capable of recognizing in
Shakespeare elements which it could not see before.

We must acknowledge also that Shakespeare's work was the
product of a specific era, and that some elements in it can be fully
understood only from the perspective of that era. Shakespeare was

a poet of the English Renaissance, a period which for historical convenience we may regard as having begun with the accession of King Henry VII to the English throne in 1485. This is not a date to be taken too precisely, for historical eras come into being over long periods of time, and each one carries on the traditions of the past, to which it adds and which it modifies or discards only partially. It is possible for present historians to see that there were in the time of Shakespeare certain distinctive attitudes which were not equally present in the age of Geoffrey Chaucer, and which they can relate to political, economic, and intellectual changes taking place throughout Europe. But Shakespeare's age probably shares more with that of Chaucer than it does with our own time.

With the accession of Henry Tudor in 1485 began the rule of the dynasty with which the English Renaissance must be closely associated. During his reign and that of his son, King Henry VIII, arts and learning, hindered from growth during the long years of the Wars of the Roses, became for the first time an important royal concern. In the reign of his granddaughter, Queen Elizabeth I, English poetry and drama reached what may have been the highest peak of excellence they have ever attained. Of this artistic and intellectual flowering, the plays of Shakespeare may have been the greatest as well as the most distinctive product.

It is difficult to say just when the English Renaissance came to a close; some may argue that it has never ended, that it is alive today. We may mark its fading with the death of King James I in 1625 — although John Milton, who was then only seventeen years old, was still to be very much a poet of the Renaissance. But by 1625 the greatest literary achievements of the English Renaissance had been written, distinctive attitudes which we associate with the age of Elizabeth were being challenged by new ones often beyond the conception of Shakespeare, and the modern world had come into being.

The term "Renaissance" seems to have been first used by the French historian, Jules Michelet, in his *Histoire de France*, published in 1855. It was immediately taken up by other scholars, and while all have recognized its general value as a description of a unique historical era, none have really been able to define it; the debate over its meaning continues to this day. Generally, we may agree that it was an age of rapid expansion in commerce, of new scientific discovery, of intense political nationalism and religious controversy. Perhaps the most salient characteristic of its intellectual life was a quality of uncertainty — the breaking down of ancient convictions, the groping for new conceptions, and a strong defence of the old against the new.

It is easy to speak of the preceding Middle Ages as a period when Augustinian and Thomistic philosophy provided the answers to most of man's most vital questions, when the church was a universal one, when the political order was rigidly established, with society neatly stratified from the lowliest serf to the king himself, and when there was little question of movement from one level to the next. But the supposedly settled notions of the medieval world were at no time exempt from challenge, and new vistas of human potential were constantly being opened to view. Thus historians often speak of "Renaissances" rather than a "Renaissance." They point to "Renaissances" of the ninth century and the twelfth century. Some go so far as to argue that no distinction between the medieval and the Renaissance worlds can really be supported by evidence.

The Renaissance which came to England with the accession of the Tudors was a culmination of all of these earlier movements. It was a product of medieval society as fully as it was a reaction against it. It began in Italy almost two centuries earlier, with a revival of classical learning which has come to be called "humanism." It may have been aided by the fall of Constantinople to the Turks in 1453 and the consequent movement into Italy of Greek scholars bearing their long-preserved classical manuscripts, although the study of Greek had begun in Western Europe some time earlier. It was certainly forwarded by the development and growth of printing which made possible a dissemination of learning, ancient and contemporary, such as the world had never known before. It carried an essentially medieval view of the physical universe and of man's place in the universe — a view which came to be persistently challenged in Tudor England. Indeed, it has been argued that out of this clash between new heresies and old certainties the plays of William Shakespeare emerged. Shakespeare's plays may be the finest mirror that we possess of the conflicting visions of the Renaissance world.

The Medieval Universe

The notion of the universe which medieval philosophers fashioned out of classical learning and Christian interpretation of it was primarily one of an ordered creation, planned and executed by God. Every part was related to every other part and served some function in a universal plan. The benevolence and perfection of this plan, however, had been modified by man's own original sin, which also rendered him forever incapable of more than a limited view of what God had created. Crucial to any medieval view of the universe were the twin conceptions of a benevolent and ordered creation of God as opposed to a disordered and chaotic world which was the creation of man. In the eternal conflict between order and disorder medieval philosophers reflected the disparity between the ideal world and the real one in which they lived, between the divine and the human. The goal of human life was one of ultimate union with divine perfection which could come only by salvation of the soul. To live the virtuous and truly Christian life on earth, it was necessary for man to adapt himself, in the highest degree of which he was capable, to the orderly plan of God.

The universe had been constructed in a system of hierarchies. Every form of life was arranged in a scale beginning with the lowliest plant and extending through man and the angels up to God himself. Social organizations, in the same way, began with the individual and extended in degrees of importance to the family, the state, the universal church, and finally to the kingdom of God himself. All matter was arranged in a hierarchy of excellence which culminated in the gold of which the towers of heaven were constructed. All human institutions were related to one another as part of the divine scheme, and the ultimate goal of learning as well as of art was to illuminate God's perfect plan for the benefit of man. This is one reason why allegory became a dominant mode of medieval literature. A story was worth telling only for the eternal truths it might illustrate. Virgil's *Æneid* was read in the Middle

Ages as an allegory of the human soul, and Virgil himself was revered as a prophet who had predicted the birth of Christ.

This way of idealizing the universe in an ordered, fixed, and stratified pattern was inherited by Renaissance men. It was the body of certainty which very slowly disintegrated under the force of new discovery, of developing political and religious institutions—nationalism, commerce, the Reformation—and a heightened spirit of questioning. But men do not easily abandon the comfortable convictions of the past, and we can be sure that to most of Shakespeare's contemporaries this certainty was as much a part of everyday assumed and unquestioned belief as it had been to men of earlier centuries. In creative literature especially, the cherished values of the past tend to be carried over into the present.

The astronomical system formulated by Ptolemy of Alexandria in the second century A.D. provided a map of the universe for the Middle Ages. Even though it was being challenged by scientists in Shakespeare's day — the *De Revolutionibus Orbis Cœlestium* of Nicholas Copernicus having been published in 1543 — the Ptolemaic system of astronomy is assumed in virtually all of Renaissance poetry. Indeed, John Milton, who had himself looked through the telescope of Galileo, made it the basis of his *Paradise Lost*. The Ptolemaic system accorded with medieval and Renaissance Christianity in a way that the Copernican theory never could. The new astronomy raised questions to which men were still not entirely willing to seek answers.

The earth, according to Ptolemy, was the centre of the universe. Around it moved perpetually nine concentric spheres, each containing a heavenly body or bodies which moved within it. Medieval commentators had elaborated upon Ptolemy's work, and there were inevitable disputes over details of the cosmological system, some writers holding that there were as many as eleven spheres in all. Generally it was believed that the closest sphere to the earth was that of the moon. Then came those of the planets Mercury and Venus, then that of the sun or Sol, and after it the spheres of the planets Mars, Jupiter, and Saturn. The eighth sphere contained the fixed stars — fixed in relation to one another — a conventional symbol of stability and order, just as comets and meteors stood for disorder, corruption, and change. The outermost sphere was a kind of shell called the *primum mobile* or "first mover." Some writers held that between it and the sphere of the fixed stars was a crystalline sphere which contained only water, but more generally the term "crystalline" was applied to all of the spheres between the moon and the *primum mobile*. This outer shell moved the spheres within it around the earth from east to west, making a full circle every twenty-four hours. At the same time, each of the celestial bodies moved within its own sphere from west to east around the earth at a slower pace. The moon took twenty-eight days to make its orbit; the sun, Venus, and Mercury each took a year, the sun passing through the twelve signs of the zodiac; Mars took two years; Jupiter, twelve; and Saturn, thirty.

Each of these spheres, the medieval theologians believed, was controlled by an order of angels. Above the created universe was the empyrean, or heaven, where God sat enthroned. Hell was generally located deep in the bowels of the earth, although some savants though that it was outside the *primum mobile*, far below the created universe. Dante placed it in the first position, Milton in the latter.

The angels who controlled the spheres were arranged in nine ascending orders, generally following the classification of Dionysius the Areopagite, a fifth century A.D. Christian neo-Platonist, to whom was attributed the great work, *On the Heavenly Hierarchy* — although recent scholars have argued that the treatise was actually written in Syria sometime before 533 A.D. and not by Dionysius at all. This work divided the ætherial creatures into three "hierarchies," each of which was subdivided into three "species," the triune divisions corresponding, as might be expected, with the trinity. The first hierarchy consisted of Seraphim, Cherubim, and Thrones, the purely contemplative orders which were closest to God. Then came the hierarchy of Dominations, Powers, and Virtues. These orders, like those above them, were contemplative and inactive, but they had the power of action which they did not choose to exercise. The third hierarchy consisted of Principalities, Archangels, and Angels, entirely active and directed towards man. These were the supernatural creatures who served as God's messengers, who could sometimes be seen on earth, and who became involved in the affairs of men. Whether the Seraphim or the Cherubim was the order of angels closest to God was another ancient subject for dispute.

The nine orders of angels who inhabited the middle region between earth and heaven were creatures of perfect intelligence. Thus they could always perceive with unclouded vision the perfection of God above them. The precise nature of the angels, as might be expected, was widely debated in Shakespeare's time, but few doubted their existence. It was in their nature to gaze steadily upon God, whom they eternally strove to emulate and with whom they sought to unite themselves. Since, because of God's superiority and brilliance, they could never do this, they moved instead in perpetual circles around the earth, along with the celestial spheres which they controlled. Whether or not they themselves caused the spheres to move was another disputed subject.

That some of the angels had fallen with Satan was a common doctrine of faith. They were believed to have fallen because they had turned their eyes away from God and looked upon their own beautiful selves, with which they had become enamoured. They had thus been corrupted by the sin of pride. It was widely believed that these spirits after their fall had been relegated to various parts of the physical universe — to air, rivers, mountains, caves — where they continued to exist as malignant spirits, and to be the deities falsely worshipped in pagan religions. The belief in demons was still very strong in Shakespeare's day. Demonic forces, ever seeking to prey upon mankind, were most likely to appear at night, and were always ready to serve man in return for the custody of his immortal soul. Sometimes they were identified with the fairies of folklore, although fairies were conceived of in other fashions as well. There is probably no better account of the various kinds of evil spirits which haunted the imaginations of Elizabethans than that in Reginald Scot's *Discovery of Witchcraft* (1584).

Each of the planets emitted a substance called its "influence," an ætherial fluid believed to affect the lives of men on earth. Since the heavenly bodies moved at different speeds, they were never in the same relation to one another. Their peculiar conjunction at the time of a man's birth was thought to determine his personality and physical constitution, as well as to affect his future life. The positions of the stars which determined these things were not considered by medieval and Renaissance savants to be capricious or arbitrary, as pagan astrologers had usually held; they were reflections of the providential scheme of God. The ancient dispute of free will versus predestination had been given a new urgency by the advent of Calvinism and was an important issue of theological controversy, but belief in the stars did not, for most Elizabethans, preclude belief in free will. God could not be bound by the positions of the stars which he himself had created, and although His will might be the ultimate cause of things, He had left "secondary causes" in the hands of men, who by their own free choices helped to determine their own destinies.

Fortune, conceived of as a fickle goddess who showed some favours to all men but was constant to none, might seem capricious as she turned her ever-present wheel. But her apparent hostility, like the malignant force of hostile stars, was part of God's larger design. Man had incurred subjection to Fortune by his own original sin, and as Boethius had taught in his *On the Consolation of Philosophy,* a work translated by Geoffrey Chaucer and again by Queen Elizabeth herself, man had always within him the means of escaping Fortune's blows; it lay in the proper use of his reason and in submission to the will of God. The ancient art of astrology was widely practised in the sixteenth century, although there was growing skepticism, as we can see from Edmund's celebrated speech in *King Lear* (I.ii. 112–26). It was not, however, to the notion that the stars governed human life that Elizabethan skeptics generally objected, but rather to the belief that human astrologers could read what God had written in the stars by means of their horoscopes, almanacs, and other trumpery.

As the spheres moved around the earth they produced a music which reflected the perfect harmony of God's creation. The music of the spheres was an old idea which classical astronomers had explained as caused by celestial friction. For some Renaissance neo-Platonists, however, the music was believed to be made by the angels, each of whom sang a separate note, with all notes combining to make a perfect harmony. Adam and Eve before their fall could hear this music, but it was denied to fallen man on earth because of the gross non-spiritual substance of his flesh. As Lorenzo explains to Jessica in *The Merchant of Venice* (V.i. 60–5):

There's not the smallest orb which thou behold'st
But in his motion like an angel sings,
Still quiring to the young-ey'd cherubins;
But whilst this muddy vesture of decay
Doth grossly close us in, we cannot hear it.

Physical Nature

All of this vast creation was composed of four elements, but they were not elements in our modern sense of finite particles of matter. Elements in the medieval sense were combinations of the four "qualities" of hot, cold, dry, and moist. Thus earth was a combination of cold and dry, water of cold and moist, air of hot and moist, and fire of hot and dry. All matter was one in that it all consisted of these four elements in various combinations, and within all matter the four were constantly struggling against one another, striving for dominance in the composition of man, as well as of minerals and plants. Earth and water were the baser elements, confined to the physical earth; it was their nature to move downward. Air and fire were the celestial elements whose nature it was to rise. Of them, man's soul was composed; of earth, his body. Among metals, gold was considered to represent the most perfect combination of the four elements, analogous to man in the most perfect possible condition of health. The lesser metals, in a descending hierarchical order, reflected progressively less perfect combinations.

It was thus natural for men to believe that the proportions of the elements could be changed and one metal transmuted into another higher on the scale. This was the goal of alchemy, a pseudo-science which had intrigued the imaginations of men from time immemorial. Alchemists, who often displayed a surprising knowledge of chemical processes, sought for the "philosopher's stone," by which they could transmute base metals into gold. This stone, if discovered, would also produce a mysterious "elixir," called "aurum potabile," which could cure all human diseases, for these were believed to result from similar disproportions of the four elements as they comprised (in the form of humours) the human body. A study whose end was the production of gold naturally attracted quacks, as well as a perennial supply of the gullible to be fleeced. Alchemy was a common subject for satire, in Chaucer's "Canon's Yeoman's Tale," no less than in Ben Jonson's brilliant play, *The Alchemist.* The very ease with which the foolish could be duped, however, is itself testimony to the deep hold of alchemy upon the popular imagination. Alchemy provided Shakespeare with a subject for poetic imagery throughout his career. Although chemistry, as we know it today, was unknown to Shakespeare's age, Elizabethan alchemists laid the basis for much of our present chemical knowledge, and they included among their numbers some of the most respected scientists in England.

Man, the Microcosm

At the centre of everything was man. For him all nature had been created. Animals, plants, and minerals had been placed on earth merely to serve him. There was no feeling of injustice in the fact that man's original sin had caused nature to be corrupted and the animals to suffer along with him. Animals were capable only of instinct and sensory perception, whereas man was a creature of reason, created in the image of God, and ruling on earth as God ruled in heaven. In his own physical constitution man was a universe writ small, his body also being composed of the four elements of earth, air, fire, and water. He was the microcosm, a small model and reflection of the macrocosm, of the great universe of which he was a part. The analogy of the human body to the physical earth is one of the most commonly encountered in Shakespeare's plays. It is in Romeo's words as he leaps over the Capulet wall: "Turn back, dull earth, and find thy centre out" (II.i. 2). The "centre" is the flaming heart which he has left behind with Juliet, analogous to the core of fire believed to be at the centre of the physical earth. In the same play Old Capulet speaks of Juliet as "the hopeful lady of my earth" (I.ii. 15), and this same analogy is behind the striking metaphor by which King Richard II describes his body as "that small model of the barren earth/Which serves as paste and cover to our bones" (III.ii. 153-4).

In the human body the elements appeared in the form of four "humours," each of which induced special physical and mental tendencies. The particular combination of these humours within a man's body was called his "complexion," a word which described both his physical nature and his personality or "temperament." In man's body earth became black bile; its quality was cold and dry, and an excess of it caused a man to be melancholy. Water became phlegm, cold and moist; its predominance caused a man to be phlegmatic, sluggish, apathetic, and generally slow to anger. Air became blood, hot and moist; it produced what we still call a "sanguine disposition." Fire, hot and dry, produced yellow bile or choler, making one hot-tempered and quick to anger.

The primary elements were believed to enter the body through food, which naturally consisted of them. This is why the eating of certain foods was believed to cause the predominance of certain humours — too much dry beef, for instance, produced excess of choler — and this is why diet, along with bloodletting, was a primary cure for all physical ailments. From the stomach the elements passed into the liver where they were transformed by body heat into their form as humours. The stomach and the liver were thus regarded as the organs where the various kinds of human passion originated, for every passion was seen as resulting from a special combination of humours. From the liver, the humours passed through the rest of the body, transformed into various kinds of "spirits." When they passed along the veins to the heart and were there acted upon, they became "vital spirits" and governed the trunk of the body and below. When they passed along the arteries to the brain and were there acted upon, they became "animal spirits" which governed the head and consequently ruled all of man's rational activity.

The foregoing is, of course, a much simplified account of a fairly complex system of human physiology, inherited from classical antiquity and elaborated by medieval and Renaissance commentators. In spite of the work of scientists such as Andreas Vesalius and later William Harvey, it continued to provide the basic principles upon which the sixteenth- and seventeenth-century practice of medicine was built. It is the system implicitly understood by Shakespeare's audience; it provides a language for virtually all of his references to physical disease, to the human body, and to personality traits; and it is drawn upon time and time again in the poetic imagery of his plays.

The Great Chain of Being

The most common metaphor by which Elizabethans described the interrelation of all substance in a harmonious cosmic scheme was that of a great chain of being. This concept, which has been described in an important book by A. O. Lovejoy, *The Great Chain of Being* (full bibliographical data on all books referred to is included in the Select Bibliography, pp. 260–76), is one of the most basic ideas in all human intellectual history. The chain began at the foot of God's throne, and it included, as it extended downward, every physical substance and social institution God had ever created. The higher a link in the chain, the greater its perfection, importance, and closeness to God. Every link, however, contained some special quality wherein it was different from and superior to the link above it. Man, for instance, was superior to the angels in his ability to learn, for angels, with their perfect intelligence, knew all they could ever be capable of knowing. In every class of beings there was one dominant form: the lion among beasts, the eagle among birds, and the king among men. There were no gaps in the chain: every link performed some vital function in the cosmic whole. The universe was conceived of as full and active, a creation of boundless variety and of a multitude of separate duties and functions, all related to one another and all governed by the supreme law of God.

The basic principle of cosmic order was thus one of degree, in which every object had its assigned place and performed its proper and necessary function. Perhaps at no place in Shakespeare is the harmonious vision of the great chain of being, with all of its ordered relationships, expressed better than in the great speech of Ulysses on degree in *Troilus and Cressida* (I.iii. 77–137). Here all of the interrelated calamities which may beset the universe when "degree is shaken" are detailed. The same idea is expressed in *A Midsummer Night's Dream* (II.i. 88–117), where all human discord and all corruptions in nature are described as closely related to one another and as all springing ultimately from discord between the king and queen of the fairies, who are treated by Shakespeare, in one typical Renaissance fashion, as divine creatures. Discord in the heavens breeds discord on earth, and discord on earth is reflected in the heavens.

The notion appears again and again in Shakespeare's plays, and it is especially crucial in the great tragedies. Man, the family, the state, and physical nature are conceived of as corresponding planes of creation. When disorder appears on one plane, it inevitably corrupts the others. Before the murder of Julius Cæsar unnatural phenomena appear on earth. When Macbeth kills Duncan, the state is corrupted by tyranny, and nature falls into discord as the sun is blotted out and the horses of the king turn against man, their natural master in the scale of being, and at last devour one another. The turmoil in the world of *King Lear* appears in the disruption of family relations, in civil war and an invading foreign army, in the breaking forth of all nature in a violent storm, as well as in the madness of Lear himself. Elizabethans beheld disorder all around them. They were acutely aware of the imperfections of the world in which they lived. But most of them still saw this disorder in terms of man's own violation of a divine plan of which harmony, order, and degree were the cardinal principles.

Reason and Nature

Medieval philosophers made an important distinction between intelligence (or understanding) and reason. Intelligence was the natural property of angels which enabled them immediately and intuitively to grasp all truth, and this is why they never questioned the perfection of God so long as their eyes were fixed upon Him. Man had the lesser power of reason, the ability to progress by his own mental processes from one perceived truth to another. The fall of man had vitiated his rational powers so that human reason was constantly subject to error, and it was only by the grace of God that man could be led to right reason, the perception of truth — that same truth which angels could directly perceive. Reason rightly exercised by man could lead him only to the truth of revealed Christianity, and as the force which should control his will, right reason could cause him to perform only virtuous actions. The contrary force within man which, according to medieval and Renaissance moralists, worked in opposition to reason, was passion, the heritage of his fallen condition. The struggle between reason and passion for the soul of man is an Elizabethan commonplace which is well reflected in the soliloquy of Friar Laurence in *Romeo and Juliet* (II.III. 1–30). Some scholars have seen all of Renaissance tragedy in these terms, but that is something of an oversimplification.

In an age of burgeoning scientific inquiry like the Renaissance, the definition of human reason was a vital issue. If nature was to be understood, it could only be by the proper exercise of this human faculty. Although Renaissance neo-Platonists sometimes conceived of nature as standing in an intermediate position in the scale of creation, below the angels and above man, and as having an independent "soul" which controlled life on earth regardless of the powers above it, the orthodox view of medieval Christianity was that nature was entirely the creation of God, controlled by the law of God, and bound by no law other than the will of God. Man, by the use of reason, might discover much about nature, but he could no more hope to understand it fully than he could hope to know the mind of God. Really to understand nature, for Renaissance moralists, was to know how to adapt oneself to it, for nature, as the creation of God, was by definition good, beautiful, and perfect; to live by its rules was to live the most ethically satisfying kind of life. To control nature was impossible, and to seek to do so was to be guilty of the deadly sin of pride.

The Elizabethan age is marked, however, by the steady growth of a quite different conception of nature and the power of human reason which was to reach a culmination in the middle of the seventeenth century in the *Leviathan* of Thomas Hobbes. This is a conception of nature as governed by mechanical laws which operate independently of any supernatural power, and a belief that by the exercise of his own reason, man might ultimately know the laws of nature and by such knowledge be able to control his world. This belief was closely related to the growth of the physical sciences. The science in which there was most avid interest and in which Renaissance men appear to have made the most real progress was astronomy, a study which by its very nature tended to destroy the illusion of a fixed and finite universe with which men had lived for so long, and to which the ideas of order and degree were so closely related. If the universe was infinite, so also could be the potentialities of mankind. Out of

Renaissance skepticism came the idea of human progress which was to develop markedly in the seventeenth century, a rejection of the medieval assumption that social institutions were forever fixed by man's fallen condition and that his only real hope lay in the promise of salvation.

Not only the scientists were at work. Skeptics such as Giordano Bruno in Italy and Michel de Montaigne in France were attacking the philosophical foundations of the medieval system. Montaigne in his *Apology for Raymond Sebond* questioned the entire notion that man had a special place in the universe and was in any real way superior to the other animals. The writings of both these men were well known in England. Bruno lectured at Oxford and stayed at the home of Sir Philip Sidney. The influence of Montaigne's essays is apparent in many places in Shakespeare, but perhaps most obviously in Gonzalo's description of the ideal commonwealth in *The Tempest* (II.i). This demonstrates clearly that Shakespeare had read Montaigne either in the French or in the popular translation by John Florio, which there is some reason to believe he consulted in manuscript even before its publication in 1603.

When Shakespeare was writing his most profound explorations of the human condition in the early years of the seventeenth century, the belief in order and degree in a harmonious and divinely controlled universe was being subjected to ever-increasing assault; more and more men were beginning to think in terms of the animal nature of man and of human ability to control external nature. The philosophical position which conceived of man as merely a "king of beasts," who enjoyed no special position in the universe, and which regarded nature as knowable through study of its independent laws, was known as "naturalism." It is what Elizabethans often meant when they spoke of "atheism," although that term was used to apply to almost any variety of unorthodox religious belief.

The animal nature of man is one of the propositions argued by the villain of Cyril Tourneur's *The Atheist's Tragedy* (1611), a play which also illustrates the conflict between opposing views of nature and human reason. In this play is reflected some of the fear and horror with which traditionalist minds contemplated the growth of a new empirical science and the challenging of values based upon a medieval view of the world. Shakespeare mirrored the conflict in the Iago of *Othello,* who sees all human emotions in animalistic terms, and even more markedly in the Edmund of *King Lear,* who scorns the social hierarchies of the traditional order and who seeks dominance by the use of his own rational powers. The nature who is his goddess and to whom his services are bound (I.ii. 1–2) is that of the new Renaissance naturalist philosophers.

Scientific investigation, in spite of its progress, was still widely suspect in Shakespeare's day. Little clear distinction was made between it and the practice of magic. To attempt to control nature independently of divine grace — and thus to cultivate freely the powers of darkness — was to be a witch and to practise "black magic," the punishment for which was death. To study nature with the help of God — by prayer, submission, and the reading of holy books — was to be, like the Prospero of Shakespeare's *The Tempest,* a dealer in "white magic" or "holy magic." The important distinction which Elizabethans made between these two types of "scientific" activity was very real and meaningful to Shakespeare's audience.

Church and State

While ancient conceptions of man's position in the universe were just beginning to break down in the sixteenth century, the political organization of medieval Europe, which was itself related to the ideas of hierarchy and order, had long been disintegrating and in Shakespeare's age was close to dissolution. The idea of a universal church to which all the kingdoms of Europe paid homage had begun to deteriorate in England as early as the twelfth century in the struggle between King Henry II and his Archbishop of Canterbury, Thomas à Becket. King John, the son of Henry II, had brought excommunication upon himself by his defiance of the papacy, foreshadowing the excommunication of Queen Elizabeth. The coming of King Henry VII to the throne in 1485 marked the virtual end of the feudal system in which the barons of the realm, each controlling vast areas of England, accepted the vassalage of their lesser lords, as they themselves were vassals to the king, and the king subservient to the Pope of Rome. In medieval political theory, as expressed in such works as the *Policraticus* of John of

Salisbury, the king was as responsible to his feudal barons as he was to God, and they could depose and even execute him if he failed to perform his duties to their satisfaction. The barons of England had been powerful enough to force King John into submission to them and to depose King Edward II and King Richard II.

One of the characteristics of the Renaissance throughout Europe was the emergence of nationalistic states, ruled by absolute monarchs. We can see this movement in the emergence of the Emperor Charles V in Spain and Austria, and in the coming of François I to the throne of France, as well as in the accession of the first Tudor king in England. Each of these rulers established his power over a unified nation by destroying the control of his feudal lords and by amalgamating into his central authority what had been independent dukedoms. In England the task was made easier by the three decades of civil war known as the Wars of the Roses, during which the great feudal lords of England had virtually destroyed one another. Henry VII created a new nobility, dependent upon him and loyal to him. The grandfathers of many of the great nobles of Shakespeare's England — Leicester and Pembroke, for instance — had been mere country gentlemen. The Tudor kings of England were more absolute in their power than any of their medieval predecessors had been. It was almost inevitable that as absolute kings they should come at last to wield religious, as well as temporal, power, ruling a national church which was inseparable from a national state.

Although we may trace the beginnings of the Reformation in England at least as far back as the Wycliffite movement of the fourteenth century, the separation of England from the church of Rome became a reality under King Henry VIII. During the reign of his son, Edward VI, the Church of England had its real beginnings. Queen Mary, who succeeded him, attempted to return England to the Catholic faith, but that was no longer possible. Queen Elizabeth sought for a middle way, never herself claiming to be Supreme Head of the church, although the Pope accused her of so doing, and hoping always for some kind of reconciliation of England's religious differences with Rome. She ruled from 1558 to 1603 over an England in which Anglicans, Catholics, and Puritans lived in an uneasy and suspicious alliance, and she tempered the demands of each religious group in what has come to be called the "Elizabethan settlement." In Elizabethan England political and religious problems were so closely related to one another that it is sometimes impossible to separate them.

Absolutism and Passive Obedience

The end of feudalism and the emergence of the ruler as head of a national church called for a new interpretation of the rights and duties of the sovereign and of his special relation both to his subjects and to God. Tudor divines, beginning in the reign of King Henry VIII and relying heavily upon the Scriptures, particularly upon certain Old Testament injunctions, began to develop a body of political theory strongly rooted in Reformation religious principles. It was characteristically Tudor. In the reign of Queen Elizabeth it was enshrined in the official book of homilies of the Church of England and proclaimed from pulpits at regular intervals throughout the year. Its cardinal principle was that the king was God's agent on earth, responsible to God alone. He was absolute in his power, but this did not mean that he could do whatever he pleased. It was the sovereign's duty to rule according to divine law and for the good of his subjects. If he did not govern properly, God inevitably would call him to a strict account, for Tudor political doctrine was based firmly upon the supremacy of the law of God. But for the people — and this included the most powerful of lords — to rebel against their king was for them to rebel against God and thus to bring upon themselves and upon their country the worst conceivable kind of punishment, for rebellion included within itself every kind of sin of which man was capable. The homily, *Against Disobedience and Wilful Rebellion,* published in five separate editions during the year 1570, and included in the book of homilies in 1571, stated the principle in no uncertain terms:

> How horrible a thing against God and man rebellion is, cannot possibly be expressed according unto the greatness thereof. He that nameth rebellion nameth not a singular or one only sin, as is theft, robbery, murder, and such like; but he nameth the whole puddle and sink of

all sins against God and man; against his prince, his country, his countrymen, his parents, his children, his kinfolks, against God and all men heaped together nameth he that nameth rebellion.

If the king was evil, it was because God had caused him to be evil so as to punish a people for their sins; their only recourse was in prayer to God, who must inevitably remove the wicked ruler, but only when He was ready to do so. Shakespeare's aged John of Gaunt affirms this principle in *Richard II* in response to the Duchess of Gloucester's plea that he avenge his murdered brother:

> God's is the quarrel; for God's substitute,
> His deputy anointed in his sight,
> Hath caus'd his death; the which if wrongfully,
> Let heaven revenge; for I may never lift
> An angry arm against his minister (I.II. 37–41).

Passive obedience, even to the most obvious tyrant, and even to one who opposed the true church of God, was proclaimed by Tudor theorists as the most important duty of every subject. The doctrine was used to justify the Reformation, to assure the loyalty to the crown of a sometimes reluctant and rebellious clergy, and to justify the loyalty of English Catholics to Queen Elizabeth, in spite of her excommunication and the Pope's decree that she be dethroned by Englishmen loyal to the church of Rome. Some Reformation clergymen, Bishop Hugh Latimer for instance, might argue that the subject must not obey the king's law if it conflicted with the law of God, but even Latimer went on to hold that the subject must then accept punishment for his disobedience and never attempt to oppose the sovereign or his magistrates. Although Latimer, faithful to his own principle, was burned at the stake during the Catholic reign of Queen Mary, his views were much alive in the time of Elizabeth.

Of all Tudor political doctrines, passive obedience was the most commonly proclaimed, and the very vehemence and frequency with which it was expressed would tend to indicate the strength of the opposition to Tudor rule and the ever-present danger of rebellion with which Elizabethan Englishmen lived. The doctrines of absolutism and passive obedience are important in Shakespeare's history plays. They are implicit in the Bishop of Carlisle's prediction of the Wars of the Roses in *Richard II* (IV.i. 114–49); they provide the justification for the betrayal of the rebels in Gaultree Forest by Prince John of Lancaster in *Henry IV, Part II* (IV.ii. 100–23). But Shakespeare never expresses these Tudor commonplaces so clearly and unequivocally as do most of his contemporary writers of political plays. He subjects them to close examination, probes their antitheses and contradictions, and in some places, as in the scene in *Macbeth* between Malcolm and Macduff in England (IV.iii), he comes as close to challenging them openly as any dramatist could dare to come.

That there was opposition in England to the Tudor notions of absolutism and passive obedience is obvious. It came, to a slight extent, in the last years of Elizabeth, from the Catholic opposition who argued that a king who violated the law of God by opposing the true church was in effect a usurper, and thus need not be obeyed. Primarily the opposition came from the Puritans who, in such works as John Ponet's *A Short Treatise of Politic Power* (1556), held that political authority had been vested by God not in the king, but in the community of men who, in turn, placed it in their king; the ruler was responsible to his people and it was they who were, in turn, responsible to God. Some Puritan writers held that when the king did evil, it was the duty of the magistrates of the realm to depose him and, if necessary, to destroy him. This notion was formulated primarily by French Huguenots. It appeared in England in a tract called *Vindiciæ Contra Tyrannos* (1579), attributed variously to Hubert Languet and Philip Du Plessis Mornay, both of whom were close friends of Sir Philip Sidney. Puritan opposition to the absolutist position of the Tudors was to grow steadily in the early seventeenth century, and it was to culminate in such justifications for the execution of King Charles I as John Milton's *The Tenure of Kings and Magistrates*. The most widely debated political question of Tudor England was that of the terms of political obedience. Censorship made unorthodox positions extremely difficult to express, but it was these positions which the official documents obviously were designed to answer. It is thus not surprising that the question of the rights and duties of a king, and of his relation to his people, should be a crucial issue in Shakespeare's tragedies as well as his history plays.

Morality, Law, and Political Theory

Tudor political theory, in spite of its innovations, was as firmly grounded as that of the Middle Ages in the traditional view of the universe as a highly ordered creation directed by a purposeful God, in which every social division observed degree and order and performed its proper function in the great chain of being. As God's agent the king must govern according to the system of law which God had created, and which was believed to exist in three closely related forms. The first of these was the Law of Nature. This was the law which God had implanted in the souls of men, and which all men could read instinctively in their own hearts and consciences. Its highest commandment was that man love God and thus love his fellow men as children of God and do all those things which are necessary to the preservation of orderly life on earth. A second kind of law, the Law of Nations, consisted of those rules, derived from the Law of Nature and always consistent with it, by which the nations of the earth were governed and which regulated their dealings with one another. It is to these two kinds of universally accepted law that Hector appeals in *Troilus and Cressida* (II.ii. 173–86), when he argues that Helen should be returned to her lawful husband. The third kind of law was the Civil Law. It consisted of those customs which individual nations evolved for their own governments according to their own special circumstances. Thus, while England and France were both governed by the Law of Nations, each might have a different Civil Law for its internal affairs. This law must, of course, be consistent both with the Law of Nations and the higher Law of Nature. The greatest description of this essentially medieval conception of law as a reflection of the moral order of the universe and as the instrument by which the will of God is reflected in the government of men is in the Preface and opening chapter of Richard Hooker's *Of the Laws of Ecclesiastical Polity,* a monument of Elizabethan prose which provides perhaps the clearest statement of what we may call the orthodox position in Elizabethan thought.

But just as the principle of order in nature was being questioned, the neatly formulated conceptions of law and social hierarchy which had been inherited from the Middle Ages were meeting their challenges. If some men could believe that physical nature was governed by mechanical laws independent of any higher control, it was perhaps inevitable that others should look for similar laws in the operation of human society. This movement found its most important expression in Italy in the work of Niccolò Machiavelli. Although no English translation of *The Prince* or the *Discourses* was printed before those of Edward Dacres of 1636 and 1640 respectively, both of these works were widely read by Elizabethan intellectuals in Italian, in French and Latin translations, and in various English translations which were circulating in manuscript well before 1600. Machiavelli's writings in Italian were even printed in England, with false title pages to disguise the fact, as early as 1584.

Machiavelli was feared and vilified in England, and caricatured upon the English stage — perhaps most notably in the Barabas of Marlowe's *Jew of Malta* — for he struck at the very heart of the whole system of order and degree in a divinely planned universe. He denied the Law of Nature as well as the Law of Nations, for he argued that the government of a kingdom need have no relation to God's government of heaven, and that there was no law any nation need observe in relation to any other except the requirements of its own strength and security. He argued that although religion might be used to serve the purposes of a ruler, the Christian religion was harmful to a state because it taught humility, a quality destructive to political power. All human achievement he saw not as part of any divine plan, but as the product of a blind and capricious fortune against which men might for a brief time prevail if they asserted their own qualities of strength, cunning, and will, which he called *virtù*.

Machiavelli denied the relevance of politics to morality, distinguishing between the public and the private virtues, but holding that the ability of a king to preserve his state had no necessary relation to his probity in matters of private conduct. He thus countered the basic principle, derived from the *Politics* of Aristotle and elaborated in the *De Officiis* of Cicero, that the essential element of all good government was the morality of the ruler. For

Cicero the foundations of all political action had been justice and virtue; for Machiavelli they were the maintenance of power and the preservation of the state against its enemies. Political organization and conduct he saw not as divinely instituted, but as bound by mechanical laws which could be studied and mastered. The instrument he would use for this purpose was history; by careful study of past political behaviour, Machiavelli believed that one might understand certain laws of government which must inevitably continue to operate. His method was based upon the assumption that human nature was fixed and immutable and that its essential characteristics were greed, the drive for self-preservation, and the lust for power. He stands in every respect at the opposite extreme from Richard Hooker.

It is not surprising to find that Shakespeare's plays reveal an awareness of Machiavelli's position and a frequent probing of it, for no thinking man of the age could be unaware of Machiavelli or ignore the implications of what he stood for. In *Julius Cæsar*, for instance, no matter how one may interpret the fall of Brutus, one of the key elements in his tragedy is in his separation of public good from private morality, his decision to murder his friend for the good of Rome. The Duke of Gloucester, who is to emerge as Richard III, in *Henry VI, Part III* declares that he will "set the murderous Machiavel to school" (III.ii. 193). There is probably no better example of the effects of self-seeking lust for power in all of Shakespeare's plays. He is a good example of the stage "Machiavel," as shaped by the special genius of Shakespeare. Richard is the man of constantly changing exterior appearance, who can smile as he murders for sport. In this aspect — and there are many other aspects to his character — he represents a caricature of Machiavelli, but we may find some of Machiavelli's most characteristic political principles stated by the Earl of Worcester to justify his own treachery in *Henry IV, Part I,* and Henry Bolingbroke, in each of the three plays in which he appears, provides a model of Machiavellian politics.

The Elizabethan Commonwealth

Although, as the agent of God on earth, Queen Elizabeth was in theory as absolute a monarch as had ever lived, she was the custodian and executor of a system of laws which had a validity beyond the person of the sovereign, and large numbers of her subjects participated in the actual government of England. In political treatises of the time England is commonly referred to as a "commonwealth," a concept perhaps best defined by Elizabeth's learned Secretary of State, Sir Thomas Smith, in his *De Republica Anglorum* (1583), translated as *The Commonwealth of England* and published frequently throughout the seventeenth century. For Smith it was "a society or common doing of a multitude of freemen collected together and united by common accord and covenants among themselves for the conservation of themselves as well in peace as in war." In this commonwealth, the nobles and the common people had their rights and duties as fully as the queen had hers, all working together for the preservation of the realm and the common welfare. It is this interdependence of all classes of the realm that Shakespeare always stresses in his English history plays. The idea of commonwealth in one way operated against the principle of absolutism implicit in Tudor political theory, and it was only when the Stuart kings attempted to apply Tudor absolutist theory in all of its implications to the immediate problems of government, asserting the divine right of the king as superior to all other rights, that England was brought to civil war and King Charles I to the scaffold.

That Elizabeth was a strong-willed and effective queen is attested to by all contemporary accounts, and she was respected as such by all of her fellow European sovereigns. The actual details of government were performed by her Privy Council, whose members she chose, but matters of policy she decided herself, although she rarely failed to consult her ministers. Chief of these was William Cecil, Lord Burghley, her Lord Treasurer and chief support during the greater part of her long reign. She and Burghley were in essential agreement about most matters, but when they differed he deferred to her judgment. Towards the end of their forty-year association, Burghley advised his son, Robert, who was to succeed him, always to give the queen the best advice of which he was capable, but never to try to prevail over her own good judgment.

Within the queen's council there were, of course, factions and internal struggles, and it would be impossible here even to touch upon the long history of intrigues and rivalries which were a part of Elizabeth's government. Burghley, who stood for the Church of England and a middle road which would assure prosperity at home and peace abroad, was opposed most notably over the years by a faction led by Robert Dudley, Earl of Leicester, long the queen's favourite in spite of their political disagreements. With him were joined his brother, Ambrose Dudley, Earl of Warwick; and Sir Francis Walsingham, who had begun his political career as Burghley's protegé. These men drew much of their support from the growing Puritan forces in England. They were aggressive in matters of church reform and were the leading voices in favour of military engagements abroad. Their faction in time grew greater than Burghley's, but with the queen's support, the Lord Treasurer kept England upon a middle course which assured her survival against sometimes seemingly impossible odds. The struggle between the forces of moderation and their more militant opponents went on after all of these great figures were dead. It continued in the next generation with Sir Robert Cecil carrying on the policies of his father, and those of Leicester being carried on by his stepson, Robert Devereux, Earl of Essex, who drew his support from Catholic as well as Puritan opponents of the Anglican church. There is reason to believe that Shakespeare was associated with the party of Essex and his chief supporter, Henry Wriothesley, Earl of Southampton. Some scholars have found in the Earl of Essex a model for various of Shakespeare's characters, most notably Hamlet. That Shakespeare's *Richard II* was staged before a private audience on the eve of Essex's ill-fated rebellion against the queen in 1601 has long been known. Shakespeare's company was examined in Star Chamber and exonerated of any complicity in the rebellion. Although such matters may intrigue our imaginations, we know virtually nothing of Shakespeare's relations to the various political factions of his time.

In addition to her council, Queen Elizabeth's government depended heavily upon the ancient English institution of Parliament. Ignored by the strong kings Henry IV and Henry V, Parliament had been reconvened by the weak king, Henry VI, and throughout the reigns of the Tudors it grew steadily greater in power. It is paradoxical that while the Reformation in theory made the king absolute ruler of church and state, it also strengthened Parliament and made it a more vital institution of government than it ever had been before. Henry VIII had relied upon his great Reformation Parliament for support in opposing the power of the church. He kept it in session long beyond its normal terms. In emphasizing its wishes, he had, in effect, contributed to a lessening of the power of the crown which was steadily to continue.

Parliaments traditionally had been called by the king to deal with the great issues of the times — to institute changes in religion, to express the people's support in time of war, and, most significantly, to provide for the payment of armies. The English Parliament, with its Lords and Commons, unique in the politics of contemporary Europe and scorned by many foreign observers, theoretically represented the totality of the English commonwealth. As Sir Thomas Smith explained, it was an institution which "representeth and hath the power of the whole realm both the head and body. For every Englishman is intended to be there present, either in person or by procuration and attorneys, of what preeminence, state, dignity, or quality soever he be, from the prince (be he King or Queen) to the lowest person of England. And the consent of the Parliament is taken to be every man's consent." Elizabeth's relations with her parliaments, which among other things persistently demanded that she either marry or name an heir to the throne, were often difficult. They have been treated at length in the two volumes of J. E. Neale's *Elizabeth I and Her Parliaments*. Elizabeth could not control the members of Parliament as she controlled the lords of the Privy Council whom she appointed. Suffice it to say that, in spite of the theoretical absolutism of the queen, by the end of her reign Parliament was exercising a high degree of influence in state affairs, and that of its two houses the Commons had emerged as the more important.

Anglican, Catholic, and Puritan

The most crucial problem of Elizabethan England, at the root of most of its internal conflicts and a basic issue in all of its foreign relations, was that of religion: the precarious situation of the Church of England, threatened by Catholics who opposed

it out of allegiance to their ancient religious practices, and by
Puritans who opposed it for its failure to embrace more fully the
extreme positions of the Reformation. As a church which sought
a middle way, it was faced with hostility from both extremes, but
at the same time it secured for all Englishmen a higher degree of
personal liberty than was known in any other country of Europe.
Elizabeth's government was most interested in outward conformity
of action and in the security of the state, rather than in matters
of private belief, in spite of its persecution of dissidents. So long
as Catholics and Puritans — many of whom continued to hold high
positions throughout her reign — did not make themselves con-
spicuous or threaten her government, they were not greatly interfered with. This was different from the situation in Catholic
Spain and France or in Protestant Geneva.

Elizabeth's first Parliament, meeting within months of her accession to the throne in November of 1558, by the two acts of
Supremacy and Uniformity, confirmed her position as head of the
church, ratified the changes in religious services made by Edward
VI, and decreed Anglican church attendance as obligatory for all
Englishmen, with fines to be levied for every instance of absence
from services. The new church replaced the Latin missal with the
Book of Common Prayer, ordered the destruction of vestments,
shrines, and icons, and while it reformed church services in line
with many of the ideas of continental reformers and abolished many
traditional Catholic practices, in key matters of religious doctrine
it did not really depart radically from what had always been held
to be the Christian faith. Changes in the constitution of the
clergy were largely on the higher levels in the great cathedral cities
and in London; there was no disruption such as had taken place
during the brief reign of Queen Mary. Most of the bishops swore
allegiance to the new order with little difficulty, and it is likely
that for most of the Elizabethan country clergymen the changes
in church structure meant relatively little, and that they continued to
perform their routine parish duties as they had always performed
them, omitting specifically Roman practices and acting under
bishops who now professed allegiance to the queen rather than to
Rome.

In actuality many of the proposed changes of the new church

were extremely difficult to put into effect, in spite of the royal commissioners who were charged to visit the various parishes of England to see that they were. Protestant feeling was strongest in London and in the neighbouring counties of Essex and Kent. But in the more distant regions of England, including Shakespeare's Warwickshire, the old Catholic ways kept a tenacious hold. Many people no doubt believed that the changes instituted under Elizabeth would prove as temporary as those instituted under Mary, although the crushing of the northern rebellions of 1569 signified an end to any real hope of Catholic resurgence in England. Those who continued to profess the old faith, usually in secret, were called "recusants." Their number was never very large, and only in one county, Lancashire, did they possibly comprise a majority of the population.

In the early years of Elizabeth's reign little effective action was taken against Catholic recusants. The queen was anxious to preserve the loyalty of her Catholic subjects, and she seems to have been proud of the lack of real religious repression in England. The trouble began in 1570 when Pope Pius V issued his bull which declared Queen Elizabeth a bastard and a heretic and which absolved her Catholic subjects from obedience to her and urged them actively to rebel against her. The internal threat of a Catholic minority could then no longer be ignored, and repressive measures began to be taken. These became increasingly more severe as Jesuit priests, trained at newly established continental seminaries and determined to restore the old faith in England, began to make their way back to England in increasing numbers. There were also constant plots against the queen's life and a growing threat from Spain which was to be dispelled only with the defeat of the Armada in 1588. Performance of the mass and the teaching of distinctively Catholic doctrines after 1580 were subject to the severest of punishments, but these acts were punished as treason against the state and not as religious heresy. The distinction, though subtle, was a very real one to Elizabethans.

With the help of her Archbishop of Canterbury, the learned antiquarian, Matthew Parker, who had risen from humble origins to be the friend of her mother and her own childhood tutor,

Queen Elizabeth struggled against the forces which pressed with ever-growing demands for further church reform. These were led by Reformation-minded clergy who had fled from England during the reign of Queen Mary, unable to accommodate themselves to her restoration of Catholicism. For the most part they had lived with Reformation congregations on the continent, in Germany, the Netherlands, and under John Calvin in Geneva. With the accession of Elizabeth these Maryan exiles, as they are called, trooped back to England, fired with reforming zeal. They called for the stripping from English churches of all vestiges of what they termed popish idolatry; they rebelled against episcopal control, attacking the hierarchy of Anglican bishops and all the institutions of church government; they flouted the regulations which called for the licensing of preachers; they stressed the literal interpretation of the Bible and the paramount authority of individual conscience. They cited the Old Testament in urging the death penalty for adultery, blasphemy, and heresy, and they were the most vehement force in the persecution of Catholic priests. Many had embraced the Calvinist doctrine of predestination and had come to see themselves as the "elect" of God in a world generally marked for eternal perdition. Their struggle with the Anglican church, however, was never so much over theological principles as it was over church organization and government. These rebellious reformers came generally to be known as Puritans, but there was wide diversity among them in religious as well as political beliefs. Before the end of the seventeenth century, they had split into a multitude of sects — Brownists, Anabaptists, the Family of Love, and so forth.

With their doctrines of prudence, thrift, and hard work, these dissenters appealed strongly to the rising commercial classes of England. Although they were present in some numbers in every part of England, London was their centre. In the House of Commons they found their special voice and before the end of Elizabeth's reign exercised a decisive control. Their dominance in London caused constant problems for the theatres, which they opposed vociferously. Ultimately they comprised a greater threat to the Anglican church than did the Catholic opposition, and it was a Puritan revolution which was to bring about the first example in all European history of the trial and execution of a king by his own people.

It is obvious that a writer such as Shakespeare, alive as he was to all of the conflicting issues of his age, could never entirely ignore in his plays the crucial problems posed by these religious struggles, in spite of the censorship which made religious controversy one of the most dangerous of all issues upon which a dramatist might touch. His religious sympathies accordingly have been one of the longest and most acrimoniously debated of all subjects. Most commentators have argued that he wrote firmly in the Anglican tradition, but we must recognize that this tradition also has dominated Shakespeare scholarship of the last four centuries, and that those who have approached the question with Catholic sympathies have often come to quite opposite conclusions. About all we can say with certainty is that Shakespeare's plays are generally free from the virulent anti-Catholicism we may find in the work of such contemporaries as Thomas Nashe or Robert Greene, and that when Shakespeare does appear to be deriding the Puritans — and the ever-mounting Puritan assault upon the stage might have given him ample reason to do so, whatever his personal religious sympathies — he does so in a relatively gentle fashion, and never with the scornful satire of Ben Jonson or Thomas Middleton. But these facts may be reflections merely of the "gentle" nature of Shakespeare to which some of his contemporary writers have given witness. The truth is that we cannot come to any final agreement about Shakespeare's religious beliefs through the study of his plays, but it is everywhere apparent that he was concerned with the great religious issues of his age, and the many places where he touches upon them will, no doubt, continue to inspire conjecture and debate.

2

The Life of Shakespeare

◇◇◇◇◇ We do not know as much about the life of William
◇◇◇◇◇
◇◇◇◇◇ Shakespeare as his position as chief of English poets would
warrant, but we know more about him than we do about virtually
any other of his contemporary dramatists, with the exception of
Ben Jonson. That we know as much as we do about Shakespeare
is in itself remarkable. Ben Jonson wrote with an eye to posterity.
He was three times imprisoned. He associated with noblemen and
was deeply involved in court entertainment, activities which leave
records behind. But there was nothing remarkable about the life
of William Shakespeare, aside from the fact of his genius. When
the aristocratic poet Sir Philip Sidney died in 1586, the event
was marked with eulogies which provide ample information for
biographers. No one in Shakespeare's day would have thought
of recording facts about the life of a humble actor and writer of
plays for the public theatre — all that Shakespeare was to his
immediate contemporaries.

As a dramatist, however, Shakespeare acquired a considerable
reputation during his own lifetime. It continued to grow in the
century following his death in 1616, accumulating as it did so an
accretion of legend and anecdote, sometimes the result of vague
recollection, sometimes of second-hand report, and often of mere
imagination. When Nicholas Rowe in 1709, some ninety-three
years after Shakespeare's death, prepared a biography of the poet
to accompany his edition of the plays, he thus had a vast body of
legend upon which to draw. Of this material he made ample but
uncritical use, so that he perpetuated ancient anecdotes about
Shakespeare which survive into our own time and which render
extremely difficult the separation of fact from fiction. The desire

to know more about the life of a man of so overpowering a genius as Shakespeare is a natural and seemingly unquenchable one. Thus speculations and inferences about him continue down to our own day.

Even if it were possible in these brief pages to examine and evaluate all the surviving legends about Shakespeare, there would be little profit in doing so. The basic facts about his life, in spite of the apocryphal matter, are known, and it is only with these facts that we need be concerned. We know them as the result of the patient efforts of a legion of scholars, mainly of our own century, who have carefully explored every scrap of evidence, and most notably the extremely well-preserved town records of Stratford-on-Avon. This market town in Warwickshire, where William Shakespeare was born, was a thriving community of about two thousand people, which, under a charter granted by King Edward VI in 1553, had been made a corporate borough. It was thus responsible for its own government, its affairs being administered by a corporation of citizens, which at one time included the poet's father, John Shakespeare.

Stratford was the center of a rich agricultural region. To it farmers brought their produce from a wide area. Within the town itself, with its half-timbered and thatched houses on broad and straight streets, tradesmen prospered. Except for the medieval city of Coventry, with its great cathedral and its religious drama still being performed yearly on Corpus Christi day, and the county seat of Warwick, with its magnificent castle, Stratford was the most important urban centre in Warwickshire. Shakespeare, unlike many of his fellow dramatists who left provincial towns for London, retained a close relation to it throughout his life. The kind of people he must have known in Stratford appear often in his plays, and the Warwickshire countryside with its distinctive plants and animals is in everything he wrote. To Stratford he returned regularly during his London years. There he retired and died, making the Church of the Holy Trinity on the banks of the Avon, where he is buried and where his monument looks down upon the altar, a mecca for lovers of Shakespeare the world over.

Although the name Shakespeare, spelled in various ways, appears often in the records of Warwickshire, we do not encounter it in specific connection with the borough of Stratford until 1552. On April 29th of that year John Shakespeare, along with Adrian Quiney and Humphrey Reynolds, was fined for keeping an unauthorized dunghill on Henley Street where all three men apparently resided, each being assessed the sum of one shilling for the offence. This John Shakespeare appears to have been the son of Richard Shakespeare, of the neighbouring village of Snitterfield, a farmer who held part of his land on lease from Robert Arden of Wilmcote, which was a hamlet about two miles from Stratford in the parish of Aston Cantlow. In 1556 John Shakespeare purchased a tenement in Greenhill Street in Stratford, as well as a house and garden in Henley Street, and at some later date, probably in 1575, he purchased the house adjoining it. In one of these houses — we are not certain which — was the shop in which he dealt in wool and practised the trade of glove making. In this house the dramatist was born. By 1557 John Shakespeare had apparently prospered sufficiently to marry Mary Arden, the daughter of his father's landlord. He thus further increased his fortune, for in 1556 Mary had inherited from her father sixty acres of land in Wilmcote and the revenue from it. To John and Mary Shakespeare, following the birth of two daughters who died in infancy, William Shakespeare was born in April of 1564. We do not know the exact date of his birth, but since the parish register at Stratford records his baptism on April 26 and since three days usually elapsed between birth and baptism, we assume that he was born on April 23, a particularly felicitous day because it is also the feast day of St. George, patron saint of England.

Five more children were to be born to John and Mary Shakespeare. By the time of William's birth the Shakespeare family had begun to attain a position of some prominence in Stratford. Soon after becoming a property owner by the purchase of the house in Henley Street, John Shakespeare was named one of the two "tasters" of the borough of Stratford, whose function it was to see that bakers and brewers abided by government regulations in the making of bread and ale. This was but the first of his various municipal appointments. He served as a juror, a constable, and an assessor of fines. In October of 1561 he was appointed one of the two chamberlains whose duty it was to superintend municipal finances. In

1566 he was elected Alderman and in 1568 he was named High Bailiff of Stratford, the highest possible office in the municipal government. When his term expired in 1571, he was elected Chief Alderman to his successor in the office. His rise in civic prominence, and presumably in economic status as well, continued until about 1577 when he began to have financial difficulties. After some twenty years of faithful attendance at council meetings, John Shakespeare absented himself from the meeting on January 23, 1577, and, except for one possible occasion, never attended a meeting again.

Just what was behind John Shakespeare's sudden reversal of fortune we do not know, but the evidence that it occurred is ample. In 1576 he had been sufficiently prosperous to apply to the College of Heralds for a coat of arms and the right to call himself a gentleman rather than a yeoman. As a man of property who held important municipal offices, he had a strong claim to the honour. He was married, moreover, to the daughter of Robert Arden, a gentleman and landowner with roots in Warwickshire going back to the time of William the Conqueror. His petition appears to have been either dropped or denied, for it was not granted until twenty years had passed. In 1578 John Shakespeare mortgaged his wife's estate, and he was himself declared incapable of paying the assessment of 3s. 4d. required of aldermen to support the levy of troops. That he was relieved by the council of various other financial obligations, such as a contribution of 4d. a week to the poor, gives further evidence of a fallen financial condition.

He suffered a severe blow in June of 1580 when he and a certain hat maker from Nottingham, named John Audley, were bound over to the court of the Queen's Bench to give surety against a possible breach of the peace. We do not know the details of this episode, but both men failed to appear in court, and John Shakespeare was fined £20 for defaulting on his bond and another £20 for failing to bring John Audley into court. Forty pounds in Shakespeare's day was a considerable loss to be suffered by a man in an already weakened financial position, but the very fact that so large a fine was levied against him indicates also that John Shakespeare was regarded by the justices of the Queen's Bench as a man of some means. In the summer of 1582, John Shakespeare himself appeared before a justice of the peace to request "sureties of the peace against

Ralph Cawdrey, William Russell, Thomas Logginge and Robert Young, for fear of death and mutilation of his limbs." We do not know what caused this quarrel of John Shakespeare with his neighbours, as all of these men were, Ralph Cawdrey being bailiff of Stratford. It should be noted that whatever financial losses John Shakespeare may have suffered, he retained his business and his property in Henley Street, and he retained his position on the corporation council until 1587, when a new alderman was appointed to replace him because "Mr. Shaxspere dothe not come to the halles when they be warned nor hathe not done of longe tyme." By this time his son William may have already arrived in London, but there is no reason to assume that he left Stratford to escape a life of poverty, or that he was destitute during his early London years.

It has been suggested that John Shakespeare's financial difficulties and his failure to attend council meetings may have had some relation to the persecution of Catholic recusants which became particularly severe in 1577 when John Whitgift, an ardent Protestant reformer, was made Bishop of Worcester, a diocese which included Stratford-on-Avon. All those who did not regularly attend Church of England services were subject to fine, imprisonment, or both. It has been conjectured that John Shakespeare's appearance before the court of the Queen's Bench in 1580 may have had some relation to these persecutions. In 1592 his name appeared on a list of Warwickshire persons who were not attending church services, with the additional note that John Shakespeare was among those who were not attending because of fear of being arrested for debt. Since such arrest on Sundays was legal, this is not an implausible reason. Although Whitgift's zeal for religious conformity extended to Puritans as well as Catholics, it is quite clear that the list of names in question was of persons suspected of Catholic recusancy, although it is not at all clear that all persons on the list were in fact recusants. Whether John Shakespeare had or had not returned to the old faith and risked the consequent civil liabilities has been the subject of much debate, and the matter probably never will be resolved with finality.

It has sometimes been argued that John Shakespeare could neither read nor write because he regularly made a mark rather than signing his name to indicate his presence at council meetings. But this is no evidence of illiteracy. It was the custom for the town clerk to write out the names of the council members and for each of them to put his mark next to his name. Adrian Quiney, in whose handwriting letters are preserved, made such a mark. The extensive record-keeping required by John Shakespeare's various municipal offices makes it certain that he was fully literate. He lived on until 1601 and was buried on September 8 of that year, leaving no will behind him. Of all of the pieces of property which are known to have passed through his hands, only the adjoining houses on Henley Street are known to have been inherited by the dramatist.

The Stratford Grammar School

While there are records of the affairs of John Shakespeare, there are no records at all of his son William, until we find him applying for a license to marry at the age of eighteen. And indeed there is no reason why anyone should expect to find records of the doings of a Stratford schoolboy. We know absolutely nothing about William Shakespeare's boyhood, although, since he was the son of a citizen of some prominence, we can conjecture with reasonable certainty that at the age of six or seven he was enrolled in the Stratford grammar school, and the chances are that he remained there until 1580, when he was sixteen. While no list of the students attending school in sixteenth-century Stratford has survived, we know a good deal about the school itself.

A free school and an almshouse had been established in Stratford in the thirteenth century by the religious Guild of the Holy Cross, when the town itself was part of the vast manorial holdings of the bishops of Worcester. Following the accession of King Edward VI in 1547 the Guild was suppressed and the church lands taken over by the crown. When Stratford was granted its corporate charter in 1553, the school was reorganized as the King's New School of Stratford-Upon-Avon. Students were generally admitted at the age of seven if they could demonstrate an ability to read and write English and an aptitude for the study of Latin grammar. They were expected to have acquired these at an elementary school, where young boys were taught by a schoolmaster licensed by the bishop, usually at the same time that his wife taught needlework to the girls. They learned to read from a "hornbook," a single sheet of paper containing the alphabet and some prayer, usually the Paternoster in English, mounted on a wooden board for protection and covered with a sheet of transparent horn. From this the child passed to the Absey book or *ABC with Catechism,* which contained in addition to the alphabet various religious exercises and a series of precepts governing the duties of subjects.

Shakespeare presumably had completed this training by the age of seven and entered the grammar school in 1571 when its master was Walter Roche, an Oxford B.A. Roche resigned to become a lawyer in town towards the end of 1571, and was replaced by another Oxford graduate named Simon Hunt. Students were divided into two groups, the older boys under the supervision of the master and the younger under that of an usher. Shakespeare may never have come under Hunt's influence, for by the time he was ready for the upper school, probably in 1575, Hunt may already have espoused Catholicism and fled to Douai in France where he entered the seminary for the training of missionaries. From Douai he went to Rome where in 1578 he became a member of the Society of Jesus. Shakespeare was certainly taught by Hunt's successor, a Welshman named Thomas Jenkins who had taken his B.A. at St. John's College, Oxford, in 1566 and his M.A. in 1570. Jenkins remained as master of the Stratford grammar school until 1579, and it has been suggested with some probability that it is he who served as a model for the Welsh schoolmaster, Sir Hugh Evans, in Shakespeare's *Merry Wives of Windsor.* The masters of the Stratford grammar school were learned men, well trained in the classics, and under their tutelage Shakespeare could become an excellent Latin scholar.

The school day was long, beginning at 6:00 A.M. in summer and at 7:00 in winter, and ending at 5:00 P.M. There was a brief interval for breakfast at 9:00, and a period between 11:00 A.M. and 1:00 P.M when the boys went home for lunch with their families. Fifteen minutes of play were allowed at 3:00 P.M. Discipline was very strict and punishments were severe, but on Thursdays and Saturdays there were sports in the afternoon, and there were holidays at Christmas, Easter, and Whitsuntide, comprising about forty days in all throughout the year. The first year of the lower school was devoted to the memorization of the principles and illustrations in William Lyly's

Latin Grammar, and the following years to Latin speech, composition, and reading. The speaking of Latin was learned by memoriz-
ing sentences out of standard phrase books, some of which Shakespeare holds up to ridicule in his early comedies. In the upper
school there was training in logic and in rhetoric.

As a schoolboy Shakespeare would have read the *Bucolica*
(1502) of Mantuan, Christianized pastoral poems written in imitation of Virgil's *Eclogues.* He would have read the *Eclogues* and
the *Æneid* of Virgil as well, the poems of Horace, and particularly
the *Metamorphoses* of Ovid, upon which he was to draw throughout his career as a dramatist. He would have read Cæsar and Livy,
and he would have studied Cicero intensively as a particular model
for his own Latin prose composition. His first experience with
drama might have come from his study of the ten tragedies attributed to Seneca and of the comedies of Terence and Plautus,
which he was later to imitate in *The Comedy of Errors.* It is possible that he may have acted, for the performance of Latin plays
in the schools was a firmly established custom by Shakespeare's time.
It is likely that while he was making the acquaintance of Latin
drama at school, he was able to see the English interludes which
were being performed in Stratford from time to time by visiting
companies of professional actors. The earls of Leicester, Worcester,
and Warwick all had companies of players who appeared in Stratford.

In the light of the training which a normal schoolboy would
have undergone at the Stratford grammar school, it is difficult to
understand why the extent of Shakespeare's learning has been so
much a subject for debate. When Ben Jonson wrote of Shakespeare's
"small Latin, and less Greek," he seems to have been exhibiting
his own sense of superiority more than any real knowledge of
Shakespeare's attainments. In 1767 the Cambridge scholar, Richard
Farmer, inaugurated more than a century of debate when he published his *Essay on the Learning of Shakespeare,* in which he
argued that any knowledge of the classics which Shakespeare may
have had was derived from English translations. Today almost
all scholars are agreed that Shakespeare was a well-educated man
for his time, that he certainly continued to further his education by
wide reading throughout his lifetime, and that there is no display

of learning in any one of his plays which could not have been acquired at the Stratford grammar school.

Anne Hathaway

Since so little real evidence of Shakespeare's early days in Stratford has survived, it is perhaps natural that a vast body of anecdote and legend should have sprung up about this period of his life. Stories say that he was withdrawn from school because of his father's poverty; that he was apprenticed to his father's trade; that he showed a particular talent as a butcher; that he was widely known for his wit; that he engaged in deer poaching and was whipped for it; that he was forced into an unwelcome marriage; and that he left Stratford to escape his wife, to escape punishment for poaching, to escape impressment into military service, and for a whole host of other reasons, none of which will stand the test of close examination. A difficult duty of the serious biographer has involved the examination of the origins of each of these legends and their consequent dismissal as either impossible or, at best, impossible to prove.

The verifiable record begins in November of 1582, when the office of the Bishop of Worcester issued a license for the marriage of William Shakespeare and Anne Hathaway of Temple Grafton, a tiny village some six miles from Stratford. Most Elizabethan marriages did not require licenses; they were simply performed by the parish priest (of either the bride or the groom if they did not reside in the same parish) and recorded in the parish register. The priest was required to pronounce banns for the wedding — so that any legal impediment might come to light in time — on three successive Sundays or holidays before the marriage ceremony was performed. Banns could not, however, be proclaimed during the seasons of Advent or Lent, and thus an observance of the full three readings could sometimes result in a considerable delay of the marriage. In 1582–1583 the Advent prohibition lasted from December 2, 1582 through January 13, 1583, and that of Lent from January 27 through April 7, 1583. During the period from December 2 to April 7, there were thus only two weeks during which banns could be announced in church. The reading of banns could be curtailed or eliminated entirely, however, if a license was obtained from the bishop, and this is almost certainly what occurred with William Shakespeare and Anne Hathaway, for their license permitted them to be married after only one reading of the banns. Such special licenses were not unusual; the Bishop of Worcester issued some ninety-two of them during the same year that Shakespeare's was issued.

There is thus no need for further speculation about the suspension of the banns. A confusion in the records, however, has led to some additional and quite unnecessary conjecture. Before a license could be issued a bond had to be posted to guarantee that there were no legal impediments to the marriage. A bond for £40 was accordingly signed by Fulke Sandells and John Richardson on November 28, 1582, lest there "appeare any Lawfull Lett or impediment by reason of any precontract consanguinitie affinitie or by any other lawfull meanes whatsoeuer but that William Shakespeare on thone partie, and Anne Hathwey of Stratford in the Dioces of Worcester maiden may lawfully solemnize matrimony together." This document is extant in the archives of Worcester, and it is our only documentary evidence of the marriage, for neither the request for the license nor the license itself has survived. The license, however, was issued, and a clerk duly entered a record of it in the bishop's register, which has survived. He referred to the bride as Anne Whately rather than Anne Hathaway. This cannot possibly represent anything other than a scribal error, and there is certainly no need to search for an "other woman" in the life of young Shakespeare. We have no record of the actual marriage. It was probably performed in the church of some parish whose register has not survived, perhaps that of Temple Grafton.

We know very little about Anne Hathaway or of Shakespeare's relations with her. Anne must have been pregnant at the time of the marriage, for their first child, Susanna, was baptized in Stratford on May 26, 1583. Some biographers like to speculate that Anne and William had lived together on the basis of their marriage contract or *sponsalia de præsenti,* a declaration of marriage before two witnesses with no clergyman necessarily present, a practice which was quite common in Shakespeare's day, which carried no social stigma, and which he himself made an issue in his play,

Measure for Measure. There is no evidence, however, that they ever lived together before their actual marriage.

Anne Hathaway was probably the daughter of Richard Hathaway of Hewland Farm in the neighbouring village of Shottery, about a mile from Stratford, which is today shown to visitors as "Anne Hathaway's cottage." He had married twice and Anne, his daughter by his first wife, was twenty-five years old when he made his will in September of 1581. She was thus some eight years older than her husband. Fulke Sandells and John Richardson, who posted bond to allow the marriage license, were probably friends of her father, for they were farmers of Shottery and both are named in Richard Hathaway's will. Richardson was a witness and Sandells was named as overseer. This will, dated September 1, 1581, provided for a sum of ten marks (£6. 13s. 4d.) to be paid to Anne (or Agnes) on her wedding day. Richard Hathaway apparently died some days after the preparation of his will.

In 1585 the twins, Hamnet and Judith, were born and christened in the church at Stratford on February 2. It is likely that the godparents were a Stratford baker named Hamnet Sadler and his wife Judith, apparently close friends of the Shakespeares, since Hamnet Sadler later served as a witness to Shakespeare's will and was granted a legacy in it. Hamnet Shakespeare died in 1596 at the age of eleven, but both daughters lived to maturity. Susanna married a physician named John Hall and continued to live in Stratford. Their single child, a daughter who became Lady Bernard, was Shakespeare's last living descendant at the time of her death in 1670. Judith married Thomas Quiney and had three sons, all of whom died young. Judith herself died in 1662, and, like her sons, was buried in Stratford.

Of the details of William Shakespeare's life with Anne Hathaway we have no evidence — and we could not possibly expect to have — but, as we noted, during his years as a dramatist in London he returned to Stratford regularly. Although Anne and the children did not accompany Shakespeare to London, for which he left shortly after the birth of the twins, there is some possibility that they may have lived with him there for a time, for in 1596 Shakespeare was paying taxes in the Parish of St. Helen's in London on a house which must have been far too large for a man living alone. Following the death of Hamnet he moved into smaller lodgings in Southwark. When Shakespeare in 1597 bought New Place, the largest house in Stratford, his wife and daughters were comfortably installed in it, and at New Place he lived with his wife from his retirement in 1611 to his death in 1616. That he bequeathed to her his "second best bed" in his will may indicate nothing more than that the "best bed" was already hers as part of her widow's dower. Anne died at New Place on August 6, 1623, at the age of sixty-seven and was buried in the churchyard of Holy Trinity. Apparently she had expressed a desire to be placed in her husband's grave, but the sexton was afraid to open Shakespeare's grave because it was marked with a warning inscription.

The "Dark Years"

By 1592 Shakespeare was living in London, was connected with the theatre, and had written some plays which had earned him recognition as a dramatist and the envy of at least one of his fellow writers for the stage. Just when he left Stratford, how he became connected with the theatre, and how he supported himself before his first successes as a dramatist we do not know; these matters accordingly have been the subject of much speculation. The seven or so years for which we do not know how to account have been labelled the "dark years," but there is nothing very "dark" about them. Shakespeare may have made his first contact with the theatre through one of the many travelling companies which visited Stratford and may have returned to London with the players after demonstrating his ability as an actor. In 1583 Stratford was visited by the Earl of Worcester's Men, the Earl of Oxford's Men, and the Earl of Essex's Men. An unidentified company played in the town in 1585, and both the Earl of Essex's and the Earl of Leicester's Players were there in 1587, the year in which Shakespeare is most likely to have left for London.

There is also some reason to believe that he may have served for a time as a schoolmaster in some country town. His education at the Stratford grammar school would not have qualified him for the position of master, but it would have made him capable of serving as an usher or assistant to the master, in charge of the education of the younger boys. The biographer and antiquarian John Aubrey (1625–1700), who was an assiduous collector of data about great Englishmen of the past, in the account of Shakespeare which he included in his *Brief Lives* (published from his notes after his death), reported learning on a visit to Stratford that Shakespeare had practised his father's trade as a butcher, that "when he kill'd a calfe, he would do it in a high style, and make a Speech," that he had become an actor in London at about the age of eighteen, that he was "a handsome well shap't man: very good company, and of a very readie and pleasant smooth witt." In some of these details Aubrey was wrong, for Shakespeare's father was a glover and not a butcher, and "killing a calf" seems to have been some kind of parlor game with no relation to the trade of butchering. But Aubrey adds another bit of information which has the ring of plausibility:

> Though as Ben Johnson sayes of him, that he had but little Latine and lesse Greeke, He understood Latine pretty well: for he had been in his younger yeares a Schoolmaster in the Country.

This information Aubrey reports that he had had from William Beeston, a theatrical figure whose father, Christopher Beeston, had begun his career as an actor in Shakespeare's company, probably in 1596, and had remained with it until 1602 when he left it for Worcester's Men. He had thus spent some six years in close association with Shakespeare. William Beeston is a reliable authority, for there can be no doubt that his father had spoken often of the most illustrious of his fellows. If Aubrey is right — and we have every reason to believe that he was a careful reporter of what he heard — we might explain the many allusions to Elizabethan schoolbooks in such early plays as *Love's Labour's Lost* as reflecting Shakespeare's recent experience in teaching from these books, rather than as his less likely recollection of them from his own days in the Stratford grammar school.

One of the most persistent of the legends concerning Shakespeare's departure from Stratford was told by Nicholas Rowe, who presumably heard it from the actor Thomas Betterton, although it seems to have been first told by Richard Davies, a Cotswold clergyman who died in 1708. Shakespeare, according to this account, had stolen deer in a park belonging to Sir Thomas Lucy at Charlecote.

He was whipped and imprisoned. In revenge he wrote a ballad in mockery of Sir Thomas, as a result of which he was so severely persecuted that he was forced to flee from Stratford. There was no deer park at Charlecote in the sixteenth century, but this fact of itself does not disprove the story, for the surrounding woods had many deer, and Sir Thomas Lucy was concerned with preservation of the game of Warwickshire. That there may be some germ of truth in the legend is not impossible. Davies further suggested that Lucy was ridiculed as Justice Shallow in *The Merry Wives of Windsor* and *Henry IV, Part II.* It is now more generally believed, however, that Shakespeare's ridicule in those plays was directed against one William Gardiner, a Surrey justice of the peace with whom Shakespeare and his company had some difficulties in 1596.

There are many other stories and conjectures. Worthy of some notice is the fact that Alexander Houghton of Lea in Lancashire, in a will prepared in 1581, left his brother Thomas his musical instruments and "al maner of play clothes yf he be mynded to keppe and doe keppe players." If his brother chose not to "keppe players," he was requested to befriend, take into his service, or find a new master for "William Shakeshafte nowe dwellynge with me." Since Shakeshafte was a variant form of Shakespeare, which the dramatist's own grandfather is known to have used, it has been conjectured that William Shakespeare, before his marriage, had already served as an actor in the service of a Lancashire gentleman. Some scholars accordingly believe that the "dark years" were spent by Shakespeare as a player in various provincial companies, from which he naturally made his way to the greater opportunities of London. There were, however, Shakespeares and Shakeshaftes in Lancashire as well as in the Midlands, and there may be nothing further involved than coincidence.

The "Upstart Crow"

Edmund Malone in 1790 stated without supporting evidence of any kind that Shakespeare's first job in the theatre was that of assistant to the prompter. If true, this would have been as good an introduction as any into the craft at which he was soon to excel. Of Shakespeare's early associations in London we know nothing, although it is more than likely that he quickly renewed acquaintance

with a fellow townsman named Richard Field, who had left Stratford in 1579 and by 1586 was well established as a printer in London.
It was Field who printed and published Shakespeare's *Venus and
Adonis* in 1593 and *The Rape of Lucrece* in 1594. Our first clear
reference to Shakespeare in London comes from the pen of Robert
Greene, a prolific writer of prose romances, poems, and pamphlets
of various kinds, as well as plays. Greene's experiences with the
theatre companies had apparently embittered him, and as a university graduate, proud of his "M.A. from both universities," he
looked down upon the actors. Shortly before his death in 1592 he
expressed his regret for his own bohemian life in a pamphlet
called *Greene's Groats-worth of Wit bought with a million of
Repentance,* and to it he appended a letter in which he warned
his fellow university men to beware of trusting the actors. It was
addressed almost certainly to George Peele, Thomas Nashe, and
Christopher Marlowe, and in it he singled out for special invective
a new writer, who can be none other than William Shakespeare:

> Base minded men, all three of you, if by my miserie you be not warnd:
> for vnto none of you (like mee) sought those burres to cleaue: those
> Puppets (I meane) that spake from our mouths, those Anticks garnisht
> in our colours. Is it not strange, that I, to whom they all haue bene
> beholding: is it not like that you, to whome they all haue beene be-
> holding, shall (were yee in that case as I am now) bee both at once
> of them forsaken? Yes trust them not: for there is an vpstart Crow,
> beautified with our feathers, that with his *Tygers hart wrapt in a
> Players hyde,* supposes he is as well able to bombast out a blanke
> verse as the best of you: and beeing an absolute *Iohannes fac totum,*
> is in his owne conceit the onely Shake-scene in a country. O that I
> might intreat your rare wits to be imploied in more profitable courses:
> & let those Apes imitate your past excellence, and neuer more acquaint
> them with your admired inuentions.

Greene did not live to see the publication of his tract, for he had
been dead for seventeen days when it was entered in the Stationers'
Register on September 20, 1592. That the "onely Shake-scene in a
country" refers to Shakespeare there can be no doubt, and the
"Tygers hart wrapt in a Players hyde" is Greene's attempt to
ridicule a line in Shakespeare's play, *Henry VI, Part III*: "O Tiger's
heart wrapp'd in a woman's hide" (I.iv. 137). The reasons for

Greene's attack, and just what he is accusing Shakespeare of, however, have been matters of great controversy among scholars.

Edmund Malone in *A Dissertation on the Three Parts of Henry VI* (1790), argued that Greene was accusing Shakespeare of plagiarism, and since a line from *Henry VI, Part III,* is chosen for derision, that this plagiarism must have included the second and third parts of *Henry VI,* which Malone held to have been originally written by Robert Greene, perhaps in collaboration with one or more of the other dramatists to whom he had addressed his letter. These original plays, Malone argued, were extant in two quartos, *The First Part of the Contention betwixt the two famous Houses of York and Lancaster* and *The True Tragedy of Richard Duke of York,* printed in 1594 and 1595 respectively and resembling very closely *Henry VI, Parts II and III,* which were printed for the first time in the Shakespeare folio of 1623. Samuel Johnson had argued, on the other hand, for Shakespeare's sole authorship of all three of the *Henry VI* plays, and in this he has been followed by a long line of scholars, most notably by Peter Alexander in *Shakespeare's "Henry VI" and "Richard III".* These scholars have argued that Greene is not charging Shakespeare with plagiarism but instead mocking a mere actor who has had the effrontery to compete with university men in the writing of plays.

A key part of Alexander's argument lies in his belief that *The Contention* and *The True Tragedy* are not source plays for *Henry VI, Parts II and III.* He holds that they are "bad quartos" of Shakespeare's plays, derived from them by memorial reconstruction. That this is their true nature and that Malone was wrong in seeing them as Shakespeare's sources are premises now generally accepted by scholars, and most are inclined to believe that it is the upstart actor rather than the plagiarist whom Greene is deriding. But the fact that Malone was wrong about one matter does not necessarily mean that he was wrong about the other. Some scholars, most notably John Dover Wilson in his New Cambridge editions of the *Henry VI* plays, still maintain that Shakespeare began his career as a dramatist by revising the work of older playwrights.

Greene's *Groats-Worth of Wit* was printed after its author's death by Henry Chettle, himself a dramatist and hack writer. Apparently the publication of Greene's scurrilous attack, not only against Shakespeare but also against Marlowe, whom he called an atheist, had some repercussions. Important persons appear to have attacked Chettle for his hand in the affair, and Thomas Nashe (a close friend of Greene's) appears to have been accused generally of having had a share in Greene's pamphlet. Chettle accordingly felt the need to clear himself of complicity. In the Preface to a pamphlet called *Kind-Harts Dreame,* entered in the Stationers' Register on December 8, 1592, he took pains to exonerate Nashe of any complicity in Greene's work and to limit his own responsibility to the mere preparation of Greene's work for the press. Chettle's apology is important for its indication of the high esteem in which Shakespeare by 1592 was held in London, and for its suggestion that at this early date Shakespeare already had powerful friends who were willing to come to his assistance and to vouch for his character when he was falsely slandered. Of Marlowe and Shakespeare, Chettle writes:

> With neither of them that take offence was I acquainted, and with one of them [Marlowe] I care not if I neuer be: The other [Shakespeare], whome at that time I did not so much spare, as since I wish I had, for that as I haue moderated the heate of liuing writers, and might have vsde my owne discretion (especially in such a case) the Author beeing dead, that I did not, I am as sory as if the originall fault had beene my fault, because my selfe haue seene his demeanor no lesse ciuill than he exelent in the qualitie he professes: Besides, diuers of worship haue reported his uprightnes of dealing, which argues his honesty, and his facetious grace in writting, that approoues his Art.

The body of plays upon which this reputation of Shakespeare's rested must have included the three parts of *Henry VI,* which some scholars would date as early as 1588, and it is probable that they included the sequel play, *Richard III.* Thus Shakespeare at this early date had not only begun his career as an historical dramatist, but in this great tetralogy he had raised that kind of drama to a higher artistic level than that achieved by any previous dramatist.

It may well be that the *Henry VI* plays were the very first that Shakespeare wrote, a widely held notion which stems in part from Malone's interpretation of Greene's attack. Some scholars think that Shakespeare began not with history, but with Plautine comedy, and that the earliest of his plays may have been *The Comedy of*

Errors, completed around 1589. This was followed by *The Taming of the Shrew, The Two Gentlemen of Verona,* and *Love's Labour's Lost.* Shakespeare appears also to have begun his career as a writer of tragedy at this early stage. In *Titus Andronicus,* unquestionably the earliest of his tragedies, he imitated and surpassed the popularization of Seneca which Thomas Kyd, sometime before 1591, had made fashionable in *The Spanish Tragedy.* The dates of all these plays are uncertain, but there is a strong likelihood that they were all completed before June 15, 1592, for in that month the London theatres were closed because of the plague, and they did not open again, except intermittently, until the beginning of 1594. During this period Shakespeare turned to non-dramatic poetry and produced his *Venus and Adonis* and *The Rape of Lucrece,* both of which he dedicated to Henry Wriothesley, Earl of Southampton, whose patronage he apparently was seeking; whether or not he actually enjoyed it we do not know. Although there is probably nothing in Shakespeare scholarship more disputed than the date of his sonnets, it is possible that he was writing them during these years. Some scholars think that they had been completed as early as 1589.

The Lord Chamberlain's Men

When the theatres reopened in 1594 Shakespeare had already become a member of the Lord Chamberlain's Men, one of the two great companies which were, under various names, to dominate the London theatres until their closing by the Puritans in 1642, the other being the Lord Admiral's Men. On March 15, 1594–1595, payment of £20 from the royal treasury was made to "Will Kempe Will Shakespeare & Richarde Burbage seruantes to the Lord Chambleyne" for the performance of two plays at court on December 26 and 28 of 1594. That Shakespeare should have been one of those delegated to receive payment for the company indicates how important a member of it he had become, and it suggests that his importance was as a dramatist, for certainly he could not be coupled with either Will Kempe or Richard Burbage on the basis of acting ability. With the Lord Chamberlain's Men, Shakespeare was to spend the rest of his career, never writing for any other company, and doing much to insure its paramount position among its rivals. How he came to be associated with this company, however, we do not know.

One widely held theory is that Shakespeare began with Lord Pembroke's Men, a company for which Kyd and Marlowe wrote and which included Gabriel Spencer as its principal actor. The company was under the patronage of Sir Henry Herbert, second Earl of Pembroke, the husband of Mary Sidney (sister of Sir Philip Sidney), and father of the young lord to whom many scholars believe that Shakespeare's sonnets were dedicated and to whom, along with his brother, the First Folio of Shakespeare's plays was dedicated in 1623. This company toured the provinces during the plague of 1592 and 1593 and apparently encountered great financial difficulties, for the players were forced to sell some of their play books, and the company disbanded upon its return to London in 1594. If Shakespeare was a member of this company, he did not accompany it on the provincial tour.

Others believe that Shakespeare began as a member of Lord Strange's Men, although the extensive records of this company's doings between 1592 and 1594 contain no mention of his name. In 1591–1592 it combined with the Lord Admiral's Men for six performances at court, and Edward Alleyn, leading actor of the Admiral's Men, accompanied it on a tour of the provinces. The license for this tour, issued on May 6, 1593, lists as members of the company, "Edward Allen, servant to the right honourable the Lord High Admiral: William Kemp, Thomas Pope, John Hemminges, Augustine Phillipes and George Brian, being all one company, servants to our good Lord the Lord Strainge." That Shakespeare is not named in this license has been taken as evidence that he was not a member of the company, but he could not have gone on the tour with it if he had been in London writing his nondramatic poems.

After September 25, 1593, when Ferdinando Stanley, Lord Strange, became Earl of Derby, the company was known as the Earl of Derby's Men. In April of 1594 the earl died and the company was left without a patron. By June of 1594 the tie with the Lord Admiral's Men was broken, Alleyn remaining with that company, and the remnants of Derby's Men secured the patronage of the Lord Chamberlain, Henry Carey, and became known as the Lord Chamberlain's Men. To replace Alleyn the company acquired Richard Burbage as principal actor. It has been suggested that if Shakespeare was not already a member of the company, he joined it at this time. Upon the death of Henry Carey in 1596, the company passed into the service of his son, George Carey, Lord Hunsdon, and was known as Lord Hunsdon's Men until 1597 when Lord Hunsdon succeeded his father as Lord Chamberlain and the company resumed its former title.

Richard Burbage was the son of James Burbage, the leader of the Earl of Leicester's Men, who in 1576 had built the Theatre, the first of the English public playhouses. Here, in the liberty of Holywell in Shoreditch, north of the city of London, Shakespeare's plays now came to be performed, as well as at the Curtain, a neighbouring theatre which had passed into the hands of the Burbages in 1585. James Burbage had leased the land upon which the Theatre was built from one Gyles Alleyn, and this lease expired in April of 1597. In February of 1597, during the course of negotiations with Alleyn over the renewal of the lease, James Burbage died. Alleyn apparently was not anxious to come to any agreement, for a clause in his lease provided that if the Theatre was not removed from its site upon the lease's expiration it would become Alleyn's property.

On December 28, 1598, while Gyles Alleyn was absent in the country, James Burbage's sons, Richard and Cuthbert, who now assumed the management of the family's financial affairs, gathered a group of friends and after forcefully driving off Alleyn's servants, tore down the Theatre. They transported the lumber across the river to the Bankside, where a plot of land already had been leased from one Nicholas Brend, and there they built the theatre which they called the Globe. Since Richard and Cuthbert Burbage were not able to finance this venture by themselves, they formed a syndicate, keeping half ownership of the new theatre for themselves and dividing the other half among five of the chief members of the Lord Chamberlain's Men: John Heminges, Thomas Pope, Augustine Phillips, Will Kempe, and William Shakespeare. Kempe, however, appears to have had some kind of quarrel with the company at this time, for he did not take up his share.

That Shakespeare already had sufficient wealth to join in this project would by itself be evidence that he was a man of some property. This is corroborated by the tax roles which indicate that he was living in a comfortable house in Bishopsgate in 1596 (perhaps with his family) and by the fact that in May of 1597 he was able to purchase for the goodly sum of £60 New Place, the largest house in Stratford, built by Sir Hugh Clopton in 1496, when he was Lord Mayor of London. Some evidence of Shakespeare's prosperity is provided also by an extant letter from a Stratford neighbor, Richard Quiney, written on October 25, 1598, from the Bell Inn in Carter Lane, while Quiney was in London on Stratford business. He requests that Shakespeare raise for him the sum of £30 that he needs for his affairs in the city. In 1596 the coat of arms for which John Shakespeare had applied twenty years earlier was finally granted, and in 1597 William joined with his father in an unsuccessful chancery suit in which they sought to regain lands mortgaged at the time of John Shakespeare's financial troubles in 1578. William Shakespeare maintained close ties with Stratford while he prospered in London. He bought property in his native town, and remained for the rest of his career a part owner of the theatre where his plays were performed. This too contributed to his growing prosperity.

On the Bankside, south of the Thames, what was soon to be the principal theatre district of London had already begun to develop. There is strong reason to believe that Shakespeare was already living on the Bankside before the construction of the Globe, having moved from the house in Bishopsgate soon after the death of his son Hamnet in August of 1596. Here were the Rose theatre and the Swan, built by Francis Langley, probably late in 1595. In this new theatre Shakespeare's company may have been acting in 1596, for the records reveal Shakespeare as involved with Langley in a legal squabble. Langley apparently had quarrelled with a Surrey justice of the peace named William Gardiner, whose jurisdiction covered the theatre district. Gardiner, possibly in retaliation, attempted to drive the theatres from the Bankside, and he was joined in this enterprise by his step-son, William Wayte. On November 29, 1596, Langley, apparently fearing physical violence from his foes, demanded sureties of the peace against Gardiner. William Wayte, in turn, on November 29 demanded sureties against "William Shakespeare, Francis Langley, Dorothy Soer, wife of John Soer, and Anne Lee, for fear of death." We do not know any further details of the affair, and we know nothing of the two women involved. It has been suggested that William Gardiner was ridiculed by Shakespeare as the Justice Shallow of *Henry IV, Part II* and *The Merry Wives of Windsor.*

When Ben Jonson prepared the text of his play, *Every Man in His Humour,* for inclusion in the folio edition of his works published in 1616, he appended a list of the actors who had performed the play in 1598. Heading this list is the name of William Shakespeare. But it was as a writer of plays rather than as an actor in them that Shakespeare was making his mark. In the years immediately preceding the opening of the Globe, we see him finding new directions in all of the dramatic genres. For a noble wedding in 1595 or 1596 — for which specific wedding we cannot be sure — he wrote *A Midsummer Night's Dream.* This must have been followed shortly by *The Merchant of Venice.* At about the same time he returned to tragedy with *Romeo and Juliet,* and began his great period as a writer of history plays. Just when *King John* was written we do not know, but it is likely that it preceded *Richard II,* which was probably in existence by December of 1595. This was followed by the two parts of *Henry IV,* which must have been completed early in 1597, and it is likely that they were followed shortly by *The Merry Wives of Windsor,* written probably for performance at a feast of the Knights of the Garter in April of 1597. By 1598, Francis Meres in his *Palladis Tamia* could give eloquent testimony to Shakespeare's reputation:

> As the soule of *Euphorbus* was thought to liue in *Pythagoras:* so the sweete wittie soule of *Ouid* liues in melliflous & hony-tongued *Shakespeare,* witness his *Venus and Adonis,* his *Lucrece,* his sugred Sonnets among his priuate friends, & c.
>
> As *Plautus* and *Seneca* are accounted the best for Comedy and Tragedy among the Latines: so Shakespeare among the English is the most excellent in both the kinds for the stage; for Comedy, witnes his *Gentlemen of Verona,* his *Errors,* his *Loue labours lost,* his *Loue labours wonne,* his *Midsummers night dreame,* & his *Merchant of Venice:* for Tragedy his *Richard the 2. Richard the 3. Henry the 4. King John, Titus Andronicus* and his *Romeo and Iuliet.*

Meres is not necessarily listing all of Shakespeare's plays, since he is merely illustrating his genius. What he referred to by *"Loue labours wonne"* continues to puzzle scholars. Probably the first play to be performed at the Globe was Shakespeare's Roman tragedy, *Julius Cæsar*. Thomas Platter, a traveller from Switzerland, recorded in his diary that he had seen it there on September 21, 1599. It is likely that *Henry V* was performed there in the same year. Between 1598 and 1601 Shakespeare achieved his greatest successes as a writer of romantic comedy, for to these years belong *As You Like It, Much Ado About Nothing,* and *Twelfth Night.* Although we cannot be certain of the date of *Hamlet,* it seems to have been written at the turn of the century. *Troilus and Cressida* may have followed in 1602.

Bellott vs. Mountjoy

Some light upon Shakespeare's life in London around the turn of the century is provided by the records of a lawsuit, which was brought in 1612 by one Stephen Bellott against his father-in-law, Christopher Mountjoy, and in which Shakespeare gave testimony as a witness. Christopher Mountjoy was a Huguenot tiremaker (maker of elaborate jewelled headdresses in silver and gold), who had his house and shop in Silver Street, in the northwest of London between Cripplegate and St. Paul's. His customers included Queen Elizabeth herself. It is likely that he had supplied the theatre companies with wigs and headdresses of various kinds. Stephen Bellott was his former apprentice, and the dispute involved promises which Mountjoy had made to Bellott so as to induce him to marry his daughter. He was to have received a dowry of £60 and a bequest of an additional £200 in Mountjoy's will. The marriage between Stephen Bellott and Mary Mountjoy took place on November 19, 1604. Following the death of his wife in 1606, Mountjoy apparently began to squander his money, and Bellott brought suit in the Court of Requests to insure that his bequest would be paid. Shakespeare was called upon as a former lodger in Mountjoy's house who had been involved in the negotiations culminating in the marriage.

Various witnesses were called upon to give depositions in the

Bellott vs. Mountjoy suit, and Shakespeare appears to have come down from retirement in Stratford so as to be among them. Joan Johnson, who had been a maid in the household of the Mountjoys, Daniel Nicholas, William Eaton, and Nowell Mountjoy, brother of the defendant, all testified. The gist of their evidence was that Shakespeare, as a highly regarded friend of both parties, had been asked by the Mountjoys to approach Bellott concerning the marriage and had been a witness to Mountjoy's promises. Shakespeare's own deposition in the case immediately makes his identity as the dramatist beyond dispute:

> William Shakespeare of Stratford vpon Aven in the Countye of Warwicke gentleman of the age of xlviij yeres or thereaboutes sworne and examined the daye and yere abouesaid deposethe & sayethe . . .

The essence of his testimony is that he had indeed approached Bellott over the marriage at the request of Mrs. Mountjoy but that he failed to remember the details of the financial arrangements. Since he speaks of having known Bellott throughout the period of his apprenticeship, and since that apprenticeship began in 1598, Shakespeare may thus have been living with the Mountjoys in that year. He certainly lived with them between 1602 and 1604, and perhaps for a longer period, since he testifies that he had known Bellott and the Mountjoys for about ten years. It is interesting to speculate that Shakespeare may have acquired in the household of these French Huguenots the knowledge of French which he displayed in *Henry V.*

The lawsuit was referred from the Court of Requests to a tribunal of the elders of the Huguenot Church in London. Mountjoy was ordered by them to pay Bellott twenty nobles, but a year later they had not yet been paid. In 1614 Mountjoy was excommunicated from the Huguenot Church for "licentiousness." He died in 1620, leaving a will with no bequest to his daughter or son-in-law. Bellott himself lived until around 1646. The matter is of no importance other than for what we may glean from it about Shakespeare's life in London and for the signature of Shakespeare which appears at the bottom of his deposition, an undisputed signature, and one of the best that we have, since it was made when he was in good health.

The Booke of Sir Thomas More

Around the turn of the seventeenth century we find Shakespeare also involved in an interesting relation with some of his fellow dramatists — a relation which gives further evidence of the importance among them which he had achieved. He appears to have been called upon to make additions to a play which its authors were having difficulty in revising to the satisfaction of the Master of the Revels, one of whose duties it was to censor all plays before they could be publicly performed. This play is *The Booke of Sir Thomas More* which was never printed in Shakespeare's lifetime, but which has come down to us in British Museum Harleian Manuscript 7368. Although the date of the first writing of the play is uncertain and has long been a subject for scholarly dispute, most commentators are today inclined to place it around 1601 or 1602. The manuscript consists of the original version of the play, plus six additions to it inserted at various places and each in a different handwriting. Of the seven hands one is now generally believed to have been that of William Shakespeare. It is that of the second addition to the manuscript, and scholars refer to it as "Hand D." The other handwritings are those of Anthony Munday, who wrote out the original draft, of Thomas Dekker and Henry Chettle who collaborated with him, of a third playwright who may have been Thomas Heywood, of an unknown playhouse scribe, and of Sir Edmund Tilney, Master of the Revels, who made marginal annotations.

Sir Thomas More by the beginning of the seventeenth century had become a virtual folklore hero, and apparently a play about him was written by Munday, with some help from Chettle and Dekker, but with Munday serving as copyist for the entire play. Upon completion, it must have occurred to the authors that the play would never pass Sir Edmund Tilney's censorship, largely because of its opening scenes, which dealt with the dangerous subject of insurrection against foreigners residing in London. The play was thus revised, probably before it was submitted for censorship. It was at this time that Shakespeare appears to have been called in, preparing his three pages of addition which constitute the only notable poetic achievement in the play. The manuscript was then submitted to Tilney who, probably as he read along, wrote directions in the margins which called for further revisions. When he had completed his reading, however, it must have been obvious to him that the play would need really extensive alteration before it could be made politically acceptable. He called for a complete deletion of the insurrection scenes. His orders may have persuaded the authors that the possibility of receiving a license for the play, no matter what they did, was extremely slight, and they may thus have abandoned the project entirely. It is virtually certain that the play was never staged. It has been suggested that it may have been submitted to Tilney for censorship twice, and that its rejection for a second time was what led the authors to abandon it.

Shakespeare's authorship of the lines in question has been argued effectively in *Shakespeare's Hand in the Play of Sir Thomas More,* in which A. W. Pollard (the general editor), E. M. Thompson, W. W. Greg, J. D. Wilson, and R. W. Chambers each devote a chapter to arguing Shakespeare's authorship on the grounds of paleography, bibliography, spelling, and intellectual content. This volume was published by the Cambridge University Press in 1923, and its evidence has since been augmented by later scholars. The survival of the manuscript has been an exceedingly fortunate accident, for not only does it provide us with an important example of Shakespeare's artistry which otherwise we would not have, but in providing a clear example of Shakespeare's handwriting it has added immeasurably to our ability to establish the text of Shakespeare's plays.

The King's Men

When Queen Elizabeth died and James VI of Scotland came to England in May of 1603 to succeed her as King James I of England, the Lord Chamberlain's Men were taken under royal patronage and became known as the King's Men. Thus Shakespeare's troupe was recognized as supreme among English acting companies, and the honour afforded its members many new privileges, such as wearing the royal livery and appearing more frequently in court entertainments. As the king's servants they were called upon to participate in royal pageants and processions and were often given new livery for the occasions. When they took part, for instance, in the great coronation procession with symbolic tableaux — delayed a year because of the plague — on March 15, 1604, Shakespeare and his fellows were each presented with four yards of red cloth, according to the records of Sir George Home, Master of the Great Wardrobe. The records of the Audit Office reveal that later in 1604 Shakespeare's company was paid for participation in a celebration in Somerset House in honour of the new Spanish ambassador. Many of Shakespeare's plays were performed at court, *A Midsummer Night's Dream* in 1603, *Othello, The Merry Wives of Windsor,* and *Measure for Measure* in 1604, *Henry V, Love's Labour's Lost,* and *The Merchant of Venice* in 1605.

Various records have survived of Shakespeare's doings, both in London and in Stratford, in the early years of the seventeenth century. On May 1, 1602, Shakespeare had made the sizeable purchase of one hundred and seven acres of farm land in Old Stratford from William and John Combe for the sum of £320, and on September 28 of the same year he acquired from Walter Getley a cottage and a quarter acre of land in Chapel Lane across the garden of New Place, thus considerably augmenting his holdings in his native town. In July of 1604 he sued Philip Rogers for a debt of 3s. 10d., and in July of 1605 he paid the very large sum of £440 for a quarter interest in the lease of Stratford tithes. In that same year of 1605, Augustine Phillipps, who had long been his fellow actor, died. His will, prepared on May 4, 1605 provides a bequest "to my Fellowe William Shakespeare [of] a thirty shillings peece in gould."

On May 5, 1606, the name of Shakespeare's daughter, Susanna, appears on a list of recusants who had failed to receive communion on Easter Sunday. On June 5, 1607, she was married to John Hall in Holy Trinity Church at Stratford. The christening of their daughter, Elizabeth, was recorded on February 21, 1608. In the burial registers of the church of St. Saviour's in Southwark, close to the theatres, under the date of December 31, 1607, appears the entry, "Edmond Shakespeare a player in the Church." Another entry in the church fee book records that he was buried with "a forenoone knell of the great bell" and that 20s. were paid for his interment and knell. This was almost certainly William Shakespeare's younger brother Edmund, who had been baptized on May 3, 1580, and who had followed William to London and also had become an actor. It is likely that he died of the plague, which caused the theatres to be closed between July and November 1607. It is also likely that an "Edward sonne of Edward Shackspeere, Player, base-borne," who was buried at the church of St. Giles Cripplegate on August 12, 1607, was the child of this actor (the names Edward and Edmund often being confused) and that he too died of the plague.

During the winter of 1603 William Shakespeare acted with the King's Men in a performance of Ben Jonson's *Sejanus*. This is our last record of Shakespeare's acting. It is likely that he never performed in a play again, for he was now the chief supplier of plays for the most important troupe in London; he must have had little time for other pursuits. He had already entered upon the period of his greatest achievement as a writer of tragedy, for *Othello,* which was performed at court in 1604, had probably been completed by 1602. *King Lear* must have been written before its Whitehall performance before King James on December 26, 1606. *Macbeth* was probably among the plays performed at court in July and August of 1606 for the entertainment of the king's brother-in-law, King Christian IV of Denmark. It may well have been written specifically for that occasion. Around this time, possibly soon after *King Lear,* *Timon of Athens* was begun and abandoned before completion. At the end of 1606 or early in 1607 Shakespeare returned to Roman tragedy with *Antony and Cleopatra*. This play must have been followed closely by *Coriolanus*. Soon after the accession of James I, Shakespeare also seems to have found a new direction in comedy with *Measure for Measure,* which was acted at court on December 26, 1604, and with *All's Well That Ends Well,* which must have been written shortly before it. *Troilus and Cressida,* which is usually included among these "problem plays," must have been written by the end of 1602, and it may well have been written specifically for performance at one of the Inns of Court.

Blackfriars

In August of 1608 Shakespeare's company gained possession of Blackfriars, an indoor theatre which catered to a select upper-class audience. A theatre in Blackfriars, the old Dominican priory about a hundred yards to the southwest of St. Paul's cathedral, had been constructed first in 1576 when Richard Farrant had remodelled some rooms in the abbey to be used for performance by the Children of the Chapel Royal. After Farrant's death in 1580, legal difficulties caused the theatre to close. In 1596 James Burbage purchased a section of the building and attempted to remodel it as a theatre. He was opposed by powerful residents of the area and died before he could complete his plans. But in 1600 Richard Burbage succeeded in opening the theatre his father had projected, and he rented it for twenty-one years to Henry Evans, whose children's company performed in competition with the adult companies of London. In 1608 the Children of Blackfriars were suppressed for performing George Chapman's *Byron* plays, which had offended the French ambassador. Evans was pleased to get out of his difficulties by turning the remainder of his unexpired lease over to Richard Burbage, who now formed a syndicate to manage what was to be the winter headquarters of the King's Men. The seven partners (or Housekeepers) in the enterprise were Richard Burbage, Cuthbert Burbage, Henry Condell, John Heminges, William Sly, Thomas Evans, and William Shakespeare. When William Sly died on August 17, his share was divided among the other partners, making each a one-sixth owner.

For the three years that he was to remain in London Shakespeare wrote for the audience at Blackfriars as well as that at the Globe. He now turned to pastoral romance and to the themes of rebirth and reconciliation in plays reflecting a new serenity in contrast to the dark world of the tragedies. These plays included *Pericles, Cymbeline, The Winter's Tale,* and *The Tempest.* His place as chief writer for the King's Men was gradually taken over by Francis Beaumont and John Fletcher, upper-class gentleman themselves, who knew the tastes of the refined Blackfriars audience. Under their direction English drama moved farther and farther away from the popular drama which Shakespeare had helped to establish in the last decade of the sixteenth century.

Sometime in 1611 Shakespeare left London for Stratford. We know this because, when he came to Westminster in 1612 to give evidence in the Bellott vs. Mountjoy case, it was Stratford and not London that he gave as his place of residence. He seems, however, to have returned to London from time to time. He may have returned for the performance of his *Henry VIII* on June 29, 1613. This was the last play he was to write and the last ever to be played at the Globe. On its first performance the roof thatch of the theatre was set aflame when a cannon was fired, and the Globe burned to the ground.

To what extent Shakespeare collaborated with other dramatists in his final years we cannot be sure. It has long been held, although without certain evidence, that he was joined in the writing of *Henry VIII* by John Fletcher. Aside from his part in *Sir Thomas More,* the only play that we are certain he wrote in collaboration with another person, if he had any share in it at all, is *The Two Noble Kinsmen,* which was not included in the First Folio of 1623. It was published in 1634 as the joint work of Shakespeare and Fletcher and later included in the 1679 folio of the works of Beaumont and Fletcher.

Return to Stratford

When Shakespeare retired to Stratford, he was not only a wealthy and prominent citizen, but one who had brought fame to his native town. Many records of his activities in his final years have survived, and many legends and anecdotes as well. His mother, Mary Arden, had died in September of 1608. His younger brother, Gilbert, was buried on February 3, 1612, and in the following year on February 4, 1613, his last remaining brother, Richard, was buried. According to Nicholas Rowe, one of Shakespeare's closest friends in his retirement was John Combe, a money-lender for whom Shakespeare supposedly wrote a not very complimentary epitaph, but who bequeathed Shakespeare a legacy of £5 upon his death in January of 1613.

Shakespeare continued to be involved in London affairs until the very end of his life. On March 10, 1613, he bought the Black-friars Gate House from one Henry Walker for the sum of £140, apparently as an investment, for there is no indication that he ever meant to reside in it. In the same month he and Richard Burbage each received a sum of 44s. from the Earl of Rutland for a special emblem and motto they had designed for a shield which the earl carried at a court tournament on March 24.

A fire in Stratford in 1614 destroyed fifty-four houses, but
Shakespeare's was not among them. In this year Shakespeare, along
with various other wealthy citizens of Stratford, became involved
in a rather complicated controversy involving a plan to enclose
farming lands in the area of Welcombe, a village a mile north
of Stratford, where Shakespeare owned tithe rights. The corporation of Stratford was opposed to the plan, and Thomas Greene,
the town clerk of Stratford who was also Shakespeare's cousin,
kept a record of the proceedings in the affair in a kind of commercial diary which has survived among the papers in the birthplace museum at Stratford. In these records the name of William
Shakespeare occurs several times. On September 5, 1614, Greene
included Shakespeare's name in a survey of landowners in the
Welcombe area. On October 14 William Replingham, one of
those proposing to enclose the land, signed an agreement to repay
Shakespeare and Greene if either of them should suffer financial
loss because of the enclosures. Greene recorded that when he was
in London in November of 1614 he visited Shakespeare, who had
come to the city in the company of his son-in-law, John Hall, so
as to discuss the matter. The controversy continued throughout
the last two years of Shakespeare's life, and although the affair
is of slight importance and Shakespeare's name appears in the
records infrequently, it does supply evidence of Shakespeare's
prominence in the community and of the care with which he
continued to look after his business investments.

That Shakespeare was accompanied to London by his physician
son-in-law in 1614 may indicate that he was already in ill health.
Sometime in January of 1616 his will was drawn up for him by
Francis Collins, the lawyer who handled his real estate dealings.
On February 10 his daughter, Judith, was married to Thomas
Quiney, and on March 25 Shakespeare revised his will so as to
provide for this new development. It is interesting to note that on
March 12 Judith and Thomas Quiney were excommunicated by the
Bishop of Worcester for having been married in church during
Lent without a special license from the bishop to do so. Why
they neglected to secure this license we do not know. Perhaps
there was some impediment to the marriage which would have
made impossible the posting of the customary bond. Two weeks

following the excommunication Thomas Quiney was summoned into court to answer charges of having had illicit relations with one Margaret Wheeler.

Shakespeare's will, preserved in Somerset House, London, is in no significant way different from the will of the usual country gentleman of the early seventeenth century. It begins, following a regular form for wills, with a bequeathal of "my Soule into the handes of god my Creator, hoping & assuredlie beleeving through thonelie merittes of Jesus Christe my Saviour to be made partaker of lyfe everlastinge. And my bodye to the Earth whereof yt ys made." It then disposes of all of the property we know Shakespeare to have owned at the time of his death. There are bequests to the surviving members of his family, to various relatives and friends in Stratford. To Mr. Thomas Combe is bequeathed his sword, and to his old theatre associates John Heminges, Henry Condell, and Richard Burbage, goes a sum of 28s. 8d. each, with which to buy mourning rings. Ten pounds go to the poor of Stratford. New Place was left to Susanna and John Hall. The much discussed bequest to his wife of "my second best bed with the furniture" is her only mention in the will, but her dower rights were otherwise provided for. There is no doubt that she continued to live in New Place with her daughter and son-in-law until her death. This building was demolished in 1702 by Sir John Clopton, a descendant of its original builder, into whose hands it had passed following the death of the last of Shakespeare's descendants. It was rebuilt but demolished again in 1759 by its then owner, Francis Gastrell, because of a quarrel with the city officials of Stratford. An engraving of it, however, has survived and is reproduced in Edmund Malone's edition of Shakespeare (1790).

John Ward, who was vicar of Stratford from 1662 to 1681, recorded in his diary many years after the event that "Shakespear, Drayton, and Ben Jhonson, had a merry meeting, and itt seems drank too hard, for Shakespear died of a feavour there contracted." Although Ward is hardly a reliable authority, this legend has persisted, and it may well be true. What we do know is that on April 23, William Shakespeare died. His burial within the chancel of the church of the Holy Trinity was recorded on April 25. On

June 22 his will was probated in London by John Hall, and early in 1617 John Hall paid a "fine of admittance" for occupying New Place.

Sometime between Shakespeare's death and the year 1623 a monument to the poet was created by an Anglo-Flemish stone cutter named Gheerart Janssen, who lived in Southwark close to the Globe theatre, and thus may have known Shakespeare. It is the familiar bust of the poet writing with a quill, flanked by Corinthian columns supporting a cornice, on which are two small nude figures representing Rest and Labour. Between them are carved Shakespeare's arms, helm and crest, and above all is a skull. The monument is a typical one for the time, designed originally to be painted in life-like colours, not unlike other monuments of the period which may be found in many English churches. We must remember that it was the creation of a professional tomb-maker, not that of a skilled sculptor. Nevertheless it and the Droeshout engraving in the First Folio of 1623 are the only two unquestionable likenesses of Shakespeare which have come down to us, although there are in existence dozens of other portraits of questionable authenticity.

A tablet under the bust bears the following epitaph:

Judicio Pylium, genio Socratem, arte Maronem:
Terra tegit, populus mæret, Olympus habet.

Stay, Passenger, why goest thou by so fast?
Read, if thou canst, whom envious Death hath plast
With in this monument Shakspeare: with whome
Quick nature dide; whose name doth deck this Tombe
Far more than cost; sith all yt He hath writt
Leaves living art, but page, to serve his witt.
Obiit anno domini 1616. Ætatis 53. Die 23 Apr.

Inscribed over Shakespeare's grave itself, near the north wall of the chancel, is a familiar quatrain of verse which according to legend was composed by Shakespeare himself. It is addressed to sextons, warning them against taking his bones out of the grave and placing them in a charnel house, as was often done after a body had lain in a grave for some years:

Good frend, for Iesus sake forbeare
To dig the dust encloased heare!
Blest be ye man yt spares thes stones,
And curst be he yt moves my bones.

3

Life in Shakespeare's England

◇◇◇◇◇
◇◇◇◇◇ When Shakespeare arrived in London he found a bustling
◇◇◇◇◇ city of about two hundred thousand people, a vast
metropolis for its time, for no other city in England could then
boast more than fifteen thousand inhabitants. Built on the
banks of the Thames, the city depended upon the river and the
sea for its existence, and these had already made it a thriving
commercial centre. At its centre was the ancient walled city of
medieval times, but although the walls still stood, the city had
now stretched beyond them. It was a place of narrow streets and
alleys running haphazardly in all directions, crowded with half-
timbered houses and shops. Over all towered the great cathedral
of St. Paul's, not only the principal place of worship but also a
centre of commercial life. On the walks of St. Paul's unemployed
servants and workmen looked for new masters and were engaged,
lawyers met their clients, and a thousand and one other legal and
illegal transactions could be made. Here also the booksellers of
London had their shops and displayed their wares. At the eastern
end of the old city, within the wall, on the river Thames, stood
the massive Tower of London, believed by many to have been
built by Julius Cæsar, although its earliest building, the White
Tower, was actually built by the Norman invaders with stone they
brought across the water from Caen. The Tower had been used
as a fortress by William the Conqueror. In Shakespeare's day it
still contained the greatest arsenal of weapons in England and
was actively used as a prison for political and other offenders

against the crown. Although the Angevin kings of England had lived within its walls, it was no longer a royal palace, but still continued to be London's dominant symbol of royal supremacy.

London was ruled by a Council of Aldermen, elected for life by the citizens of the city's twenty-six wards. The Aldermen in turn elected a Lord Mayor who served for one year. The city was in effect controlled by merchants. It was jealous of its many ancient prerogatives. The Queen of England could not enter London except by invitation of the Lord Mayor, and when she did so she usually came by barge down the river Thames from the royal city of Westminster which lay about two miles upstream and was the seat of English government. Here was the great palace of Whitehall where the queen and her court resided, and here was Westminster Abbey (then called the Abbey Church of St. Peter) where English sovereigns were crowned and where most of them were buried. Also in Westminster were the Parliament House and Westminster Hall, built by the Norman King Rufus, in which the great law courts of the realm held their sessions. Around the government buildings of Westminster sprang up the houses of lesser officials, and the area came to include many persons without real occupations, who were often a source of civic disturbance. London and Westminster, although they grew closer and closer as each extended its population, were entirely separate municipalities, and there was often intense rivalry between their inhabitants. The commercial city of London and the government centre of Westminster were joined by the Strand, a fashionable avenue which ran for two miles along the Thames, and which in Shakespeare's day was lined with great houses and fine shops.

To the north were suburbs under the jurisdiction of the magistrates of the County of Middlesex. Under this more permissive control they tended to become centres for activities looked upon with disfavour by the London civic authorities. Here, prostitution flourished, along with sports and amusements of every kind, and here the first public theatres were built. Across the Thames from Westminster in the County of Surrey, was Lambeth, where the Archbishop of Canterbury had his palace, and further downstream was the suburb of Southwark. Here were the prisons of the

Marshalsea, the Clink, and the Queen's Bench, and here, as in the northern suburbs, was a home for the more disreputable occupations — prostitution, and the disagreeable trades of soap-making, tanning, and brewing. Paris Garden in Southwark was England's greatest centre for bullbaiting and bearbaiting, and close by the theatres came to flourish. With the building of the Globe on the Southwark Bankside in 1599, this area became the unquestioned theatrical capital of England. Connecting Southwark to the city was London Bridge, the only span across the Thames. A wooden bridge had existed on its site almost since time immemorial. We know that King Harold led his troops across it to meet William the Conqueror at Hastings in 1066. The first stone structure was completed in 1209, and in Shakespeare's day London Bridge was one of the wonders of England, lined with shops and houses on either side, with a busy commerce of small boats passing beneath its arches, and with a section which could be raised and lowered for the passage of larger vessels. On the bridge the heads of traitors were regularly displayed. From this city where Shakespeare spent his productive years he was to draw inspiration throughout his career as a dramatist.

Sanitation and Disease

In the crowded streets of the city disease was rampant, for public sanitation was so primitive as to be virtually nonexistent. Sewers were unknown. Down the middle of the streets, and along the sides of some of the larger ones, were ditches into which garbage and other waste was thrown and allowed to accumulate until heavy rains carried it down to one of several large ditches — Fleet ditch and Moor ditch were the most prominent — notorious for their foul odours, and thence on into the Thames. Although householders were required to carry their refuse to the ditches, often they threw it from windows above, to the peril of passersby. Even with the coming of rains, the flow of sewage was heavily obstructed, partly because of floor rushes which were thrown into the ditches when they had become too soiled for further use in houses. Dung heaps and dirty straw were deposited from stables, along with the refuse of butcher shops and the stale fish discarded by fishmongers. Birds of prey and other scavengers were actually a welcome relief, since they carried off some of the offal, but matter from the sewage ditches had regularly to be loaded into carts and taken away to depositories in the suburbs or carried out to sea in barges, though this service was extremely inefficient and did little to relieve the general filthiness with which Elizabethan citizens were obliged to live.

Water supply was a constant problem. A great conduit, made of lead and reinforced with stone, had been constructed in Cheapside as early as 1285. By Shakespeare's time, there were various conduits throughout the city from which water was carried in tankards. In 1580, at the suggestion of a German engineer, a pumping system was constructed under London Bridge based upon water wheels operated by the tides, so that water could be drawn from the river, and this system was later augmented. In 1609 Sir Hugh Myddelton began work on an elaborate system of pipes and tunnels which would bring water into the city from the springs of Hertfordshire. The project, in spite of enormous difficulties, was finally completed in 1613, but as the city expanded the need for water could not adequately be met, and the search for new sources of supply was a continuing and worrisome one.

As the city grew and the problems of crowded slums became worse, ordinances were passed to restrict the building of new houses, but this only aggravated conditions, for existing structures were simply broken into smaller and smaller units, and the crowding of people grew ever worse. The filth of the streets made rats inevitable, and rats brought with them the bubonic plague, the black death which had ravaged medieval Europe and which continued to return frequently in Shakespeare's day. There was no year during Shakespeare's lifetime in which there were no deaths at all from the plague, but two great epidemics, one in 1592 and 1593 when some twenty-two thousand persons died, and one in 1603 in which about thirty thousand perished, decimated the population, bringing with them not only panic and terror but a host of economic problems.

Bubonic plague tended to attack the poorest elements of society, but there were other maladies which made no economic distinction. One was a mysterious fever called "the sweating sickness" which began to appear in England in the early years of the sixteenth century and tended to attack the wealthy and well-fed. Its signs were a high fever, head and stomach pains, and a violent sweating which lasted for about twenty-four hours, although usually the patient was dead before that time had elapsed. It attacked with extraordinary suddenness. A man might be going about his affairs in perfect health and be dead a few hours later.

Although plague houses were boarded up, the belongings of victims burned, and other drastic measures taken to confine the disease, it was carried inevitably from the city into the provinces, where any visitors from London were greeted with fear and suspicion. Into London it came from the provinces as well. It is likely that the great plague of 1603 was brought to the city by some of the many people who flocked to London from all parts of England to behold the coronation of King James I, although it is also possible that it was brought in from the Low Countries where it had raged for some years before. Whenever deaths from the pestilence reached the number of thirty a week, the theatres were closed. Although nothing was known of germs, it was obvious that the sickness was spread in crowds, and since the plague was generally regarded as God's punishment for human wickedness, the theatres, long under attack by Puritans as centres of vanity and blasphemy, were the first to feel the effects of public terror and the search for blame.

Leprosy, the dreaded scourge of the Middle Ages, had declined by Shakespeare's day. While the disease continued for at least another century in the English provinces, only isolated cases appeared in London, largely because of the stringent measures taken in the fifteenth century to see that sufferers were strictly confined and their possessions burned. There were no longer any lazar houses in London, for sufferers were sent out of the city to such ancient houses as Burton Lazars in Leicestershire. London was, however, fairly well provided with hospitals for a city of its time. St. Bartholomew's and St. Thomas's catered to a wide variety of human ills, and the hospital of St. Mary's of Bethlehem (Bedlam) was a place of confinement for the mentally ill. Patients here still earned their keep by entertaining visitors, for Elizabethans generally had not ceased to regard madness as a source of amusement. It was the accepted belief that madness was caused by demons who could only be driven out of the patient's body by physical means. It should be noted that all of these London hospitals were places for the poor. Sick persons of the more respectable social classes were treated in their homes.

London was full of quack doctors of every kind and description who preyed upon the poor and the gullible. The practice of medicine had been under the loose control of the church, with no real regulation until 1512 when, under King Henry VIII, an act of Parliament attempted to suppress quackery by prescribing that medical practitioners be licensed by a bishop after approval by a licensing board of qualified persons. In 1518 the College of Physicians was founded, with the requirement that only those with the degree of M.D. from Oxford or Cambridge be admitted. The College was given supervision of medical practice in London and within a seven-mile radius around it, but it had so few members that only the court and the noble residents of great houses could be treated. Medical training at Oxford and Cambridge, which consisted almost entirely of the reading of classical medical treatises, was so poor that the best doctors were those who had studied abroad at the great medical centres of Bologna, Padua, or Montpelier. Great noblemen often had foreign physicians in their service, among the most notable being Roderigo Lopez, a Spanish Jew, who served as personal physician to Queen Elizabeth. For humble people there were only quacks or magicians; and in the provinces perhaps the parish curate, who may have read some of Galen or Hippocrates. Childbirth was entirely in the hands of women, very few of whom had any license to practise midwifery, and it was not uncommon for five or six neighbour women to be present at the birth of a child. Infant mortality was extremely high, probably well over fifty per cent, but the birth-rate was also high, it not being unusual for women to have had by the time they were thirty as many as ten children, with only two or three of them surviving the first weeks of life.

Surgery was performed by members of the Company of Barber-Surgeons which had been established by a royal charter in 1540. Members were apprenticed for seven years, beginning at about the age of seventeen, usually after some years in a grammar school. They were supposed to work only under the supervision of a physician, but as a matter of fact they practised for themselves, and since they treated ordinary surface wounds and fractures, they were the medical practitioners with whom the ordinary person was likely to have the widest contact. Each year the company was granted the bodies of four recently executed criminals, from which they learned a good deal about anatomy. Sometimes they were able to cure battle wounds quite efficiently, and occasionally they attempted more difficult operations, but few of their patients survived the dangers of infection. For the most part, their practice consisted of treating venereal diseases, which were extremely common, and various skin infections.

Life was difficult and precarious, and death was an omnipresent reality which could strike at any time with lightning rapidity. Even the best of medical practice depended upon an utterly false conception of human physiology, and remedies for disease were still prized by doctors as secrets to be passed on to their children, just as Helena in *All's Well That Ends Well* inherited the recipes of her noted physician father. All of these conditions colour and affect the vision of human mortality in Shakespeare's plays, his treatments of sickness and death, his portraits of doctors as diverse as the Pinch of *The Comedy of Errors* and the Cerimon of *Pericles*, the smell of crowds, and the horror of ever-impending plague, whose ominous spots, "God's tokens," as they were called, are drawn upon frequently in the imagery of his plays.

Commerce and Industry

The river Thames which swallowed up the waste of London and provided much of its water supply was a busy artery of commerce, the lifeblood of an expanding economy. In spite of the difficulties of life, Elizabethan London led the rest of England in a period of remarkable economic growth. The city was the centre for internal as well as foreign trade, and for exploration of new lands — which made it the hub of what was one day to be the British Empire. Much of the impetus for Renaissance economic expansion came from the exploitation of the new continent of America. In this the Spaniards had taken the lead, but their pouring of silver and gold into Europe from their American mines caused prices to rise in England as well as elsewhere and created a great supply of new capital for investment. A fleet of English privateers, led by such illustrious seamen as Francis Drake, Walter Raleigh, Martin Frobisher, and John Hawkins, regularly looted the Spanish treasure ships and poured wealth into England. Largely from this source, Queen Elizabeth was able to support her military campaigns in the Low Countries. Trading companies were established not only to develop the wealth of the new world, but to bring England into commercial relations with Eastern Europe and the Orient as well. It was a time also of phenomenal growth in manufacturing and in the mining of copper, tin, lead, iron, and coal. Protestant refugees from the continent brought with them new skills, and the growth of science and engineering led to methods of production unknown a century before.

In such a time of economic expansion capital for investment was in great demand. In satisfying it, usurers, while they were scorned and berated for their activities, served a valuable function. Unfortunately, money lenders victimized the poor while they served the needs of business, and the poor were many. The great new wealth poured into the hands of the upper classes and merely trickled to those below, so that the Elizabethan age is actually one in which stratification between classes on the basis of material wealth became more marked than it had ever been before. Great merchant princes emerged, including most notably the Gresham family. Sir John Gresham was Sheriff of London, at the same time that his brother, Sir Richard, was Lord Mayor. Both were members of the Mercers Company, and both rose to positions of great wealth, lending money to King Henry VIII and to his nobles with whom they maintained close relations, both social and economic. The brothers were rewarded with grants of monastic lands which added to their wealth. New and more efficient methods of farming, while they led to the exploitation and misery of the rural poor, were also a source of great wealth.

Sir Thomas Gresham, the second son of Sir Richard, continued in the Mercers Company, but most of his efforts were devoted to public affairs. In 1551 he was appointed by the government of King Edward VI as financial agent for the crown in Antwerp, at that time the principal money market of the world and a great centre of international trade. His financial dealings — based, in part, upon a widespread private intelligence service — restored the value of the English pound which had fallen drastically in the early years of the Reformation. He served as principal financial adviser to Queen Elizabeth, working closely with her Lord Treasurer, William Cecil, with whose family the Greshams had close connections. On June 7, 1567, he began construction at his own expense of the Royal Exchange. This great building became, like St. Paul's, one of the landmarks of London. In its courtyard merchants conducted their affairs; on its first floor were shops of every kind. It was a symbol of English commerce and the glory of the middle classes. Its building was commemorated by the dramatist Thomas Heywood in the second part of his bourgeois play *If You Know Not Me You Know Nobody* (1603–1605), ostensibly devoted to the glory of Queen Elizabeth, but actually a panegyric in praise of Sir Thomas Gresham.

The career of the Gresham family illustrates the close relation of the merchant princes with the established landed nobility. The great trading companies all received their financial backing from the sovereign as well as from the great nobles of the realm, including the Earl of Southampton, who may have been Shakespeare's patron. These companies were more than sources of great financial profit; they brought all of the known world into England and greatly enriched the variety of English life. They included the Russia Company, founded in 1553 to develop trade in the northern regions not pre-empted by Spain, and to explore sea routes throughout the eastern world. The Levant Company, which became the East India Company in 1600, sent its ships to the Middle East and brought back not only wealth but tales of exotic lands and customs which inevitably found their way into the plays of the time. The Virginia Company led to the colonization of America, and upon its voyages to the new world Shakespeare was to draw in *The Tempest*.

Soldiers and Sailors

The economic expansion at home, with its struggle for new capital and for new markets abroad, was only one of many factors which brought England into conflict with its more powerful continental neighbours. From at least the year 1585 until Elizabeth's death in 1603, England was engaged in a bitter struggle with Spain, and there were few periods when English soldiers were not fighting abroad or when English fleets were not engaging Spanish vessels on the seas. Shakespeare lived in a time when military matters were a concern of every Englishman, and it has even been suggested that Shakespeare's remarkable knowledge of military life may have resulted from his own service with the English forces fighting against the Spanish in the Netherlands. Although it is not impossible that he may have spent some time as a soldier abroad in the years immediately before his arrival in London, this has never been proven and it is unlikely.

The struggle in the Low Countries, which continued to the end of Elizabeth's reign, was only one of her military engagements. In 1589 Elizabeth sent an army to France to fight in support of the Protestant Henry of Navarre in his struggle for the French throne. English troops remained there until 1593 when Henry concluded the French civil wars by embracing Catholicism and assuming the crown. A struggle against Irish rebels supported by Spain raged intermittently throughout Elizabeth's reign. In 1598 the English forces were disastrously defeated. An expedition of sixteen thousand men led by the Earl of Essex in the following year suffered similar defeat and may have been a factor in Essex's ill-fated rebellion upon his return to England. Only in 1603 were the Irish rebels finally defeated by an English army under the command of Charles Blount, Lord Mountjoy, who was made Duke of Devonshire as a reward for this great service. In 1603 all of England's wars came to an end, for warfare was to a large extent a matter of personal quarrel between sovereigns, and with Elizabeth's death, the hostilities with Spain subsided.

Of naval engagements, the defeat of the Spanish Armada in 1588 was the most spectacular. Later historians can see that it actually marked the end of any real threat from Spain. Elizabethans could not realize that, however, and there were many other naval adventures, among the most notable being an expedition to Portugal under Sir Francis Drake which led to the sacking of Lisbon and Corunna, and the several expeditions led by the Earl of Essex — against Cadiz in 1595 which succeeded in sacking that city and burning the Spanish merchant fleet in the harbour, and against the coast of Spain in 1597 which succeeded only in the raiding of the Azores.

Military service for the common soldier was hard and disagreeable. Falstaff's recruiting methods in the *Henry IV* plays hold up to ridicule what was actually a widely practised system of abuse. The basic army unit consisted of a company of one hundred men commanded by a captain who was commissioned by the queen and assisted by one lieutenant and by one ensign who was little more than an orderly. Although a captain might find volunteers if the prospects for looting were good — and he preferred looters, for they were the best fighters — he had to conscript men to fill up his allotted ranks. Like Falstaff, captains would march through the countryside with the queen's commission to raise men. Rarely was a company up to full strength, and since the captain drew from the treasury the pay for all of the men on his muster roll and was entitled to keep ten per cent of it for himself, corrupt captains padded their lists with fictitious names. These came to be called "shadows." Sometimes checks were made, but to avoid detection a captain had only to borrow men from another company for the occasion, and in Ireland even enemy soldiers were borrowed. When soldiers were released from service, they had little means of supporting themselves other than begging or crime.

The generals were, like Essex and Leicester, the great noblemen of the realm, and they were usually accompanied by troops of lesser gentlemen representing the great families of England. To these young gallants, war was still a matter of honour and glory; they were the men of "name" whose deaths on the battlefield were the only ones really to be lamented or to be taken into account in estimating the costs of a victory.

Sailors enjoyed a very low social status in Shakespeare's England, for they were usually regarded as ruffians, thieves, and pirates, and that in truth is what a great many of them were, although there were some who, after beginning as seamen, worked themselves up to become owners of vessels and even fleets of vessels. Life aboard ship was incredibly difficult, quarters being cramped, food poor and often spoiled, and medical attention entirely inadequate. When ashore, seamen tended to congregate in settlements along the Thames, such as Limehouse and Rotherhithe, which were notorious for their disorder and violence. After 1585 a great many English merchant ships were actually privateers, and part of the sailor's duty was to engage in combat with ships out of virtually every other port of Europe. Spanish, French, and Flemish privateers lurked in the English channel. For a time there was little distinction between friend and foe, any vessel appearing on the horizon being regarded as a likely source of booty. Privateering came to an end with the accession of James I and the concluding of foreign treaties to protect the rights of vessels at sea. This left the field to acknowledged pirates who had always been very much a part of the picture.

Privateering under Queen Elizabeth brought with it great financial profit, for the crew shared in the spoils, and thus idle adventurers with little knowledge of sailing often joined the crews of vessels. Many of those who were seized by the ever-present press gangs were equally inexperienced. Although rigid discipline was maintained on the ships of the queen's navy, the crews of merchant privateers tended to be difficult to control, drinking much of the time, and constantly fighting over the booty seized from other vessels. The captains in these respects were sometimes little better than their crews. Musical instruments were carried aboard most ships, not only for the relief of monotonous hours but also to be played during battle. It has been said that no English sailor would fight without the sound of martial music. Shakespeare, in general, does not show as much interest in seafaring men as he does in soldiers, although he is accurate in what references to shipboard life he does make. Only in *The Tempest* does he draw to any extent upon the maritime life which was so much a part of his environment.

Crime and Punishment

Discharged soldiers and idle seamen provided a large part of the criminal population of Elizabethan England. Highwaymen added to the danger of travel on roads which were poorly constructed and in constant need of repair, since every local parish was responsible for the maintenance of its own roads, and parish officials were notoriously negligent. Statutes were designed to curb the activities of many kinds of vagabonds who haunted the highways, including unlicensed actors and such Bedlam beggars as Shakespeare depicted in the Tom o' Bedlam of *King Lear*. These released inmates of the London hospital for mad folk could often be quite dangerous, and along with other wandering marauders they preyed upon rural housewives whose husbands were at work in the fields. Crimes of violence were common in every part of England, and every gentleman carried a sword for his protection.

Within the city of London more sophisticated criminals were at work. These were organized into fraternities, worked closely together, observed a social hierarchy, and had their own rules and regulations. Young gallants arriving in the city from the provinces were a tempting prey for card sharps and confidence men of various kinds. Robert Greene in a series of pamphlets published in 1591 and 1592 described the activities of these "cony-catchers," as they were called. Burglary was a skilled craft, and its practitioners used various techniques such as thrusting hooked rods through the open windows of houses. Pickpockets, who included "nips" who cut purses with a knife, and "foists," who used only their hands and enjoyed a higher social status, could be found wherever crowds gathered, notably at public hangings and among those standing in the pits of the public theatres.

Laws against crime were extremely harsh. Murder and all other kinds of felony were punished by public hanging at Tyburn, providing spectacles to which Londoners thronged with great eagerness. After sentencing to death, however, it was possible for a man to be reprieved if he had enough friends and influence. It was also possible for a condemned man who could recite in Latin a certain portion of the Vulgate Bible which came to be known as "the neck verse" to claim "benefit of clergy" and be spared from death. This was a relic of the ancient principle that only the church courts could administer punishment to clerics, and those who could read Latin were assumed to be members of the clergy. The formality of handing such persons to the bishop for punishment had long been dispensed with, however. Ben Jonson took advantage of this privilege in order to escape execution for his killing of the actor Gabriel Spencer in a duel. Such persons were branded on the thumb with the letter "T" for "Tyburn," and sometimes they were obliged to spend a year in prison. The brand was a guarantee that they would not be offered "benefit of clergy" for a second offence.

Traitors were dragged to the place of execution on carts called "hurdles" and then hanged, drawn, and quartered. This was a gruesome method of execution, since the bodies were cut down before death, disembowelled, the entrails burned in a fire, and the trunk cut into four parts, dipped in tar, and sent to be displayed in various parts of the city. The heads were often impaled on London Bridge. Noblemen, however, were beheaded by axe in the courtyard of the Tower of London. Burning at the stake was the penalty for witchcraft, religious heresy, and for women who had poisoned their husbands.

There were some eighteen prisons in London and its suburbs alone, some under the jurisdiction of the city authorities and others under that of the crown. They were unlike our modern prisons in that they were places of detention rather than punishment. Their inmates were not usually committed after a trial or for specific periods of time. They were incarcerated while awaiting trial, sometimes for exceedingly long periods, and upon conviction they were sentenced to some kind of corporal punishment ranging from whipping for misdemeanours to hanging for felonies. Any person involved in an affair which required some kind of disposition by the courts could be committed to prison if there was any fear that he might escape jurisdiction. Debtors were imprisoned until their debts had been settled, often to the disadvantage of the creditor, for once a man was imprisoned for debt there was no further means by which the money he owed could be collected, and when he died the debt was cancelled. This system led to many abuses. It was not unknown for a man to purchase large sums of material on credit, pretend bankruptcy, and live well in prison, passing on his ill-gotten gains to his family upon his death, while his creditors had no redress at all.

Conviction for any crime meant the confiscation of the criminal's property by the crown, but a brave man wishing to protect his family estate might avoid this by refusing to plead either guilty or not guilty and thus avoiding trial. In such cases he was punished by *la peine forte et dure* or pressing to death. He was placed upon a bed of spikes, and heavy weights were laid upon his chest until he was crushed. An extraordinary number of poetic images in Shakespeare's plays are drawn from this practice.

The most important of the city prisons was Newgate, where felons of all kinds were incarcerated, and in its press yard pressing to death was carried out. Other city prisons included Ludgate, which was reserved for citizens of London accused of any crimes other than felony or treason and thus in actuality became a debtors' prison; and the Poultry Counter and Wood Street Counter, which were kept open all night to receive offenders committed by the two sheriffs of London — chiefly debtors, and those accused of petty disturbances of the peace. Of the crown prisons, the most important were the Fleet and the Marshalsea. To both of these were committed Catholic and Puritan recusants and other offenders against the crown, although pirates seem to have been lodged exclusively in the Marshalsea, probably because of its proximity to the admiralty courts. Noblemen and others committed by the Queen's Privy Council tended to be lodged in the Fleet, and that is probably why Falstaff is sent there after his rejection by Prince Hal. In the middle of the seventeenth century, after the abolition of the Star Chamber, it became a debtors prison. Of the five prisons in Southwark, the most important were those of the Clink and the Queen's Bench. The northern suburbs included a prison at Finsbury. Bridewell was not a prison like the others, but a place of physical punishment for beggars, vagabonds, runaway servants and apprentices, whores and their keepers. The Tower of London was used as a place of detention for noblemen and high church officials who had offended the crown or were accused of treason. It was here that Sir Walter Raleigh was imprisoned for eighteen years and wrote his *History of the World*.

Prisoners were not only obliged to pay fees upon committal and release, for the privilege of going unfettered and for other purposes, but they had to pay for their board and lodging as well. Keepers of prisons often grew quite wealthy and regarded their positions as sinecures to be sold or passed on to their children. Debtors who could not make terms for their release and who were entirely without funds often starved to death, although various charitable services provided some help. If a prisoner was on good terms with his keeper and had sufficient funds, he could often live

fairly well, but otherwise his lot was very miserable and he was
not likely to live very long. Prisoners who could pay for them
might have private rooms and comfortable beds; others might be
placed together in dark holes without beds at all. How they were
fed depended upon similar factors, the more fortunate eating with
the keeper at his own table; the less fortunate depending upon an
almsman who walked through the streets of London with a basket
strapped to his back, begging for food for the prisoners and receiving whatever refuse the townspeople chose to donate.

Courts and Lawyers

Elizabethan England had developed a fairly complex legal system which affected the lives of ordinary people to a remarkable
degree. Few of Shakespeare's contemporaries went through life
without some contact with the courts. Shakespeare himself was
several times involved in litigation, and in this he was not alone
among his fellow dramatists. Scholars have long recognized that
one of the surest places in which to hunt for biographical information about Elizabethan writers of every kind is in the voluminous
records left by the Elizabethan law courts, now partially preserved
in the Public Record Office in Chancery Lane. Lawyers were very
important people in the life of Shakespeare's England, and it is
no wonder that they should appear as characters in so many of the
plays of the period.

It is not simply that Elizabethans were very litigious people,
which in fact they were, but that the legal machinery extended
into areas which today it does not ordinarily affect. The admin-
istration of estates, the supervision of workmen in home industry,
the passing on of family property, and even matters of religion and
personal belief, all came under the direct supervision of various
courts, for courts performed many functions which today are performed by local government agencies. An Elizabethan gentleman
could not administer the ordinary affairs of life without a fairly
extensive knowledge of legal procedures. This is one reason why
Shakespeare's plays, like those of his contemporaries, are so full
of legal references; these indicate no extraordinary legal competence
or experience on the part of the authors (although some dramatists,
such as John Marston and John Ford, had been trained in the law),

but merely reflect the legal diction and habits of thought which were the common property of all Elizabethans.

A highly involved system of courts was designed, in its various branches, to administer three kinds of law: the Common Law based upon the precedent of a body of cases, modified by statute and constantly being reinterpreted, which primarily governed matters of property; the Civil Law imported from continental Europe, which established a procedure by which injured persons could seek redress from wrongs; and Canon Law, the ancient legal system of the Roman Church which had been weakened and modified under the influence of the Reformation, but which still continued to regulate many of the personal affairs of life through a system of ecclesiastical courts. Every county of England had its Quarter-Sessions and its visiting Assizes to administer criminal justice, and there were local courts to handle civil matters of various kinds, but the great bulk of civil litigation was handled in the courts in Westminster Hall, to which Elizabethans journeyed from every part of the realm.

Of these courts, that of the Queen's Bench was originally designed to handle criminal matters and that of the Common Pleas civil matters, but in practice both were civil courts in the sixteenth century with overlapping jurisdiction. The Court of Chancery was a court of appeal from the decisions of either of these. It was a court of direct appeal to the Lord Chancellor, who could provide justice or equity in cases not directly covered by either common or civil law. In addition to these, there were the Court of the Exchequer, which dealt with financial matters involving the crown; the Court of Requests, which administered equity judgment to those too poor to bring their suits in the regular courts; the Court of Wards and Liveries, which had control of the estates of minors; and a Court of the Admiralty, which dealt not only with piracy but with all matters involving international trade and was governed by a body of international law to which all the trading countries of Europe conformed. The courts were at constant rivalry with one another over matters of jurisdiction, and it was not uncommon for suits and counter-suits to be brought simultaneously in rival courts. Each court was eager to secure as many legal fees as possible.

A distinctively Tudor instrument was the Court of Star Chamber. It consisted of the Queen's Privy Council and took its name from the fact that they met in a room whose ceiling was decorated with golden stars. It has sometimes been called an instrument of tyranny, but it was actually designed as a "prerogative court" which could remedy deficiencies in the ordinary legal system. Thus it could hear appeals from the Court of Chancery, but it could also act quickly in cases of treason or disobedience to crown orders. It thus became an instrument for the suppression of civil disorders and could use stringent methods in order to do so. It was dissolved in 1641.

Although the ecclesiastical courts were considerably weakened in Elizabethan England, they still exercised a wide jurisdiction in many fields. The Court of Star Chamber had its ecclesiastical counterpart in the two Courts of High Commission, one in London and one in York, which considered important cases of religious dissent. Lawyers who practised in these church courts were trained in the civil law, to whose procedures the Canon law conformed. They were educated at Oxford and Cambridge, where Henry VIII had established Regius professorships of civil law, and they belonged to an association called Doctors Commons which had been established in 1511. They practised also in the Admiralty Court. There seems to have been considerable rivalry between them and the common lawyers who practised in the royal courts.

These common lawyers belonged to professional organizations called the Inns of Court, where they were educated in the legal profession. To these Inns gentlemen proceeded after leaving Oxford or Cambridge, often with no intention of really practising law — for these professional societies of lawyers were great intellectual centres where any gentleman might suitably complete his education. In fact those students with no interest in the law came to exceed in number those who actually went on to the bar, and there was constant criticism of the laxity and inefficiency of the actual legal training that the Inns, in marked contrast to Doctors Commons, afforded. Since early medieval times the Inns had been presenting plays at their annual revels, often written by the lawyers themselves, but in Shakespeare's time, more and more often composed and produced by the professional thea-

tre companies of London. Among Shakespeare's plays produced before the law students were *The Comedy of Errors, Twelfth Night,*
and almost certainly *Troilus and Cressida.* The Inns were, in effect,
literary centres, many of whose members achieved distinction as
poets, and some of whom abandoned the law to devote themselves
to writing for the public stage. The principal Inns were the Inner
Temple, the Middle Temple, Gray's Inn, and Lincoln's Inn. Of
somewhat lesser social status, and perhaps more seriously devoted
to legal study, were the Inns of Chancery, which included Fur-
nival's Inn and Clement's Inn, where Shakespeare's Justice Shallow
had studied. Although there were attempts to restrict the Inns of
Court to the sons of gentlemen, as most of the lawyers were, inevitably, more and more persons of lower social status gained
admission and went on by their learning and intelligence to succeed
at the law. The practice of law became one of the means of social
mobility in Tudor England, and there are many instances of men
of humble origins who were able to rise by means of it to high
social position and acquire estates which made them landed gentry.

The evidence of witnesses in civil cases, which was taken only
after the passing back and forth of bills of complaints, answers,
replications, and rejoinders, was taken in the form of written depositions. When the issues of a case had been narrowed, the lawyers
for both parties agreed in advance upon a set of "interrogatories" or
specific questions, to which the witness in each instance prepared
written answers to be studied at leisure by the master of the court
before he rendered his decision. The exception was in Star Chamber proceedings where testimony was given orally and recorded,
as the witnesses spoke, by a court reporter. This is one reason
why depositions in Chancery, for instance, carefully penned by a
scrivener, are relatively easy to read, whereas depositions in Star
Chamber cases, full of the shorthand and abbreviations of the court
scribe, are extremely vexing for the modern scholar who must de-
cipher them. While criminal cases usually were quickly concluded,
most of the business of the courts was slow and inefficient, the law's
delay being a constant source of ridicule and complaint. Litigants
on both sides of an issue were often impoverished by legal fees
long before the case in question could be decided, if it were ever
decided at all. The entire judicial system of Shakespeare's day

was, in fact, outmoded, much of it being the relics of institutions of earlier ages, and badly in need of reform.

Students and Apprentices

Throughout England there were schools such as Shakespeare attended in Stratford-on-Avon. Their masters, as we have seen, were learned men, and their graduates were well educated by any standards. There were thus many men of taste and learning among the artisans and merchants of rural England, and when these people came to London, as many did throughout the year on legal and other business, they provided an appreciative and knowing audience for Shakespeare's plays. London had its schools of various kinds, but three great grammar schools, all founded in the sixteenth century, stood supreme among them. Of these Westminster School and St. Paul's were connected with the great cathedrals and their choristers comprised the childrens' companies of players who were such formidable rivals for the adult actors. The Merchant Taylors School had been founded by one of the richest and most powerful of the London guilds.

These schools were important centres of English humanism. St. Paul's had been founded by the great humanist, John Colet; William Lyly, author of the *Latin Grammar,* had been its headmaster; and among the more illustrious of its pupils it was to number the poet John Milton. The Merchant Taylors School, under the guidance of the learned Richard Mulcaster, was not only famous for its classical learning, but also as a nursery of the drama, for its children often gave performances at court. Among its illustrious graduates it included the poet Edmund Spenser and the dramatist Thomas Kyd. The distinguished headmasters of Westminster included the dramatist Nicholas Udall and the learned antiquarian William Camden, to whom his pupil, Ben Jonson, avowed that he was indebted for all of his learning. To these schools must be added Christ's Hospital, founded by the corporation of London in 1552 for the education of orphans. Among its students was the poet and dramatist George Peele, son of the master. The Tudor age is, in fact, marked by the founding of grammar schools in all parts of England and of colleges at Oxford and Cambridge such as no earlier age had witnessed. This was in part a reflection of the humanist faith in the power of education to conquer the ills of mankind and of the Reformation conviction that it had been the ignorance of the people which had for so long enabled the papacy to endure. The curriculum of the Elizabethan grammar schools was carefully regulated so as to be uniform throughout England.

The free grammar schools of England drew their students from a fairly broad spectrum of English society. To this the career of Shakespeare gives evidence, as does that of Christopher Marlowe, who went from the King's School at Canterbury on to Cambridge; or that of Ben Jonson, the step-son of a London bricklayer, who was able to study under William Camden at Westminster. Those excluded from education tended to be the children of those whose physical labour was needed to support their families, largely in working the land. Grammar schools, like law practice, were thus an important means by which a gifted boy might begin his rise to an eventual position of greatness and power. The career of Cardinal Wolsey, the son of an Ipswich butcher, provided a graphic example. Although their training had been almost entirely in Latin composition and oratory, not all grammar school graduates went on to the universities. Some like Shakespeare and Jonson devoted themselves to literary pursuits without further training. Many others became apprentices to various occupations.

The crafts and trades of England were in control of the licensed companies which were the descendants of the medieval guilds. These companies usually possessed considerable wealth, as we can see from the ability of the Merchant Taylors to found a great public school. To become a freeman of a company one had to serve an apprenticeship of no less than seven years, which could not be terminated before the age of twenty-four. Such service would usually begin between the ages of fourteen and seventeen. These and other regulations were established by Parliament in 1563 by its Statute of Artificers, and they were strictly enforced, in addition to whatever rules individual companies made for their own government. An apprentice, in exchange for training in the craft of the master in whose household he lived, undertook to serve him faithfully for the seven-year period. Apprentices tended to be the sons of merchants and craftsmen, often with a grammar-school education and with some family wealth, for many companies required that the master be paid, and the Statute of Artificers itself established property qualifications for entry into the more prestigious crafts, although these came to be enforced less and less frequently.

Much of the regulation was designed to prevent the loss of farm labourers and those who could perform other unskilled tasks in industries such as mining. Apprenticeship was virtually the only means of entry into the skilled crafts or the lucrative trades; an important goal of middle-class families was to have their sons taken into the home of an eminent and wealthy tradesman. Young men came to London from all over England to take up apprenticeships, for training in the great city offered advantages of many kinds. They usually opened shops in their native cities when their training had been completed. They provided an eager and receptive audience for the plays of the London theatres.

Those who went on from grammar schools to the universities at Oxford and Cambridge found institutions which had developed considerably under the Tudor monarchs. Not only had new colleges been founded, but many of these, such as St. John's College, Cambridge, under Sir John Cheke, had been established to embody the new humanistic principles of learning. No longer was the curriculum organized around the study of Aristotelian logic, with its primary goal the preparation of clergymen to engage in scholastic disputation. Sixteenth-century Oxford and Cambridge carried on the study of classical literature, which had become the staple of the Tudor grammar schools, adding Greek to the traditional Latin. There were readings also in the new scientific learning, in contemporary history and political theory, and in modern languages. Although theology was still an important discipline and the training of clergy still a vital function, the universities were rapidly being transformed into training grounds for gentlemen in a broad spectrum of the liberal arts. A university graduate in Shakespeare's day was ready to enter the church, but he might just as easily move on to one of the Inns of Court or take his place in government service. Many university graduates, with no important political connections to aid them in church or state, came down to London to make their way in the burgeoning literary world. Some, such as Edmund Spenser, Michael Drayton, or Samuel Daniel, were taken into the patronage of great nobles, with whose support they wrote their poetry, sometimes while serving also as secretaries or as tutors to children. Other university graduates, such as Christopher Marlowe, George Peele, or Robert Greene, turned their talents to the public stage, drawing often upon their university experience, for Oxford and Cambridge had long been centres for the performance of plays. That William Shakespeare never attended a university placed him at no disadvantage, but may have done much to shape the direction of his art. His plays are precisely such as university men would not be likely to have written, for they are remarkably free from rhetorical ostentation and display of classical learning for its own sake. T. W. Baldwin has demonstrated that there is nothing in any of the plays of Shakespeare which can be attributed to university training; whatever learning his plays contain is no more than might be expected from a graduate of the Stratford grammar school.

Sports and Amusements

The middle class Elizabethan Englishman worked long hours, attended church regularly, and thought much about the salvation of his soul. As Puritan sentiment grew stronger, particularly in the city of London, the emphasis upon the salutary effects of hard work increased, and the idle vanities of life were subjected to ever greater scorn. But the theatres flourished in spite of that, and there were amusements both in the country and in the cities which continued to be fully enjoyed, for, in spite of all they endured, the Elizabethans were a happy people, full of the zest for living.

In rural England springtime was still a season for the traditional May games, morris-dances, and folk festivals with which the end of winter had been celebrated since time immemorial, and the Chrismas season was still marked by many of the Yuletide customs descended from pre-Christian times. The rural sports in which Shakespeare must have participated as a boy in Warwickshire are called upon frequently in the imagery of his plays. There are references to fishing, which may well reflect his own experience in Avon waters, and there are countless references to those most frequently engaged in of all rural sports, hawking and hunting.

Hawking was an especially popular sport with gentlemen, and

it had a distinctive vocabulary which was drawn upon frequently by Shakespeare. Hawks were captured wild and then trained while in captivity. Those taken directly from the nest were called "eyasses"; if captured in maturity they were called "haggards" and considered of little value, for such birds were extremely difficult to tame or "man." Only the female bird was ever referred to as a "falcon"; the male was called a "tassel" or "tercel." When a bird had been captured, its eyelids were "seeled"; that is, a thread was passed through them so that they could be raised and lowered at will by the falconer, enabling the bird to see only when he wished it to behold the artificial bait or "lure" with which he trained it. Since the hawk could be handled only when it was blind, in the field it was hooded, and leather straps or "jesses" were fastened to its legs so that it could be controlled. Bells were also attached so that the falconer could locate his bird and the quarry it had brought down, particularly in wooded areas. When the bird flapped its wings wildly, it was said to "bate," and when a broken feather was replaced with a new one, the wing was "imped." When the bird soared upwards, the highest point it reached was called its "pitch," and there it hovered until it was ready to "stoop" downward on whatever prey it sighted. When it left its quarry to pursue a passing bird it was said to "check."

What we today call hunting (and the Elizabethans generally called "venery") was practised in various forms, each of which also had a technical vocabulary upon which Shakespeare drew with great frequency. Shooting at deer was generally done with crossbows after the animals had been driven into enclosures (or "pales") from which they could not escape; sometimes the hunter stood upon a concealed platform called a "stand." Various terms used to distinguish kinds of deer—hart, sorel, pricket, and rascal, a deer so skinny as to be worthless—are common sources of Shakespearian puns. Many primitive customs associated with the killing of deer were still current in Shakespeare's day, such as the practice of adorning the chief huntsman with the hide and antlers of the animal after the hunters had smeared their own arms and faces with its blood. The pile of dead deer amassed at the end of a hunt was called a "quarry."

The pursuit of deer, hare, and fox on horseback with the aid of dogs was called "coursing." The pack of hounds was called a "cry"; to unleash was to "uncouple" them. A break in the scent they followed was called a "fault," and when they followed a false scent away from the game, they were said to "run counter." Birds were not only hunted with small crossbows, which shot "bird-bolts," but they also were trapped with a great variety of mechanical devices. Shakespeare often refers to the kind of noose called a "springe" which was used to catch woodcocks, regarded as especially foolish birds, easy to snare. A steel trap was called a "gin." A common method used to catch young birds was to spread a sticky substance called "birdlime" on twigs. All of these practices, and the terms associated with them, are part of the language of venery which is so marked in Shakespeare's plays.

Another favourite sport, both in the city and in the country, was the game of bowls, which could be played either on a green or in a bowling alley. In this game a small white ball called the "jack" or "mistress" was placed at the end of the green or alley. Towards it each of the players rolled larger wooden brown balls, their object being to come as close as possible to the jack; to touch the jack was to "kiss" it. The balls could not be rolled directly at the jack, however, for each had a lead weight on one side of it which would cause it to curve away. This weight was called the "bias," and the skill of the game involved rolling the ball in such a way as to compensate for this bias. Any impediment which interfered with the ball on its way towards the jack, usually a lump in the green, was called a "rub."

The suburbs around London provided amusements of many kinds, most of which were forbidden within the city limits. There were many forms of gambling, both with cards and with dice; there was cockfighting, and there was pleasure-boating on the Thames. But the most popular of all the bankside pastimes was the baiting of bears and bulls, the great centre for which was at Paris Garden in Southwark, close to the principal London theatres. At least one of the theatres, the Hope, built in 1614, was so designed that it could be used for bearbaiting, as well as plays, and although the original stipulation was that it was to be used for this purpose only once in every two weeks, this was soon disregarded as the managers found bearbaiting to be far more profitable than stage plays.

The building of Paris Garden in 1526 had actually been sponsored by King Henry VIII, for the sport of animalbaiting was frowned upon only by the Puritans, who drove it out of London as they gained power in the city government. They were opposed not only to its cruelty but to the fact that it was often indulged in on Sundays. The bull or bear was chained to a stake, and four or five mastiff dogs were turned loose upon it. One bout between the chained animal and his attackers was called a "course," and it usually ended with several of the dogs dead or disabled and the rest standing back, howling and barking. Then another course would begin with a fresh team of dogs. Such courses might continue until darkness. Although many dogs were usually killed, the bear or bull rarely was seriously injured. Sometimes the day's baiting was concluded with a comic spectacle in which a monkey was set upon the back of a horse or donkey and the two pursued around the ring by yelping dogs. The sport was apparently as noisy as it was cruel. Shakespeare must not have been particularly horrified by it, however, for there are probably more allusions to it in his plays than to any other amusement of the time. It is interesting that the theatre and animalbaiting were often thought of as similar enterprises. The theatre manager, Philip Henslowe and his son-in-law, Edward Alleyn, one of the greatest actors of his time, seem to have spent at least as much effort in managing bull- and bearbaiting matches as they devoted to theatrical affairs. It may well be that the theatre was the less profitable of the two kinds of enterprises.

Of court entertainments, the most important and the one most intimately connected with drama was the masque. In its earliest form it appears to have grown out of a kind of mumming in which ordinary citizens disguised themselves on public holidays and, in their fanciful costumes, usually emphasizing the grotesque, went to serenade their neighbours. Among the upper classes it was common for such masquers to appear, accompanied by musicians, at a party. The masquers would put on some kind of skit, and then either unmask and dance with guests or else depart as they had entered. In Renaissance Italy masquers became a part of court entertainment. When the custom was introduced into England, the costuming and the accompanying dance and music grew more and more elaborate until the masque became an allegorical spectacle, the masquers playing symbolic roles and reciting poetry especially written for the occasion.

The masque had its greatest development under King James I and his queen, Anne of Denmark. Vast sums of money were spent on stage settings designed by Inigo Jones, the greatest architect of his day, who had himself been trained in Italy. The poetic speeches were written by Ben Jonson, one of the greatest of poets. In its final form the masque was a fusion of music, dance, and poetry adapted to a central unifying theme, usually closely related to the interests of the court audience before whom it was performed.

Although Shakespeare's ordinary audience might never see a masque at court, the dramatist provided them with masques within the plays themselves. Shakespeare drew upon the masque in various forms in plays so diverse as *Romeo and Juliet* and *The Merchant of Venice,* where masquers play an important role in the action; in *Love's Labour's Lost, Much Ado About Nothing, Cymbeline, The Tempest,* and *Henry VIII.* In a play such as *A Midsummer Night's Dream,* the tone and technique of the masque are made to pervade the whole work. Although Shakespeare himself never wrote a masque for court performance, the tradition of the masque fulfils a very important role in his achievement.

Music and dance were not only important features of the masque, but were closely associated also with the performance of plays in Shakespeare's theatre. Many of the comedies end with a dance, and names of dances such as the galliard, lavolta, and cinquepace occur frequently in the dialogue. The playing of musical instruments was regarded as a necessary accomplishment of a Renaissance gentleman, and in many middle-class homes dinner was usually followed by a session of singing and the playing of instruments. Almost every instrument of the time, with the exception of the virginals, was employed in the theatre. The boy actors, of course, were skilled choristers, and such clowns as Robert Armin in Shakespeare's own company were accomplished singers and dancers. It is thus not surprising to find that not only the names of musical instruments, but technical musical terms as well, should occur often in Shakespeare's plays and be an important source of his poetic imagery.

The English Drama Before Shakespeare

◇◇◇◇◇ When Shakespeare began to write his plays a tradition of
◇◇◇◇◇ public theatre was already firmly established in England.
◇◇◇◇◇ It was a theatre which, while it catered to the needs of no one social
or intellectual class, embraced in its various forms the interests
and needs of all. It was distinctively English, although it had
originated in a medieval world in which national cultures had not
been of primary importance. As England had participated in the
intellectual revival of Western Europe, its drama had absorbed
the influences both of the classical world and of contemporary
Europe and had developed a richness and diversity. When Shakespeare came to London, this dramatic tradition was on the verge
of bursting into greatness. To its efflorescence, Shakespeare contributed more than any other dramatist of his time. He absorbed
what he had inherited from the past, shaped it by his own genius,
and gave it new directions, so that his distinctive contribution was
to mark the work of his successors.

One important source of this tradition was in the liturgy of the
universal church, which from its very beginnings had been dramatic
in nature. The Roman mass itself was a dramatic representational
act, and it has been argued that in the five or six centuries following
the fall of Rome, church service satisfied for Western Europe that
need for drama which has always been a part of the human spirit.
The movement from the religious liturgy of the medieval church to
the secular drama of Shakespeare's age is a long and difficult one, and
the evidence from which we are forced to draw conclusions is frag-

mentary and inadequate. While the liturgy is only one of the wellsprings of Elizabethan drama, it is nevertheless the one about which we know most and the one whose continuing influence can be most surely traced.

The Liturgical Drama

In the ninth century in the Abbey of St. Gall in Switzerland, under the influence of the great Carolingian revival of church liturgy, the monk, Notker Balbulus, developed the wordless Halleluia; and his friend, Tutilo, wrote semi-dramatic tropes. These were simple embellishments of the liturgy, not dramatic in themselves, but sometimes with a potential for dramatic development. Manuscripts dating from the beginning of the tenth century reveal that in various cathedrals of Europe the introit to the mass for Easter morning was prefixed by a brief dialogue in which one choirboy, representing an angel and standing over the altar which represents the tomb of Christ, chants the line *"Quem quæritis in sepulchro, O Christicolæ,"* and three other choirboys, representing the three Marys who have come to the tomb, sing in response, *"Jesum Nazarenum crucifixum, O Cælicolæ."* This *quem quæritis* trope, as it is called, is identifiable as dramatic, and it was to provide the seed for fuller dramatic development, but we cannot know with certainty whether it was something entirely new or a relic of an even larger dramatic quality in the liturgy from which it sprang.

What is clear is that liturgical embellishments can be found in increasingly more sophisticated and elaborate — and thus more dramatic — forms, although at what date these more sophisticated forms came into being and how they are related to seemingly more primitive ones we cannot be sure. It appears that in the service for Matins on Easter morning, which was somewhat less solemn an occasion than the Easter Mass, more and more lines appear in the tropes, and biblical figures are impersonated to a greater degree. Sometime between A.D. 965 and 975 Ethelwold, Bishop of Winchester, prepared a set of instructions for services to be performed in the Benedictine monastaries in England. It is the *Regularis Concordia,* and it is probably our earliest dramatic document. It describes in detail one method of performance of the *Quem quæritis* trope. In other versions of the Easter trope we find four little scenes:

the visit of the Marys to the tomb, a race by Peter and John to the sepulcher, the appearance of Christ as a gardener to Mary Magdalene, and His appearance to the wayfarers on the road to Emmaus. In some other versions we have also a scene of lamentation by the Marys and one showing the purchase of ointment for the body of Christ from a spice-merchant, the first character in liturgical drama of whom there is no mention in the Bible.

Liturgical plays appeared at seasons of the year other than Easter. The Christmas season, a time for festivity and merriment even in pre-Christian times, was a natural time for play making, but whether Christmas plays sprang from extension of the Easter plays or were a simultaneous development we cannot be certain. At Christmas time the dialogue between the Marys and the Angel is paralleled by a dialogue between shepherds coming to adore the Christ child and the midwives, or *obstetrices,* who vary only slightly the opening line of the Easter play: *"Quem quæritis in præsepe, o pastores, dicite."* The altar which had stood for the *sepulchrum* of Christ in the Easter plays stands for the *præsepe* or cradle of Christ in this Christmas play.

There are other scenes as well. A little play was performed which represented the Magi and their gifts. Another represented the slaughter of the innocents by Herod, giving us what is probably our first stock character type, the ranting tyrant. As the final play of the Christmas season, we have an *Ordo Prophetarum* in which the various Old Testament patriarchs prophesy the birth of Christ. Among them is Balaam with his ass, a natural subject for comic elaboration. It is interesting that this play is based not upon scripture, but upon a sermon directed towards the conversion of the Jews, long attributed erroneously to St. Augustine.

This liturgical drama in Latin was not particularly an English phenomenon, for it seems to have developed simultaneously throughout Europe. Nor was it for long confined to the Easter and Christmas seasons. Biblical stories other than the birth and resurrection of Christ were dramatized for performance at services throughout the year. On the Sundays following Epiphany there were *lectiones* or lessons devoted to the lives of Old Testament patriarchs. To accompany these services, we find plays based upon Old Testament stories, of which perhaps the most important which have survived are the *Ordo Joseph* in a thirteenth-century manuscript at Laon, with its depiction of the selling of Joseph by his brother; and the Anglo-Norman *Mystère d'Adam,* with its scenes of Adam and Eve and Cain and Abel, a work whose stage directions are in Latin and whose dialogues are in Anglo-Norman French. There are at least two plays on the prophet Daniel, one of them probably written by the wandering scholar, Hilarius, who may be the earliest known dramatist of Western Europe. Also, a *Ludus de Sancta Katarina* was written by Geoffrey, Abbot of St. Albans, for performance at Dunstable in Bedfordshire, sometime before the year 1119. Although this work has not survived, its author is the earliest known dramatist to have worked in England.

Other material for dramatic treatment was found in the lives of saints, to whom special services were devoted on regular days of the year. St. Nicholas and St. Catherine, the patrons of schoolboys and schoolgirls respectively, were particularly popular subjects. Hilarius wrote a *Ludus super Iconia Sancti Nicolai.* There were plays on the conversion of Saint Paul, on the raising of Lazarus, and on other New Testament subjects. These we call "miracle plays." Since they dealt with the lives and miracles of people who had actually lived, they allowed a scope to the dramatist's imagination greater than that permitted by the simpler Easter and Christmas plays.

Thus we have within the very church itself a kind of drama devoted ostensibly to religious instruction, but which satisfies also the need for entertainment known by every people in every age, and which the early Christian Church had done so much to stifle. Indeed, the growth of Christianity had been an important factor in the extinction of Roman drama following the collapse of the Roman empire. The fathers of the church had bitterly denounced dramatic entertainment, and it must be remembered that they were censuring the barbarous and decadent shows of the later empire. In the centuries following the fall of Rome, the Greek drama was largely forgotten, and, of the Roman, little was read other than some of Terence. It is significant that while the last vestiges of a great Pagan drama which had itself emerged out of religious ritual were being stamped out by a new religion, out of this very new religion a new kind of drama was emerging.

The Anglo-Norman *Mystère d'Adam* provides evidence that at a very early date a tradition of vernacular religious drama had begun to develop alongside of the Latin plays. Similar evidence is provided by *The Shrewsbury Fragments,* discovered in 1890, which contain the roles of a single actor who had appeared in Christmas and Easter plays, his speeches being in English, and the stage directions and parts to be sung by more than one performer being in Latin. Religious plays in Latin and in English appear to have continued side by side, but the vernacular drama developed more rapidly and gradually became more secular in spirit — moving out of the church into the churchyard, and replacing the choirboys, monks, and priests of the Latin plays with guildsmen, students, and other lay performers. That secular elements came more and more to be a part of such plays does not, however, mean that such plays passed out of the hands of the church or became essentially less religious in character. The biblical drama in England, in the vernacular as well as in Latin, remained under church control until its extinction in the time of Queen Elizabeth. Its demise may have come because a Reformation church could no longer countenance and support the performance of plays which were essentially expressions of Catholic doctrine.

The Corpus Christi Day Cycles

With vernacular plays the phenomenon of an international drama gradually ended, and plays performed in England came to take on distinctively English characteristics. Plays were elaborated and developed. Crude realism and bawdy humour became more and more prominent in them. Balaam would beat his ass for comic effect; the actor who played Herod might give full expression to whatever exhibitionist propensities he possessed; and we even have one text in which Mary Magdalene sings a bawdy song to her lover. Such seeming irreverence was not really at variance with the religious nature of the plays, although it may seem so to us today, for it was a commonplace medieval notion that man's grossness and folly were signs of his need for God and thus entirely appropriate for depiction in religious art.

Lay actors began to develop the characters they portrayed, revealing facets of them unenvisioned in their biblical originals. Inevitably, lines came to be spoken rather than sung. Finally, there emerged a drama covering all of biblical story from the fall of Lucifer to the last judgment, performed in English, by lay actors, in the market squares of the great cathedral cities of England. These were the mystery play cycles which came to be performed regularly on Corpus Christi day. We do not know exactly how or when they came into being, but they were in existence by the second quarter of the fourteenth century, and were still being performed when William Shakespeare was a boy.

Corpus Christi day, a springtime festival celebrated on the Thursday following Trinity Sunday, was originally proposed by St. Juliana of Liege (1193–1258), promulgated by Pope Urban IV, confirmed by Pope Clement V, and ordered adopted by the Council of Vienne in 1311. From 1318 onward it was celebrated in England, and in many cities it came to be adopted by the trade guilds as their principal festival of the year. The papal decree establishing the holiday had required that one of its features be a procession in which five pageant scenes from the fall of man to the last judgment would represent man's need for Christ. That guildsmen should participate in these scenes was natural, for the guilds themselves were religious organizations, each with its chapel and its patron saint, and even before the institution of Corpus Christi day guildsmen had honoured their special saints in street processions. It is possible that the five scenes prescribed for the procession may have furnished the impetus which caused Corpus Christi day to become a time for cycles of plays depicting the full story of mankind. The elaborate wagons on which the guildsmen came to act their plays may have been drawn in the Corpus Christi procession.

The texts of four great cycles of plays acted in different English cities on Corpus Christi day have come down to us. Each cycle consists of a sequence of related mystery plays — each performed by the members of a particular guild — covering the events of the Old Testament and the New Testament and concluding with the last judgment. Of the authorship of these plays we know nothing, and it is extremely unlikely that any one of the cycles was the work of a single man. It is probable that in the forms in which they are extant the cycles represent accretions of revision and further revision over a period of several centuries.

Probably the oldest of the four surviving cycles is that performed at Chester. It has been preserved in a number of manuscripts, none earlier than the last quarter of the fifteenth century, but the plays themselves must date from the middle of the fourteenth. There is some reason to believe that Ranulph Higden, the author of the *Polychronicon,* who was a monk at St. Werburgh's, Chester between 1299 and 1364, had some share in their composition. The cycle consists of a set of banns (a proclamation announcing the contents of the cycle) and twenty-five plays beginning with *The Fall of Lucifer* performed by the Tanners and ending with *Doomsday* performed by the Weavers. The plays are in rhymed eight-line stanzas; they are uneven in quality, often very crude, the technique being generally one of exposition and explanation rather than the presentation of vivid realistic scenes such as we sometimes find in the other cycles.

The most strikingly realistic in their technique are the plays of the second great extant cycle, the York cycle, preserved in British Museum MS. Add. 35290. These consist of forty-eight plays and a fragment, beginning with *The Creation and Fall of Lucifer,* acted by the Barkers, and ending with the fragment, *The Coronation of Our Lady,* performed by the Innholders. It is likely that this fragment was a late addition meant to replace the forty-seventh play, the Hostler's *Assumption and Coronation of the Virgin,* and that the cycle ended, like that of Chester, with Judgment Day, here performed by the Mercers. Probably the supreme achievement of the York cycle is the play of *The Crucifixion,* performed by the Butchers of the city, which attains a stark realistic effect of Gothic horror, with Christ hanging from the cross throughout the performance.

The York cycle may go back to the middle years of the fourteenth century, although the handwriting of the one extant manuscript is, for the most part, of about one hundred years later, with additions in even later hands which give good evidence of the replacement and alteration of the plays over a long period of time. Scholars have assigned parts of the cycle to three different periods of composition, the comic elements being assigned to the second, and the more realistic plays being considered the latest in date. There is much alliteration in the verse and great metrical variety, sometimes within a single play. It is possible to count twenty-two different stanzaic forms in all. The plays were performed on movable pageant wagons which made stops at from twelve to sixteen "stations" about the city. We have evidence that the plays were being acted in York as late as 1580. Of all the cycles, the York plays are the most comprehensive in scope and probably the most important.

The third great extant cycle is preserved in a manuscript formerly at Towneley Hall and now in the Huntington Library, San Marino, California. They are called the Towneley plays or the Wakefield plays, for, although there is no external evidence that Corpus Christi plays were performed at Wakefield, topographical allusions in the manuscript itself make it clear that the plays were associated with this city. The manuscript, written in the second half of the fifteenth century, consists of thirty-two plays, some preserved only in fragmentary form. They exhibit several stages of growth and have been assigned by scholars to different periods of composition. Like the York cycle, the Wakefield exhibits great metrical variety. Some of the plays show signs of having been imitated from the York plays. Five plays, all written in the same nine-line stanza and outstanding both for their realism and their fine sense of comedy, are the work of a single writer of extraordinary genius who has come to be known as the "Wakefield master." The most notable of these, and probably the greatest single achievement of the medieval drama in England, is the *Secunda Pastorum* or *Second Shepherds' Play*. The plays of the "Wakefield master" have been dated between 1380 and 1410 and are probably closer to the later date, but some parts of the cycle must go back to at least the middle of the fourteenth century. In addition to the five plays indisputably by the "Wakefield master," parts of some seven others in the cycle have been assigned to him.

We are not certain about where the fourth great extant cycle of Corpus Christi day plays was performed. At the beginning of the seventeenth century, the single manuscript in which they are contained, now British Museum MS. Cotton Vespasian D, VIII, was in the possession of a Robert Hegge of Durham. Thus they are called *Hegge Plays* by some scholars. They are also known as the *Ludus Coventriæ* because these words were written upon the fly-leaf of the manuscript by the librarian of Sir Robert Cotton into whose possession it had passed. They were thus confused with the plays performed at Coventry, but we are certain that these are not the true Coventry plays. Some scholars have preferred to call them *N Town* plays, indicating the uncertainty as to their origin. Most recent scholars are of the opinion that they are the plays performed in the city of Lincoln, which we know from other records was an important centre for the religious drama. The cycle consists of forty-three plays, beginning with *The Fall of Lucifer* and ending with *Doomsday,* the final lines of which are missing. These plays are unique among the extant cycles in that they appear to have been performed upon a fixed stage rather than upon movable pageant wagons. Like the other cycles, the *Ludus Coventriæ* shows signs of several stages of development, and in its present form it dates probably from the first half of the fifteenth century.

That Cotton's librarian should have thought of the plays as belonging to Coventry is not surprising, for Coventry was famous as a centre for religious drama. Unfortunately the true Coventry cycle is no longer extant, although a manuscript prepared by Robert Croo in 1534 was extant until 1879 when it was destroyed in a fire at the Free Reference Library in Birmingham. Two plays of the cycle, that of the Shearmen and Tailors and that of the Weavers, have been preserved.

There is ample reason to believe that cycles of mystery plays no longer extant were performed in many other cities of England — in Beverly, Newcastle, Norwich, and elsewhere. Various individual plays have survived, such as the Brome *Sacrifice of Isaac,* the Newcastle *Noah's Ark,* and the Norwich *Creation of Eve and The Fall,* which probably were parts of larger cycles. There is reason to believe that mystery plays were performed in London and at the Universities of Oxford and Cambridge, and plays have survived in the Cornish language. The performance of mystery plays was probably the most universal in its scope of any dramatic phenomenon the world has ever known. The productions covered all of England and were put on by amateur actors, often at great expense, as their contribution to a social system in which every man had his function and in which the relation of man to God was always an immediate concern. Their audience embraced every social class, serf, artisan, student, bishop, and king, and their subject matter was the history of the entire universe from its reputed creation to its anticipated dissolution. These plays established traditions and conventions which continued to mark and shape the English drama to the closing of the theatres in 1642 and later.

The Miracle Play

The term "miracle play" has often been used to include these cyclical plays, but more properly a miracle play was based not upon scripture, but upon miraculous events in the lives of saints or the Virgin Mary. We have noted the Latin St. Nicholas and St. Catherine plays which are liturgical miracle plays. The miracle play in English is not very common — or at least, there are few extant examples. One of the most striking is the fragmentary *Dux Moraud,* preserved in the margin of a 1250–1300 assize roll for Norfolk and Suffolk (Bodleian MS. Add. 30519). Here, written in a fourteenth-century hand, is the part of a single actor, the title role, in a play which uses a story of paternal incest, going back ultimately to the Greek *Appolonius of Tyre,* to teach the moral lesson that salvation is open to all sinners, no matter how heinous their crimes. The play falls generally into the type of *Miracle de Notre Dame,* common in France, in which the hero gains salvation by appeal to the Virgin Mary. Of particular interest is the fact that this miracle play probably antedates the four extant mystery play cycles and reminds us that the distinctive forms of medieval drama did not develop in any chronological sequence.

Also remarkable as an English miracle play is *The Play of the Sacrament,* preserved in Trinity College, Dublin MS. F.IV. 20, dating from the second half of the fifteenth century. This play, as we are informed at the end of the "banns" was performed at Croxton, but there are, unfortunately for identification, many towns in England of this name. From the language and from some probable local allusions, however, it has been conjectured that the play was acted in East Anglia and that the Croxton referred to is either that in Cambridgeshire or that in Norfolk. The play is crude but interesting as an example of a medieval anti-Semitic legend which has been dramatized for performance by a travelling company of nine players. The miracle which leads to the Jew's final conversion to Christianity is his inability to destroy the holy wafer which he has bought from a Christian and which he torments upon the stage in a manner which makes a full use of the sensational and calls for much ingenuity of stagecraft. It is full of farcical humour, usually in very bad taste, and in one of its characters, Doctor Brundyche of Braban, we have not only an adaptation of the comic quack doctor of English folk drama, but also the possible influence of the stock pedant of Roman comedy. In this play religious drama has become popular lower-class entertainment.

In Bodleian MS. Digby 133 are four plays which have no real connection with one another except that, although in different handwritings, they were gathered together. One is a morality play, *Wisdom*. The other three are based upon stories in the New Testament. They are all too long, however, to have been parts of mystery play cycles, and they exhibit the same kind of imaginative elaboration of story, with a dwelling upon the sensational and miraculous, which we associate with miracle rather than mystery plays. The three plays are a *Mary Magdalene*, a *Conversion of Paul*, and a *Massacre of the Innocents*. Of these *Mary Magdalene* is the most interesting, for it is a kind of hybrid which contains within itself all ment. They are all too long, however, to have been parts of mystery play concerned with the life of Christ, and at the same time it is a miracle play which takes the life of Mary Magdalene from the *Legenda Aurea* of Jacobus de Voragine, the great medieval storehouse of the lives of saints, and dwells in detail upon the miraculous and the exotic. All of this is for the clear purpose of moral instruction, and thus it assumes also the function of the morality play and comes in fact to include as characters such morality play abstractions as the Seven Deadly Sins. It provides also a realistic portrait of medieval English life, with a tavern scene in which Mary is seduced by a gallant, the earliest perhaps of a long series of tavern scenes in which virtue is seduced by vice, culminating in the Boar's Head Tavern scenes of Shakespeare's *Henry IV* plays.

Mary Magdalene was performed on eight separate stages, each representing a specific locale, arranged around a central *platea* or unspecified area. The play is divided into two parts with twenty separate scenes in the first and thirty-one in the second; the first part, dealing with the fall and conversion of Mary, was probably acted in the morning, and the second part, dealing with Mary's voyage to Marcylle and her consequent conversion of the king and queen of that country, in the afternoon. Since there are at least forty separate characters in the first part and at least twenty-six in the second, the production of this play must have been a formidable and expensive undertaking in which a great many townspeople participated. The day on which it was performed may well have been a festival occasion not unlike Corpus Christi day.

Mary Magdalene seems designed to satisfy the various tastes and expectations of an audience conditioned by the mystery and miracle drama. Stock characters, such as the ranting Herod and the boasting Pilate, are taken over from the Corpus Christi day plays, and the usual medieval preoccupation with the assault of evil upon the soul of man is reflected in the Seven Deadly Sins who appear upon the stage to besiege the castle of Magdalene. The raising of Lazarus from the dead provides wonder and mystery. The awe and solemnity of biblical story are varied by highly romantic digressions. The scenes are arranged in an episodic series, with little continuity from one to another, thus helping to establish one tradition of dramatic construction which continues in the later drama.

The Morality Play

The personified abstractions who appear in *Mary Magdalene* remind us that the roots of the morality play, usually taken to be the final development of medieval drama in England, are implicit in the earlier mystery and miracle plays. In essence, the morality play is the dramatization of a moral sermon, as the mystery and miracle plays are dramatizations of specific events. While their subject matter is concrete and factual, that of the morality play, in spite of its realism in depicting the details of contemporary life, is abstract and allegorical. Its hero — *Humanum Genus,* Mankind, Everyman — represents not an historical person but all of humanity, and the characters he encounters on the stage are representations of moral abstractions.

Although the earliest extant examples of the morality play date from the fifteenth century, John Wyclif, writing in about 1378, alluded to a dramatic performance in the city of York which was based upon the Lord's Prayer and in which the various vices were held up to scorn and the virtues were praised. We know also that as late as 1572 such a "Creed" or "Paternoster" play, with various pageants depicting the deadly sins and their antitheses, was performed in York in place of the Corpus Christi plays. There are records of Paternoster plays performed at Lincoln and at Beverly as well. It is likely that in this kind of play, no example of which survives, lie the roots of the morality play.

The morality play has been called the last great manifestation of the medieval spirit of allegory. It came to incorporate within itself many of the dominant motifs of medieval literature, but above all it made use of three great themes. The first of these was the conflict of the vices and the virtues for the soul of man, an allegorical formulation which has its origins in the *Psychomachia* of Prudentius, a Latin writer of the fifth century A.D., and which appears in many forms of medieval literature. The second great theme was the coming of death, which appears most notably in the *Danse Macabre* paintings on the walls and windows of churches, in tapestries, in illuminated service-books, and in the early sixteenth century in the remarkable series of paintings by Hans Holbein. With these two themes was joined, as the final element in the disposition of man's soul, the debate in heaven of the four daughters of God: Mercy, Truth, Peace, and Justice. The writers of morality plays found this allegory, based upon a verse in Psalms 85.10, already fully developed in earlier ecclesiastical literature.

Only one of these themes, the coming of death, appears in our earliest extant morality play, the fragmentary *Pride of Life*, written in two hands in the blank spaces and on the back of an account roll of Holy Trinity Priory, Dublin, for 1343. It has been conjectured that this represents a preliminary stage in the evolution of the morality play, the other themes being added as the form developed. The three themes appear together in *The Castle of Perseverance*, our only example of a full-scope morality play. This work of more than three thousand lines presents a Christian view of the role of humankind from birth to final judgment. The hero, *Humanum Genus*, stands between good and evil angels who appeal to him. He is twice seduced by the Seven Deadly Sins, in spite of the offices of the virtues. After his death, his body is chided by his soul, and its final disposition is debated by the daughters of God, with Mercy, and thus salvation, finally triumphant. The play, dated usually about 1425, appears along with two other moralities, *Mankind* and *Wisdom* (of which a fragment appears also in the Digby MS.) in a manuscript at one time (1683–1769) in the possession of the Reverend Cox Macro and now in the Folger Library, Washington, D.C.

Wisdom, or *Mind, Will and Understanding,* as it is also called, is dated usually around 1460. It is a dull play, full of long, didactic speeches, but it is notable for some touches of realism and for its treatment of ecclesiastical abuses of the fifteenth century. Of considerably more interest is *Mankind,* for the form in which that play has descended to us shows that it had passed into the hands of a travelling troupe of seven professional players. It has been dated about 1475, and although it is full of coarseness and vulgarity designed to cater to a lower-class rural audience, it shows signs of having seen better days. Mercy, the only surviving virtue in the play, competes for man's soul against a variety of vices, led by Mischief and a devil named Titivillus. Evil in this play has become comic horseplay, as it is to continue to be in the moralities of the early sixteenth century. It is not unlikely, however, that *Mankind* may have at one time been a full-scale, serious morality play, such as *The Castle of Perserverance,* which was drastically abridged to suit the need of a small professional troupe and vulgarized to fit the tastes of an audience more interested in crude comedy than in moral elevation. In spite of the play's buffoonery and vulgarity, however, the simple outlines of the morality play formula for human salvation remain.

The finest artistic achievement among English morality plays is *Everyman,* printed by Richard Pynson at the beginning of the sixteenth century and reprinted three times before its end. The play presents the morality play motif of the coming of death and, in spite of the late date of our earliest text, it is possible that in some earlier version it may go back to the time of *The Pride of Life* — like it, representing the first of the morality play themes upon which the others came to be grafted as the form developed. Our play is very similar to a Dutch play, *Elckerlijc.* The exact relation between the two works has been much debated, most scholars today agreeing that the Dutch is the earlier play and that it provided the specific source of the English *Everyman* which probably was translated directly from it.

In the morality play the English medieval drama developed a vehicle by which a philosophical view of human destiny could be presented in symbolic terms. It was based upon the doctrine of free will, for the essential feature of all morality plays was the free choice of a hero between competing forces which vied for his favour. The theological principle upon which the early moralities were based was a very simple one: mankind, being vitiated by original sin, would naturally choose evil, but being endowed also with the grace of God, he could recognize his error, repent, and embrace the true means of salvation. Theologically there was very little room for development and variation, for the three basic movements of *The Castle of Perseverance* which taught this theological principle could be repeated only so many times, and soon all variations of the formula would be exhausted. In order to grow, the morality play had to move away from its theological bases, as it did in the early years of the sixteenth century when the dramatic structure designed to teach the means of attaining heaven began to be used to teach other lessons, secular lessons of vital interest to a Renaissance world of steadily expanding intellectual horizons.

The morality play, in the new forms which it now assumed, continued to influence the course of English drama until the closing of the theatres. Generic distinctions between comedy and tragedy were alien to it, for, like so much of medieval art, it mingled high seriousness with farce, usually in alternating scenes, and its stock character, the Vice, although symbolic of evil, was essentially a comic creature. As comedy and tragedy later developed into distinctive dramatic genres, the morality play continued to exercise an influence upon each. It provided a native comic tradition which absorbed the classical devices fused with it in the Renaissance. In tragedy it provided a formula for moral choice, with man's soul in the balance, which was still alive in the seventeenth century and was demonstrated in Shakespeare's *Othello,* where the tempting Iago, gloating over his own villainy, carries on the role of the Vice, just as it is carried on in other forms in characters as diverse as Falstaff and Richard III. The morality play provided a logical scheme for the organization of plot which, along with the episodic structure of the miracle and mystery play, became an essential ingredient of English dramatic tradition.

The Tudor Interlude

By the last decades of the fifteenth century, secularization of the drama had reached such a point that, alongside of religious plays which continued to be performed, we find a drama which caters to entirely different interests. A new kind of drama had evolved in seeming accompaniment to a growth of humanistic learning in England and a consequent expansion of human interests and intellectual concerns. This new drama was fostered also by the growth of professional acting companies, both those who wandered from town to town entertaining motley audiences in market squares and innyards, and those who, as servants of great nobles, began to entertain guests in aristocratic households. These professional actors performed the plays called "interludes," a term which came into fashion around 1500 and which we use to describe both the later morality plays which turned from religious to secular instruction, and certain plays, performed probably between the courses of feasts in noble houses, which almost entirely subordinated the traditional didactic ends of drama to those of entertainment as an end in itself.

We associate the beginnings of the interlude with a group of writers who have come to be known as "the circle of Sir Thomas More," for all were in some way associated with him. More himself is reputed to have been a writer of comedies in his youth, although none have survived. When, as a boy, he served as page in the household of Cardinal John Morton, chief minister to King Henry VII, Morton's chaplain at Lambeth palace was Henry Medwall, the author of *Fulgens and Lucrece,* our first important entirely secular play. This play was printed by John Rastell, the humanist and dramatist who married More's sister, Elizabeth. Of their two children, William Rastell carried on the humanistic and dramatic interests of his father, and Joan Rastell married John Heywood, the earliest known English dramatist of real talent, and the name most closely associated with the Tudor interlude. Their son, Jasper Heywood, was the first translator of Seneca into English.

Fulgens and Lucrece was unknown until 1919 when the single extant copy of the quarto printed by John Rastell was discovered. Because of this discovery, many notions about the state of English drama at the close of the fifteenth century had to be revised. Medwall had been known for a long time as the author of *Nature,* an old-fashioned morality play whose subject is the life of man from birth to old age, with all of the sins he must encounter on his earthly passage. Yet this play is different from earlier moralities in that the *Ethics* of Aristotle, rather than the traditional Christian scheme of salvation, is offered as the guide to human felicity, with reason, rather than divine revelation, exalted as the supreme power to whose rule mankind must conform. In this fact we may perceive the humanistic interests of the author which are expressed also in *Fulgens and Lucrece.* This play is based upon a humanistic tract, a translation by John Tiptoft, Earl of Worcester, of a Ciceronian imitation, the *De Vera Nobilitate* of Buonaccorso of Pistoia. It is a classical debate on an ancient subject — the meaning of true nobility, whether it be based upon good deeds or upon noble birth. Its sub-plot, in its comic commentary upon the main plot, looks forward to the practice of mature Elizabethan dramatists, and especially to that of William Shakespeare.

In *Fulgens and Lucrece* didacticism is still an end of drama, although a classical device, rather than a morality play formula, is used to illustrate not a religious affirmation, but a social principle which was a prominent subject of debate in polite aristocratic circles. In the comic interludes of John Heywood didacticism is often abandoned entirely. His plays are the work of a professional court entertainer, an accomplished musician, and probably the first poet of real ability to write plays in English. Three of his clever interludes, *Witty and Witless, The Play of the Weather,* and *The Play of Love,* are little more than comic dialogues in verse. *The Pardoner and the Friar* and *The Four P's* extend the dialogue and debate technique so that we have dramatizations of comic anecdotes. In *John Johan, Tib his Wife, and Sir John,* Heywood carries into English the tradition of French farce. Among Heywood's plays, it is perhaps the most notable for its skillful manipulation in action of three stock character types with long associations in folk literature. The hearty obscenity of the play links it also to the tradition of Chaucer as much as to Elizabethan plays to come.

The interlude flourished in the schools as well as in great houses and at court. In John Redford's *Wit and Science* we find an adaptation of the morality play form to the problems of secular learning and to the acting requirements of schoolboys. The play was performed by the children of St. Paul's school, where Redford, also an accomplished musician, served as singing master. That the form of the morality play lent itself easily to the treatment of new interests generated by the growth of humanistic learning in the early sixteenth century may be seen in other interludes as well. John Rastell's *The Nature of the Four Elements,* for instance, is essentially a lesson in world geography by a scholar who had himself embarked on a voyage to Newfoundland, only to be forced home when his ship was attacked by pirates. In Rastell's *Calisto and Melibea* we see still another direction the interlude was capable of taking. Here we have an episode from the Spanish *Celestina* (1499) adapted as a moral lesson on the rearing of children, perhaps the earliest example of the transformation into English drama of a continental secular narrative. It is so adapted, however, as to embody a moral purpose quite alien to the original.

The education of children had been the subject of a group of Latin plays written by humanistic scholars in the Netherlands, the most famous being the *Acolastus,* produced at The Hague. These plays used the biblical parable of the prodigal son to teach moral lessons, and they were soon imitated in English interludes. The *Acolastus* itself was "Englished" by John Palsgrave in 1540. Thomas Ingelond adapted his *Disobedient Child* from a prose dialogue on the tribulations and punishment of youth by the French Latinist, Ravisus Textor. Other interludes devoted to the sins of errant youth include *Nice Wanton,* based possibly upon a Latin comedy by the Dutch humanist, Georgius Macropedius, *Lusty Juventus* by Robert Weaver, *The Interlude of Youth,* and *The World and the Child.* In these plays the traditional scheme of Mankind's position between the vices and virtues has been applied to the more specific problem of rearing children.

Perhaps the most significant of the secular areas into which the morality play form intruded was that of government and statecraft, for the political morality plays were to provide one important source of the mature Elizabethan history play. The titular hero of John Skelton's *Magnificence* (ca. 1516), perhaps the earliest of such plays, stands actually for King Henry VIII. The good and evil forces vying for his favour represent specific factions in the Tudor court and particular political positions with which these were associated. *Albion Knight* (ca. 1538) uses the familiar morality play abstractions to teach political lessons given a new urgency by the Pilgrimage of Grace rebellions which had taken place in the north of England in 1536 and 1537. Sir David Lyndsay treated the economic and social ills of Scotland in *Ane Plesant Satyre of the Thrie Estaites,* performed before King James IV at Linlithgow on January 6, 1640. John Bale, Bishop of Ossory, combined morality play abstractions with real historical figures in *Kynge Johan* to express a fiercely Protestant view of the most pressing political issue of his time, the relation between the English king and the Church of Rome. This play was first written before 1536 and revised twice before it was performed for Queen Elizabeth upon her visit to Ipswich in 1561. The Catholic political position was reflected in *Respublica,* written in 1553, probably by Nicholas Udall.

As the interlude extended itself in various directions, it took different forms. Sometimes the morality formula expressed itself in farcical comedy such as we find in Ulpian Fulwell's *Like Will to Like* (1568) or George Wapull's *The Tide Tarrieth No Man* (1576). It was perhaps inevitable that allegory should soon come to support itself by the adaptation of story framework from various sources: from the Bible in *Goodly Queen Hester* (1571), from classical mythology in John Pickering's *Horestes* (1567), from traditional folk legend in John Phillips' *Patient and Meek Grissell* (ca. 1566), from Roman history in R[ichard] B[lower]'s *Appius and Virginia* (1575), and from such historical tales as had been told over and over again in various collections of moral anecdotes designed largely for the instruction of princes, as in Thomas Preston's *Cambises King of Persia.* Thus we cannot really speak of an end to the Tudor interlude. As it developed its range, the mature Elizabethan drama came into being naturally. In the first half of the sixteenth century we already find most of the dramatic movements which were to reach their fruition in the age of Shakespeare.

Early Elizabethan Comedy

Comedy had been a part of the English drama from its very beginnings. It had manifested itself in the Corpus Christi day plays in such stock characters as Noah's wife who has to be driven aboard the ark, her henpecked husband, Cain's boy who assumes the manner of a typical country yokel in the *Killing of Abel,* and the antics of Lucifer himself as he goes off to hell. In the morality plays comedy had come to centre more and more about the Vice, who soon lost much of his theological significance and degenerated into a prankster and clown. As the morality play moved away from its religious direction, in fact, the Vice's comic buffoonery, already evident in the most religious of medieval plays, came more and more to dominate the action, until in a work such as Ulpian Fulwell's *Like Will to Like* (1568) it is the centre of dramatic interest, and if the play has any didactic purpose it is quite obscured. The mingling of comedy and tragedy which was so much a part of the native English dramatic tradition continued through and beyond the maturity of Shakespeare. Thus a play of supposedly serious moral import such as Thomas Preston's *Cambises* (which Shakespeare a quarter of a century later could still mock in *Henry IV, Part I*) is full of the low comedy of the Vice, called Ambidexter, as he sports with the rustics Hob and Lob and with the comic ruffians, Huf, Suf, and Puf.

This native comic tradition, with its strong roots in the medieval drama, remained the basic stuff of English comedy, in spite of the new influences which began to appear in the second half of the sixteenth century. The classical examples of Plautus and Terence and the sophisticated romantic comedy of Renaissance Italy never replaced the native English tradition; they were absorbed by it, and out of the fusion came a kind of drama which is distinctly English.

Terence had long been read in the schools as a model for Latin conversation, and the discovery of the fourteen lost plays of Plautus towards the end of the fifteenth century aroused new interest in this somewhat cruder writer as well. That the Latin comedies studied by English schoolboys should be acted by schoolboys was natural, and it was perhaps inevitable that they should soon be acting also in English imitations of Plautus and Terence written by their more enterprising schoolmasters. The earliest English play to show the strong influence of classical comedy is *Ralph Roister Doister* by Nicholas Udall, himself a schoolmaster at Eton and at Westminster, whose most widely disseminated book was an anthology of passages from Terence to be used by students as a guide to speaking Latin.

Roister Doister preserves in English the staging of Latin comedy, with its two houses at an intersection and the movement of the various characters from one to the other, and the classical system of act and scene division with its five acts and a new scene whenever there is a change of actors upon the stage. Udall based his plot upon suggestions in several plays of Terence and Plautus. He took over from the classics such stock comic characters as the braggart soldier and the parasite. These have been transformed, however, into entirely English types, and much of the play's humour is more closely allied to that of the late English morality plays than it is to Plautus or Terence. A similar adaptation of classical form to the needs of an English audience may be found in *Gammer Gurton's Needle,* acted at an uncertain date by the students of Christ's College, Cambridge and written by a "Mr. S" whose identity has never been established satisfactorily.

In *Roister Doister* the stock courtesan has been transformed into an English housewife. In the barnyard setting of *Gammer Gurton's Needle* the Roman parasite has become a typically English Bedlam beggar. The verse in both plays consists of the crude fourteeners which had become the fashion in the late morality plays, and both plots are merely the crudest adaptations of the clever intrigues of Roman comedy. Little in these plays looks forward to the grace and sophistication, the romantic treatment of love and marriage, and the tender and elegant sentiment which we associate with the comedies of Shakespeare. For the first signs of these elements we must turn to George Gascoigne's *Supposes,* performed by the lawyers at Gray's Inn in 1566.

Gascoigne's play is based not upon Plautus or Terence, but upon an Italian adaptation of the motifs of Roman comedy to the tastes of the sophisticated court milieu of Renaissance Italy, with its glorification of women in neo-Platonic terms and with its elaborate code of courtly behaviour enshrined in the Petrarchan sonnet tradition. Gascoigne's source was Ludovico Ariosto's *Gli Suppositi*, performed in prose at the court of Ferrara in 1509 and later rewritten in verse by Ariosto himself. It was the prose version which Gascoigne translated. Thus for the first time we have an English play written in a flexible instrument, capable of a variety which the crude verse of earlier plays could not hope to attain, and soon to be followed in the court comedies of John Lyly.

The action of this play involves an ingenious combination of disguises or "supposes," all cleverly fashioned to make for a happy resolution at the end. Not only does it go beyond *Roister Doister* in the classical precision of its form and the grace of its language, but it is important also for the romantic motifs which shape and colour its action. Although the lady of the play has been living with her lover for some months and is in fact pregnant when the action opens, she is not the courtesan-prize of Roman comedy. She is the faithful sweetheart of romantic story, and her lover is the courtly gentleman enslaved by love in the full romantic sense. Into the play also comes an echo of the old romantic legend of *Apollonius of Tyre,* with the tearful reunion at the end of the father with his long-lost son, albeit in this instance the father has been transformed unexpectedly from the stock pedant of Roman comedy. These romantic elements are the stuff of Shakespeare's comedies, and he himself was soon to adapt the *Apollonius of Tyre* story in his *Comedy of Errors* and to use Gascoigne's play as the source of his Bianca-Lucentio sub-plot in *The Taming of the Shrew.*

Between *Supposes* and the comedies of Shakespeare lie the plays of John Lyly, a humanistic schoolmaster, deeply read in the classics and concerned with the elegant court behaviour, with its artificiality and its grace, codified in the courtesy books of Renaissance Italy. It is important to remember that Lyly wrote his plays to be performed by boys before audiences which often included the queen as well as her courtiers. They are court drama, and they come as the culmination of a long tradition of court entertainment extending back into the Middle Ages. For the special talents and weaknesses of boy actors, Lyly wrote plays which served the requirements of an upperclass audience and the tastes of a queen from whom throughout his life Lyly vainly sought preferment. It is thus perhaps to be expected that in his plays women should occupy important roles and be developed as distinctive and important personalities, and that love and courtship should be among his principal dramatic themes.

The refined prose of Gascoigne's *Supposes* is surpassed by the artificial elegance of the prose in which Lyly wrote all but one of his comedies — *The Woman in the Moon,* the last of his plays, in blank verse. It was the same prose style of balanced antithesis and alliteration with which he had taken the literary world by storm in his novel *Euphues,* and which was to be imitated and then parodied for decades to come. He infused into an already lively and vigorous English comedy the grace of refined and elegant language and the order of well-designed, coherent plots. Lyly's are intellectual plays; their themes are the preoccupations of the Elizabethan court. In *Campaspe,* for instance, he presents a courtly view of love, and explores the problem of whether dalliance may ever be reconciled with the noble duties of the soldier and statesman. In this play Lyly also probes such conventional philosophical problems as the relation of art to life and of reality to illusion. His plays are often cast as elaborate debates; they are full of wit combat such as we may find in *Campaspe* in the exchanges between Alexander and Apelles and between Alexander and Diogenes. Such dramatization of intellectual debate had already been foreshadowed in the early *Fulgens and Lucrece,* and Lyly follows the tradition of that play also in so far as the serious intellectual debate of his main plot is parodied in the crude comedy of a subplot. Lyly shares in the general Elizabethan fondness for allegory, both moral and historical, and thus scholars have long argued about the various figures in Elizabeth's court for whom Lyly's dramatic characters may have stood. This allegorical dimension links Lyly's plays to the *Arcadia* of Sir Philip Sidney and the *Faerie Queene* of Edmund Spenser. We are not certain that Lyly wrote the songs with which his plays are richly embellished, but if he did, he must also be regarded as among the supreme poets of his age.

Probably the first great poet among the university graduates who in the last decades of the sixteenth century turned to the stage as a means of meagre livelihood was George Peele. Unlike Lyly, he was a product of the London streets and, after distinguishing himself at Oxford, he returned to London to live by his pen, never far from beggary and prison. His *Arraignment of Paris* was performed by the Children of the Chapel Royal before Queen Elizabeth herself, and it shares with Lyly's plays in the artificial conventions of court entertainment. Peele adapted classical mythology to the ends of royal flattery in more audacious a manner than Lyly ever attempted. This courtly entertainment, moreover, is written in blank verse, of a beauty and richness approached by none of Peele's contemporaries save Marlowe.

The *Arraignment of Paris* appears to be the only play which Peele wrote for performance by children at court. Although the canon of his works is uncertain and disputed, the other plays which are unquestionably his were all written for the public stage, and cater to the popular tastes of his age. In *The Battle of Alcazar* we have heroic vaunting and the exoticism of middle eastern potentates in the manner of Marlowe's *Tamburlaine*, with the heroic celebration of a popular hero, Sir Thomas Stukeley, who had died within the decade preceding the play. In *The Old Wives' Tale* we have a conglomeration of motifs from English folklore in which Peele mocks the traditions of popular folk romance at the very same time that he exploits them. In his *Edward I* we have the most jingoistic of early history plays, spiced with a lurid episode out of popular balladry and with Robin Hood himself upon the stage. In *David and Bethsabe* Peele captured the spirit of Old Testament tragedy as no other writer of his age was able to do. Much of Peele's time was spent in writing pageants to be performed by the London guilds, and, as might be expected, *The Arraignment of Paris* preserves much of the quality of spectacle and elaborate mythological allegory associated with the masque, a prominent part of the city pageants presented annually by the guilds to honor the Lord Mayor of London chosen from their ranks.

The Arraignment of Paris is further important because it is the first clear expression upon the English stage of the pastoral mode which was to be so important in later Elizabethan and Jacobean plays. The highly artificial and stylized pastoralism of Renaissance poetry, prose, and drama exalted the native goodness of the country in opposition to the evil and corruption of civilization as reflected in city life. In its pose of "primitivism" it came to conceive of a "golden age" in which men and women, as shepherds and shepherdesses, lived a perfect existence in a land always beautiful and always new, where man's only duty was to devote himself to love on the most elevated neo-Platonic plane. Some writers came to combine this "golden age" with the notion of a time before the fall of man from Paradise, and the Arcadia of pastoralism sometimes was identified with the Garden of Eden. The pastoral world of Peele, however, is that of pre-Homeric Greece where the shepherd Paris woos the nymph Œnone among all the rural delights of an Arcadian Mount Ida.

The pastoral tradition represents only one of many expressions in the English Renaissance of the spirit of romance. Into the forests of the pastoral Arcadia came the traditional motifs of romantic legend: danger, adventure, tragic separations and tearful reunions, long-lost children and newly discovered brothers, all of the pain and tribulation of love, with the inevitable happy ending in which complications are resolved and temporary sorrows are dispelled. Pastoral romance in the Italian *Arcadia* of Jacopo Sannazaro and the English *Arcadia* of Sir Philip Sidney purveyed this traditional matter in sophisticated and elegant form to an upper-class audience, but these were motifs of popular folk romance as well, and alongside the elegant pastoralism of Peele's *Arraignment of Paris* there developed a drama of folk romance of cruder form directed to a simpler audience. In *George a Greene, the Pinner of Wakefield* (ca. 1591), we have a varied fare of traditional romantic situations presented to an audience with little interest in the shepherds of a mythical Arcadia, but full of a pride in their own rural society and eager to glory in the ability of their rustic folk-heroes to triumph over any odds by superior strength alone and to overcome no matter what evils by their simple, straightforward honesty and courage. Such yeoman heroes could be exalted as the equals of any king or noble, and while they were always loyal to their king — for folk drama always exalted the simple patriotic virtues — they were never willing to surrender their yeoman status for the rank and titles of nobility. George a Greene serves his king and outwits his king's enemies, but he resolutely refuses to be knighted for his services.

This crude play usually has been attributed to Robert Greene, and it may well be his. Greene is the dramatist perhaps most influential in bringing the romance tradition to the popular stage. Like Peele, Greene was a true poet. He was a graduate of both Oxford and Cambridge, and he was deeply read in the classics and in the romantic literature of Renaissance Italy where he claimed to have traveled. His remarkable achievement was to combine the elegant pastoralism of literary tradition with the real world of rural England to produce a kind of romantic, homely pastoral drama which is unique in its age, and which may be seen best in *Friar Bacon and Friar Bungay.* This play, with Greene's *James IV,* a history play only in its title (for it merely places an Italian novella in a Scottish court setting), represents Greene's highest achievement as a dramatist.

Both in drama and in prose romance, Greene was an inveterate borrower; he imitated whatever in the work of his English and Italian predecessors had captured public taste, but what he borrowed he made distinctly his own. He drew upon the traditional materials of medieval chivalric romance in *Orlando Furioso,* and in *Alphonsus* as well, for while this imitation of Marlowe's *Tamburlaine* retains an exotic oriental setting, it has about it also much of the sentiment and flavour of medieval romance. The Turks and Christians who oppose one another seem to be knights clashing in armour. Greene took particularly as his subject the vicissitudes of romantic love, long a subject of medieval romance and of special prominence in the Renaissance epics of Tasso and Ariosto which Greene knew. One of Greene's constant themes is the patient, suffering heroine to be restored at last to happiness with her lover — illustrated by the Margaret of *Friar Bacon,* the Dorothea of *James IV,* and the Angelica of *Orlando Furioso.* In Greene's romantic comedies the sentimental spectacle of long-suffering love at last triumphant became fully a part of the English dramatic tradition, to be echoed later in Shakespeare's Viola, Helena, and Imogen.

Greene makes full use of the romantic devices of disguise and mistaken identity, and, as in *Friar Bacon,* he exploits the supernatural, here combined with a simple, patriotic glorification of England for her ability to produce a magician superior to that of any foreign country. His plots are extravagant and far-fetched, often with little attempt at logical probability or psychological verisimilitude, elements not common to the fairytale world of romance. The effect of realism which we nevertheless find in his plays comes from the simple, ordinary, homespun settings in which the improbable stories are laid, so that we have in *Friar Bacon* a unique wedding of the fantastic and the real. As is common to the romance tradition, Greene's heroes tend to be kings and nobles, but unlike Lyly's heroes, they act in a land we always recognize as ordinary England, and they are brought into contact with characters distinctly of the soil. In the heroine of *Friar Bacon and Friar Bungay*, Fair Margaret of Fressingfield (an actual town in Suffolk), the Arcadian shepherdess has been transformed into a simple English country milkmaid, as beautiful as her forebears in Italian romance, but far more believable and real.

We must note also that in Greene's romantic plays we tend to find a simple, optimistic morality so characteristic of folk literature and romance. There are no real villains, only those who do evil out of error or through the momentary effects of passion. The Ateukin of *James IV* is more a burlesque of the Machiavellian villain than a real villain. Evildoers are always punished in accordance with their crimes, and good characters are always reconciled in accord with a system of poetic justice. The greatest of virtues are honesty, courage, patience, and chastity. These are the qualities of romantic comedy. Robert Greene firmly established the romantic tradition in English drama, and William Shakespeare was the greatest of his followers.

Early Elizabethan Tragedy

The medieval imagination had been intrigued by the spectacle of the fall of man from the heights of worldly power and felicity to the depths of ignominy, suffering, and death. Giovanni Boccaccio's *De Casibus Virorum et Feminarum Illustrium* had been imitated in Chaucer's "Monk's Tale," in Lydgate's *Fall of Princes,* and in Elizabethan England most notably in *A Mirror for Magistrates* — that great collection of stories of the falls from greatness of unhappy kings and princes, first published by William Baldwin in 1559 and augmented and reissued regularly throughout the remainder of the century. Misfortunes which overtook the heroes of such *de casibus* stories were often merely arbitrary reversals of fortune which illustrated to the medieval mind the folly of placing one's hopes in the worldly goals of power and wealth. In many of the stories — in Lydgate and in *A Mirror for Magistrates* especially — the hero was an obvious sinner, and the fate which befell him was viewed as God's punishment for his misdoings. Medieval moralists, with their strong sense of analogy and typology, could see the destructions of mortal men as reflections on a lesser scale of those two greater falls from grace which they viewed as the ultimate source of all human misery: the fall of Lucifer from Heaven, and the fall of Adam from Paradise. Thus at the dawn of the Renaissance we already have a literary tradition which conceives of tragedy as punishment for sin in a moral universe in which such punishment must be expected, and we have also a vision of disaster as the fate of all those who strive for earthly joy.

The medieval morality play had its own potential for tragedy and could easily coalesce with that kind of *de casibus* story which emphasized destruction as the wages of sin. In the earlier morality plays the hero, placed between good and evil forces which vied for his soul, always chose evil at first but came to realize his error and by the end of the play was usually restored to true felicity. As the morality play developed, however, perhaps under the influence of a steadily growing Calvinism, we find plays in which there is no escape from sin, in which the irrevocable damnation of the hero stems from his wrong moral choice. The tradition of the *de casibus* fall from greatness merges with the morality play to produce a kind of drama which depicts man's catastrophic decline through his own voluntary choice of evil and his consequent punishment in a moral universe which, while it offers the hope of salvation, nevertheless decrees that sinners must suffer the consequences of their acts.

Such a moralistic view appears in what has been called our earliest English tragedy, *Gorboduc, or Ferrex and Porrex,* written by Thomas Sackville and Thomas Norton for production by the lawyers of the Inner Temple before Queen Elizabeth at Whitehall on January 18, 1562. In this play, which Sir Philip Sidney in his *Defense of Poesy* exempted from his general condemnation of English drama, we have the basic form of the morality play applied to political rather than religious issues. The resulting play depicts the destruction of a king because of his sins of rule, but suggests at the end the regeneration of his kingdom which has profited from the lessons of his disaster and is ready for the institution of new political virtue.

The strong morality play elements in *Gorboduc* have sometimes been obscured by the more obvious influence upon the play of the tragedies of Seneca. Classical example helps give to *Gorboduc* an elegance and sophistication such as we find in no earlier English play; in this play we have our first clear evidence of the vogue of Senecan imitation which was to affect strongly the direction of Elizabethan and Jacobean tragedy. We must never suppose, however, that Senecan imitation swept the native tradition from the English stage. Seneca was subsumed and absorbed by the dramatic tradition which had long existed in England. What resulted was a uniquely English kind of tragedy in which the morality play never ceased to exert a role.

Lucius Annæus Seneca (ca. 4 B.C.–A.D. 65), the Roman statesman and philosopher who served as counselor to the Emperor Nero, wrote ten plays, nine on traditional subjects from Greek mythology, and one, the *Octavia,* based upon recent Roman history. We are fairly certain that they were closet dramas, never acted, but recited before Nero and his court. It is this circumstance which accounts for many of their distinctive characteristics. Seneca's prose writings were studied throughout the Middle Ages as examples of stoic philosophy, and his plays were read in the schools, largely as models for Latin rhetoric. Between 1559 and 1581 all of the ten tragedies attributed to him (some scholars of today doubt his authorship of any of them) were translated by five men: Jasper Heywood, the first of the group, Alexander Neville, Thomas Nuce, John Studley, and Thomas Newton, who in 1581 gathered these various translations together and issued them in one volume called *Seneca: his Ten Tragedies Translated into English.* While educated Elizabethans did not need to depend upon these translations — generally free renditions in crude fourteeners — they did much to further knowledge of Seneca in England, and they made the imitations of his plays in English an almost inevitable development.

Senecan imitation made the five-act structure a common element of Elizabethan tragedy, just as it had been brought into comedy by imitation of the classics, although we must note that John Bale had used such a structure in his *Kynge Johan* as early as 1536. Performance upon the public stage took little account of act and scene divisions, however, until at least the second decade of the seventeenth century, and this Senecan refinement was given great importance largely in the private theatres. Perhaps the greatest and most far-reaching innovation of the authors of *Gorboduc* was in their use of blank verse, which had been developed by Henry Howard, Earl of Surrey, for his translation of Virgil, and which the authors of *Gorboduc* apparently regarded as approximating more closely the Latin measures of Seneca himself than did the four-teeners of Jasper Heywood's translation. With *Gorboduc* blank verse becomes the standard poetic form for English drama. Imitators of Seneca tried to reproduce his elaborate rhetorical style, marked by the cut and thrust of stychomythic dialogue. They took over the ghost and other supernatural devices, as well as the chorus detached from the action, to set off each of the five acts. The dumb show, itself of Italian rather than Senecan origins, came to be associated with the Senecan drama, first in Italy and then in England, being used usually, as in *Gorboduc,* to introduce each of the five acts.

Many of the stock characters of Senecan drama — the confidant, the messenger, the tyrant — were adapted by English imitators. As Seneca was popularized in plays such as Thomas Kyd's *The Spanish Tragedy,* we find more and more of a tendency to imitate what would appeal most to the popular imagination: Seneca's predilection for gruesome plots, often involving unnatural crimes, hereditary sin, incest, and, most important of all, the motif of blood revenge. The revenge theme in Seneca's own plays had been a reflection of his stern morality which conceived of crime as inevitably to be punished by an unswerving *nemesis,* with blood calling to blood for satisfaction from generation to generation. In Elizabethan drama the problem of revenge came to be treated in terms of Christian as well as pagan presuppositions, and the re-sulting conflicts provided a theme for much of Elizabethan and Jacobean tragedy.

Since Seneca's tragedies were vehicles for his own stoic philosophy of life, they were, of course, highly didactic works. The sententious epigrams, the philosophical dialogues, and the long, extended soliloquies of self-analysis by which Seneca had underscored the moral lessons of his plays came to be imitated in English. A play such as Thomas Hughes' *The Misfortunes of Arthur* (1588) has scarcely a line in it which is not translated from Seneca. Later dramatists like Marston, Chapman, Jonson, and Webster seem to pride themselves upon their ability to insert characteristically Senecan epigrams in appropriate — and sometimes inappropriate — places in their own plays. The conscious moralizing of Senecan drama merged easily with the didactic tradition of the English morality play. Chorus, epigram, and neatly divided plot enabled plays like *Gorboduc* to make their moral statements more effectively than they could be made by the cruder devices of the morality drama. Certainly there was no conflict between the two dramatic traditions in this respect. It has been held, most notably by T. S. Eliot, that the chief contribution of Seneca to English drama was not in matters of form so much as in the influence of his distinctive attitude towards life which Elizabethan dramatists came to reflect in their plays. There is much truth in this, but we must note that upon the Elizabethan stage the classical stoicism of Seneca was often Christianized and that Senecan form could be used to forward moral themes not unlike those of the morality plays.

We must distinguish carefully among several varieties of Elizabethan Senecanism. First, there was the academic imitation of Seneca written at the universities and at the Inns of Court. To this tradition belongs *Gorboduc*. These plays were generally marked by deep interest in classical drama itself, a desire to "get Seneca right," and considerable pride on the authors' part in their recognizable "Senecanisms." These plays tend to be learned and sophisticated, were performed before private audiences, and presumably were of little interest to the great mass of the public who knew little or nothing about classical literature. In these plays Senecan imitation is an important end in itself, in spite of the many other concerns which the author of a play such as *Gorboduc* may have had.

Seneca was imitated also by a group of writers in the patronage of Mary Sidney, Countess of Pembroke. At her great estate, Wilton House, they devoted themselves to studying and imitat-

ing in English not so much Seneca himself as the French dramatist, Robert Garnier, who had imitated Seneca in French. Mary
Sidney herself wrote a *Cleopatra* in this tradition. Samuel Daniel's *Philotas* and Samuel Brandon's *Virtuous Octavia* are prod-
ucts of this circle. Thomas Kyd prepared his translation of
Garnier's *Cornelia* during the brief time that he was associated
with it. It should be noted that the plays of the Pembroke circle
carry on the tradition of Seneca's *Octavia* rather than that of the
nine plays based upon Greek mythology. None of the Pembroke
plays was ever staged. They were entirely academic exercises,
read only by a small circle of enthusiasts, and they have little relation to the mainstream of Elizabethan drama.

Seneca really joins this mainstream when he comes to be imitated
upon the public stage, as he is in Kyd's *Spanish Tragedy*. Here the
sensational elements of Seneca are fully exploited. The horrors
merely reported by the messengers of the academic drama are
presented in full view of the audience. While many of the popular
Senecan plays carry on the overt pretense of teaching their audiences while entertaining them, the didacticism of Senecan drama
is gradually submerged by the desire to titillate an audience by
whatever means. Forms and conventions evolved by a drama in
order to further didactic ends continued to exert their influence,
however, long after the didactic goals had been abandoned.

Kyd's *Spanish Tragedy* established the revenge play as a stock
vehicle for the Elizabethan stage. Revenge tragedy evolved and
came to have many facets, so that it is impossible to see the many
plays, which range from Kyd's fairly early work through Shakespeare's *Hamlet* and Webster's *Duchess of Malfi,* as constituting a
homogeneous group. In general they all pose the ethical problem of
a blood revenge demanded by a traditional and deeply rooted code
of honour as it came into conflict with a Christian belief that
vengeance belonged to the Lord and that to take justice into one's
own hands was to damn one's soul. Different dramatists approach
this problem in different ways, with varying degrees of sympathy
for the avenger, and with different results. We cannot say that
there is any one attitude or resolution common to them all.

In the Lorenzo of Kyd's *Spanish Tragedy* we find one of the earliest examples of the Elizabethan "Machiavel," the villain who needs no real motive for his crimes other than the joy he derives from villainy itself, the artist in evil who wears the mask of seeming virtue as he invites the audience to gloat with him over his own dissimulation and trickery. This stage stereotype appears again in Christopher Marlowe's *Jew of Malta,* where the comic aspect of his villainy is even further emphasized, and it receives its supreme and most imaginative expression in Shakespeare's Richard III. This "Machiavel" owes much to popular fear and misunderstanding of Machiavelli, fostered by such attacks upon him as the *Contre-Machiavel* of the French Huguenot, Innocent Gentillet, which was widely read in an English translation by Simon Patericke, and which linked Machiavelli with the St. Bartholomew Massacres of French Huguenots in 1578 (although these occurred more than a half century after his death). The stock character of the "Machiavel" has no necessary relation to the actual ideas of Machiavelli. We can trace its antecedents in the Vice of the medieval morality play, which had long established comic villainy as an English stage tradition, and in the villain-hero of Senecan tragedy.

When Shakespeare wrote *Titus Andronicus,* the earliest of his tragedies, he thus had a well-established tradition of tragedy upon which to build, and it is characteristic of him that he went beyond what he had inherited. Tragedies had been written in the schools and at the Inns of Court, and they long had been a staple of the public theatre companies. Probably the most impressive of the works of tragedy which ushered in the last decade of the sixteenth century, to culminate in Shakespeare's *Julius Cæsar* and *Hamlet,* was Christopher Marlowe's *Doctor Faustus.* Here the terrible fate of man seeking to aspire beyond the normal limits of humanity was treated in terms of a dramatic tradition which Marlowe, like Shakespeare, had inherited, and in which the influence of the morality play may be seen more clearly than in *Titus Andronicus.* Although interpretations of Marlowe's plays differ, and various critics have often seen *Doctor Faustus* in diametrically opposite terms, all can agree that it is the most profound exploration of the meaning of human disaster to be written in

England before the end of the sixteenth century. It was this kind of exploration which Shakespeare was to carry on in his great tragedies of the following decade.

Christopher Marlowe, born in the same year as Shakespeare but cut off by murder just as Shakespeare was on the threshold of his greatest achievement, is the greatest of the dramatists who wrote before him. That Shakespeare was influenced by Marlowe's work is obvious, particularly in what his history plays owe to the example of Marlowe's *Edward II*. But this influence must not be exaggerated. Marlowe and Shakespeare were quite different, not only in their artistry, but in their general intellectual make-up as well. Each faced in his own distinctive way the confusion and uncertainty so characteristic of Renaissance intellectual life, and Shakespeare's plays, taken together, embody a vision of reality quite different from what we may find in the seven plays which Marlowe left behind him.

The History Play

We have seen that terms such as comedy and tragedy, in the classical sense, were not a part of the native English dramatic tradition as it evolved through the morality play. The Tudor interludes were usually hybrid plays, impossible to categorize as either comedy or tragedy, and relatively few writers for the public stage before the end of the sixteenth century seem to have been much concerned about whether their plays were to be called comedies, tragedies, histories, or any of the sub-species which Shakespeare ridicules though Polonius in *Hamlet*. The term "history" was used very loosely, being equivalent to "story" and applied on title-pages to just about any kind of play. Genres came to be an important factor in English drama only under the influence of classical imitation, and only in the schools and the private playhouses were generic distinctions usually accorded some of the respect with which they were treated by the neo-classical critics of France and Italy.

This is of particular pertinence when we speak of the history play, which not even the neo-classical critics attempted to isolate as a separate dramatic genre. Such critics, in fact, treated historical drama as inseparable from tragedy, one of whose requirements they held to be what Ben Jonson in his preface to *Sejanus* called "truth of argument," by which he meant a verifiable historical source. Francis Meres in his *Palladis Tamia* included even Shakespeare's *Henry IV* among his tragedies, although it is doubtful that many other critics would have seconded him in this. In spite of this haziness of distinction among the Elizabethans themselves, it is possible for us to distinguish a fairly large group of plays which begin to appear in the late 1580's, reach their peak around 1600, and then gradually disappear, which are concerned with the history of England, and which, by the very nature of this concern and the restrictions it placed upon their artistry, stand apart from all other contemporary plays. However, we must always recognize the inherent difficulties in our distinction of the history play as a separate dramatic genre. While we may set up a norm to which the best of the history plays conform, and make it as broad as possible, there are still many plays which mingle history and romance in different degrees and which it will always be impossible for us to categorize satisfactorily.

The growth of the English history play coincides with the growth of historical writing in general in Renaissance England, a growth which in turn is connected with the complex political problems of the age. Polydore Vergil, the Italian humanist whose Latin *Historia Anglica* is the first of the great Renaissance histories of England, wrote his history in order to justify the claim of the Tudors to the throne — as he had been commissioned to do. Thus, in spite of his fastidious search for truth, he used history for immediate political ends. Among the goals of Renaissance history, as it was written in prose, in narrative poetry, and in the drama, was the need to throw light upon the political problems of the present by examination of the past. Elizabethan historiography was intensely didactic, and it rarely hesitated — in any of its forms — to alter the facts preserved in the chronicles so as to emphasize the political lessons and dramatic conflicts it saw implicit in its subject matter. Renaissance historiography — quite unlike the universalist history of the Middle Ages — was also intensely nationalistic. In England it sought to bolster patriotic feeling by explaining the greatness of England and its special destiny according to a providential scheme which has been described as the

"Tudor myth" and which viewed King Henry VII, the first of the Tudors, as a special agent of God intended to restore England to greatness after its long years of expiation for the sin of the murder of Richard II. In its political philosophy, Tudor historical writing asserted the absolute supremacy of the king as God's agent on earth and categorized rebellion even against a tyrant as a hostile act against God himself. We may define the Elizabethan history play most simply by saying that it was a kind of play which accomplished on the stage the general ends of history as the Elizabethans conceived of them, in much the same way that they were accomplished by the poetic and prose histories of the day.

The history play, while it accomplishes these ends, stands in the full line of development of the English drama. Its roots can be traced back to the mystery, miracle, and morality drama of the Middle Ages. It begins to take form during the period of the interlude in such plays as John Skelton's *Magnificence* (1516) and John Bale's *Kynge Johan* (1536). As it grows it draws fully upon the traditions of the morality play, the Senecan drama, and of the kind of heroic play best represented by Marlowe's *Tamburlaine,* which has sometimes been called the true source and original of the Tudor history play. The salient characteristic of *Tamburlaine* is its glorification in a series of episodic scenes of one heroic figure, with each scene serving to augment the hero's greatness, until at the end of *Part I* he is at the very peak of his glory. The popularity of this play caused Marlowe to write a second part which depicts the death of his hero, for implicit in the very notion of a superman hero who can control fate, as Tamburlaine does, is the corollary that such control can last only for a brief while; ultimately fate must triumph, for man, no matter how powerful, is mortal, and death must destroy him. Marlowe's hero learns at the end to accept the inevitability of death, and dies at the height of his conquest, thus achieving as much on earth as fate may allow to any mortal being.

Tamburlaine is a history play because it is based upon the life of an actual historical figure, and in depicting his career it makes explicit certain political ideals with which Marlowe was deeply concerned. Its heroic quality did much to condition the tone of history plays which followed it. Although the greatest of the history plays were written by William Shakespeare, Marlowe is also deeply involved with this dramatic genre, and his *Edward II*, from which Shakespeare learned much in *Richard II*, must be included along with Shakespeare's plays as among the greatest examples.

Edward II is a personal tragedy as fully as it is a political history. There is no conflict between the demands of these two genres — always closely related. This is true also of Shakespeare's *Richard II* and *Richard III*, where the tragedies of individual kings are inseparably tied to the political life of the state. History also could be rich in comedy, as in the *Henry IV* plays, and it might be a portrait of a hero-king such as we find in *Henry V*. The history play, with Shakespeare, as with his contemporaries, took on many forms and itself reflected the rich diversity of the Elizabethan drama as a whole. When Shakespeare began to write, history, comedy, and tragedy had all emerged as parts of a dynamic, steadily evolving dramatic tradition. In each dramatic form he had had important predecessors, but Shakespeare was to develop their work beyond anything of which the best of them had been capable.

5

Elizabethan Theatres and Theatre Companies

 Acting was an ancient profession when Shakespeare arrived in London, and the manner of performing plays upon a stage was already highly conventionalized. He himself began as an actor, although he does not appear to have been particularly distinguished, or to have spent much time, as a performer. By his dramatic creativity, however, he enlarged the conventions of theatre production and extended the possibilities of the actor's art, so that the theatre which he left for his followers was an infinitely richer artistic vehicle than that which he himself had inherited. We can have no full understanding of what he finally achieved without some knowledge of the theatre conditions with which he began.

While drama, as we have seen, had had its more fruitful early development within the medieval church, we must not suppose that there were no other medieval kinds of entertainment, or that at any time in the history of the English theatre religious plays were the only kind performed. Not only were there wandering companies of acrobats, mimes, animal trainers, ballad singers, and other popular performers, but there were folk plays and festivals of many kinds, revels in schools and universities, and civic pageants in which historical events were commemorated. The physical conditions of play production in Shakespeare's time may, in fact, have owed more to the long tradition of secular entertainment than to religious entertainment. While the liturgical drama could centre naturally upon the altar and the nave of the church and involve a kind of actor-spectator relationship similar to that of a priest and his congregation, other kinds of spectacles had to evolve their own specific conditions for viewing by an audience. When the religious drama moved from the church to the market square, it too had to develop its own kind of physical theatre. In all likelihood, the devices which it evolved for this purpose drew upon the long experience and traditions of secular entertainment.

Medieval Spectacle

A primary element of medieval entertainment was pageantry and lavish spectacle. To this the medieval church, along with secular institutions, contributed fully, not only with its plays, but with its religious services themselves, its processions, and its highly decorated churches. Pageantry was served as well by all of the institutions of kingship, nobility, heraldry, and warfare, creating tastes and habits of mind from which the Elizabethan theatres eventually were to emerge.

Among the most popular of medieval spectacles was the knightly tournament. Although this was a dangerous sport, frowned upon by ecclesiastical authorities, it seems to have been popular throughout Europe as early as the tenth century. Tournaments were specifically banned in England until the reign of King Richard the Lion-Hearted (1189–1199), but they flourished in succeeding centuries, were deliberately encouraged by the Tudor monarchs, and continued to be an important source of upper-class entertainment in Shakespeare's own time. Even in its earliest form, the tournament had within it certain elements of drama — spectacle, suspense, and physical struggle between opposing forces — in which spectators could vicariously participate. As the tournament developed, however, from a simple mock battle into more rarefied and elegant forms, involving individual combat (jousting) either on foot (at barriers) or on horseback (at tilt), it came to be a highly artistic, quasi-dramatic form of entertainment. This was connected with the development of chivalric codes of behaviour and, particularly in England, with the popularity of Arthurian romance.

As the procedures of tournaments grew more formal, the challenging knight was called upon to explain his appearance in arms. He often did so in terms of a make-believe story involving the motifs of chivalric romance. He fought for the honour of a lady who joined in the game, and when the battle was done she ceremoniously rewarded him for his victory. Often the participants wore elaborate disguises in keeping with allegorical themes by which the tournaments were governed. Settings became important, for if the knight were fighting against some allegorical force of evil, that force's habitat had somehow to be depicted; if he were fighting against the Seven Deadly Sins, the traditional iconographic associations of all seven could be made evident. Costume also came to figure largely in the spectacle, for the spectators could identify their champions only by what they wore and by their elaborate coats of arms, each element of which came to have a symbolic meaning, some of which are carried over in the poetic imagery of Shakespeare's plays. Often the knight entered the lists on a symbolically decorated pageant wagon. With ladies taking part in the pageantry, the tournament came to include music and dance, usually as part of the ceremony with which the victorious knight was rewarded.

These non-military aspects of the tournament came to have a greater and greater importance. Well before the beginning of the sixteenth century, it was in these elements that the real interest of the sport lay. Tournaments are important in dramatic history because they demonstrate the continued existence, alongside the drama of the medieval church, of a kind of quasi-dramatic spectacle whose essential element was not religious doctrine, but elaborate pageantry and romance. They illustrate one kind of long-established taste to which the Elizabethan theatre came to cater. They provide one model for the construction of the earliest English public theatres, for the arenas (lists) became ever more formalized and elaborate in structure as tournaments developed. A round, rectangular, or hexagonal yard, with doors for entry on two sides, and with a central scaffold on which the king and his party could be seen while they observed the action, is a basic design which may recognize also in the structure of Elizabethan playhouses. Lesser scaffolds for persons of lower rank, and mere standing places for the lowest, suggest the kind of audience accommodations we encounter in the later theatres.

Another kind of medieval theatrical spectacle was provided by

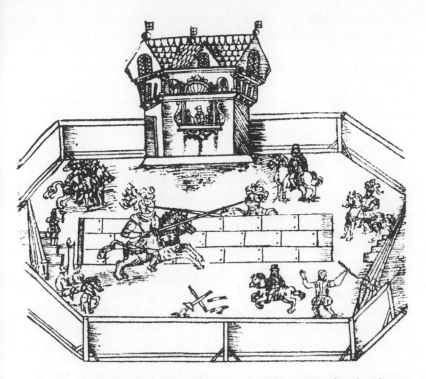

FIGURE 1   An English Tiltyard (c. 1515). From a pen drawing in British Museum MS. Harleian 69, f. 19.

the great triumphal processions and pageants which usually accompanied the coronations of kings or the welcome into cities of royal visitors and their guests, and which came to be a feature also of royal weddings, births, and great events in general. Such displays had much in common with the triumphs of ancient Rome; their object was to do homage to the ruler and his guests and to display them to the people with as much of the trappings and fanfare of royalty as possible. Unlike the tournaments, such pageants were bourgeois in nature, instituted by citizens, and provided a kind of city entertainment in which every social element of the population could participate. Stands would be erected along the route of the procession and on these citizens would present tableaux, usually allegorical in nature, in which the monarch would be praised lavishly and exhorted to acts of virtue. The speakers would be costumed and the stands decorated to represent allegorical or mythological themes. Although each stand consisted of a self-contained scene, often these scenes would be related to one another in terms of a theme which unified the entire processional pageant, so that a monarch moving through the city would be provided at his various stops with a consistent dramatic spectacle. The allegorical representation of the vices and virtues, which was a stock feature of such pageantry, links this phenomenon with the morality drama which was being acted during the same historical period, sometimes on street stands not unlike those constructed for the triumphal pageants. These were, in fact, not unlike the stands which had long been used in similar city settings by travelling entertainers, with their acrobatics, juggling, and animal acts.

In addition to such stands, the architectural features of the city were made use of. The city gates were often decorated, their arches making a natural setting for the scene to be depicted. Market crosses were similarly used, as were the great cisterns, on top of which actors could perform while the flowing waters provided realism for scenes involving water. When such performances were presented, the windows and galleries of the surrounding houses made a natural theatre.

But probably of greater importance to the evolving structure of the Elizabethan playhouse were the specially constructed triumphal arches upon and within which such tableaux were presented. These came to be a special feature of city pageants, and with succeeding years they grew more and more elaborate. When arches were supplemented by extended, raised platforms or with upper stages, as came to be done, they provided, with the surrounding houses and galleries, a theatrical structure which the buildings of public playhouses were later to imitate. The records of these royal processions and city pageants are numerous, including especially notable ones devised for the entry of Richard II into London in 1392, and in Shakespeare's day for that of James I into the city in March of 1604, an event upon which Shakespeare was to draw in *Measure for Measure,* and for which some of the most memorable of all triumphal arches were constructed.

Historians of the theatre have a perhaps natural tendency to compartmentalize these various types of medieval spectacles, to treat each as a separate phenomenon. It is not likely, however, that medieval men and women saw them as distinct from one another. The knightly tournaments and the bourgeois street tableaux have much in common, and both share features with the religious drama which furnished its own pageantry and spectacle in market squares throughout England on Corpus Christi day and at other times of celebration.

The Staging of Religious Drama

The religious drama of the Middle Ages was presented both on movable wagons and on fixed stages. The wagons were not unrelated to the ornamented chariots on which knights rode into the lists at tournaments and to the decorated pageant carts on which medieval guildsmen displayed the emblems of their professions in municipal pageants. The fixed stages were not unlike the decorated stands and ceremonial arches of civic processions. It is important to note that the guildsmen who came to perform the religious plays were long-experienced participants in medieval spectacle, and they drew naturally upon the practices with which they were familiar. But no matter what the stage, one essential element of the medieval theatre was its cosmic universality. The stage depicted not only the known world, but Heaven and Hell as well. While specific locations were indicated upon it by conventional means when the particular story made this necessary, the stage itself stood for the entire universe, and the action which occurred upon it was universal in its scope and implications, concerned always with the ultimate fate of the human soul. This feature of the medieval stage may be the most important of all those elements which the Elizabethan playhouse inherited from it. Shakespeare's theatre was also designed to represent the universe, and this is one reason why place designations rarely appear in Elizabethan texts and why the treatment of time sequence is generally so haphazard.

Only a small portion of the medieval religious drama has survived, but this is enough to assure us that it existed in many forms, in both individual plays and cycles, in plays of relative brevity and in others extending from sunrise to sunset, in plays requiring great casts of performers and in others requiring only a handful. Obviously many kinds of stages were used, and it is clear that the experience of erecting tournament lists and street pageant stands and scaffolds for related kinds of spectacles during the same historical

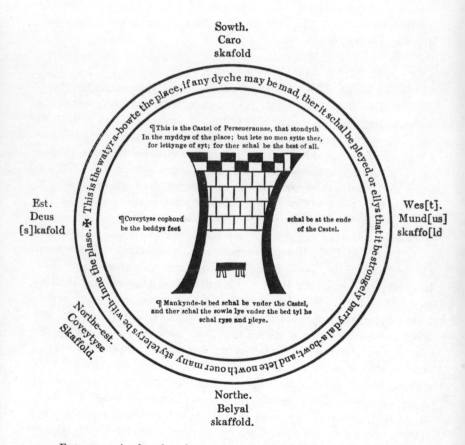

Sowth.
Caro
skafold

Est.
Deus
[s]kafold

Wes[t].
Mund[us]
skaffo[ld

¶ This is the Castel of Perseueraunse, that stondyth
In the myddys of the place; but lete no men sytte ther,
for lettynge of syt; for ther schal be the best of all.

¶ Coveytyse copbord
be the beddys feet

schal be at the ende
of the Castel.

¶ Mankynde-is bed schal be vnder the Castel,
and ther schal the sowle lye vnder the bed tyl he
schal ryse and pleye.

Northe.
Belyal
skaffold.

FIGURE 2 A plan for the staging of *The Castle of Perseverance,* from the Macro Manuscript in the Folger Shakespeare Library, Washington, D.C.

periods were heavily drawn upon. There was an important tradition, especially in Cornwall, of staging plays so that the actors were surrounded by the audience on all four sides. We know from a contemporary manuscript diagram that *The Castle of Perseverance* was staged in this manner.

One essential feature of all medieval stages was a central acting area called a *platea*. It depicted no definite locale. It could be used for any time or any place, and where specific locations (Bethlehem, Calvary, and so forth) needed to be designated, recognizable symbols of these places, either chairs (*sedes*) or canvas houses (*mansions*), were set around the *platea*. In the churches where the liturgical drama was performed, the *platea* probably included most of the length of the church floor. Spectators crowded either on the galleries above or at the end of the floor may have furnished a prototype for what was to be the gallery and pit of Elizabethan playhouses. When the plays were performed outdoors it is likely that a similar arrangement of spectacle and spectator prevailed. For important performances special outdoor arenas were built, the tournament lists providing a convenient model.

The pageant wagons used for some, but not all, of the Corpus Christi day mystery cycles were an unusual phenomenon and hardly the rule in medieval staging. They seem to have been devised for various purposes. They made it possible to transport easily all of the stage equipment and machinery for a specific play to various parts of the city, and, with cycles of plays to be performed regularly and only once a year, to avoid the expense and inconvenience of permanent theatres in congested parts of cities or the necessity for constructing new scaffolds for each Corpus Christi day performance. It is likely that the highly ornamented pageant wagons were drawn in the Corpus Christi day procession and that they added to the pageantry and splendour of that event.

Athough several contemporary accounts of pageant wagons have survived, we can only conjecture about what they looked like. There is no reason to believe that they were all of the same design. Wealthy guilds could afford far more elaborate wagons than poorer ones. The decoration and perhaps even the structure of a particular wagon would usually reflect the subject of the play to be performed upon it. If it were to be used by more than one guild, as often was the case, it had to be designed so that it could be adapted for more than one play. A representative specimen might consist of *platea* behind which was a "tiring" area where the actors could keep their equipment and remain before appearing on stage. Above was a loft containing winches and other machinery, depending upon the requirements of the particular play. We know from at least one extant stage direction that action sometimes took place in the street in front of the wagon. It has been conjectured by Glynne Wickham in *Early English Stages,* and it is highly likely, that a second wagon consisting of a flat platform on wheels was sometimes placed in front of the pageant wagon so as to create an apron stage which would considerably augment the *platea.* Whatever *platea* was available could be provided with *sedes* and *mansions* to indicate specific locales as they were required. It is likely that on some wagons the upper level could be opened to view, perhaps by drawing a curtain, so that it could be used for action, particularly when movements between earth and Heaven were called for. If a multi-levelled pageant wagon was indeed used in conjunction with an adjacent portable apron stage, the arrangement would certainly have provided a model for the stage of the Elizabethan playhouse, just as the audience watching from windows and balconies and standing in the street would suggest a prototype of the Elizabethan galleries and pit. What does seem evident is that the various kinds of spectacles by which medieval life was enriched provided conventional theatrical structures which did not differ markedly from one another in so far as the types of spectacle themselves were concerned, and that it was upon these long-established, conventional forms that sixteenth-century theatre builders were to elaborate.

The Rise of Professional Companies

While the religious drama, both within the church and outside of it, was the work of amateur performers, professional entertainers were also an important feature of medieval life. Lacking monastic and municipal chroniclers to record their activities, they have left us with scant information about them. The mimes and jugglers of the late Roman empire continued to wander throughout Europe after the fall of Rome. They came to include an ever increasing variety of performers. They organized themselves into bands or troupes, both for their own protection and so as to make possible more ambitious kinds of entertainment. During the period of the Crusades, bands of wandering singers celebrated, in castles and manor houses, the exploits of legendary heroes such as Geoffrey of Boulogne or Richard the Lion-Hearted. It is likely that some mimetic representation accompanied the ballad singing of the *trouvère* who was the leader of a troupe. Other subjects were added — subjects from Arthurian legend, from classical mythology, from earlier national history, and from local events, so that an enterprising troupe might have in its repertory a considerable number of semi-dramatic musical entertainments or actual plays. Such wandering troupes may have come to perform the folk plays about St. George and Robin Hood which were common features of rural festivals.

Throughout the medieval period there were itinerant troupes of professional performers who would set up their stands or wagons in the market places of towns all over England, and would perform whatever plays they had available, including religious plays which had come into their possession, often in a popularized form. They would support themselves by taking contributions from the crowd, either before or during their performance. These wanderers were classed as vagabonds and harassed by sheriffs, but another group of professionals was more fortunate. Wealthy landowners and merchants kept in their own houses private companies of players for their own entertainment and that of their guests. Such troupes, acting usually before the same master, must have developed a considerable repertory. Servants who could act came to be in great demand. Sir John Paston, a Norfolkshire nobleman whose letters have survived, complained in 1473 about the loss of a servant whom he had employed for two years as an actor in St. George and Robin Hood plays.

Many of the English towns maintained companies of players for service on special occasions. These companies were known to visit other towns to give performances. The most fortunate of the professional actors were those liveried servants in the households of the great lords of England who could mount their plays in great halls under the most excellent of conditions, with ample funds available for costuming and properties, and with the best writers in the land to supply them with plays. King Richard III kept his own company of players and inspired many of his noblemen to do the same. By the end of the fifteenth century the great castles of England were centres for a wide variety of dramatic activity. Such liveried professionals acted not only at home. We have records of their travels about the country well before the beginning of the sixteenth century. Under the Tudor monarchs, they continued to travel and they grew in numbers. Prince Arthur, the elder son of King Henry VII, had his own troupe. And so did Prince Henry, who, as King Henry VIII, was to greatly encourage and foster entertainment at court. Although vagabond wanderers continued to exist, under the Tudors the liveried companies of players came to dominate the theatrical world of England.

Drama in the middle years of the sixteenth century was an important weapon of religious and political propaganda. As religious conflicts in the reigns of Mary and Elizabeth grew sharper, plays came to be more and more carefully controlled by the crown. This involved an ever-increasing harassment of players who did not have the protection of a great lord's livery. An act of 1572 required that all acting troupes be licensed and it restricted the number of such licensed troupes. This meant that companies attached to the households of the more powerful lords would drive out the strolling players and finally exert a virtual monopoly over English play performance. The most important of these companies in the early years of Elizabeth was that kept by her favourite, Robert Dudley, Earl of Leicester. So attached was this earl to his players that in 1586 he had them accompany him to the Netherlands where he went to take command of English troops. The great importance of this company was that its leader was James Burbage, an enterprising and ambitious man with whose activities the great period of the English theatre may be said to have begun.

The ancient tradition of English household service required that servants receive no fixed wages but live instead by the generosity of their lords, who supposedly would not fail to reward them for faithful service. This was true of those servants who were actors. They were supposed to perform other household duties as well — although most of them actually did not — and their play acting was regarded merely as a kind of dutiful service to their lord and his friends, who might at their pleasure offer reward. In spite of this, the custom of paying liveried actors with fixed stipends for performances at various houses gradually established itself. It was perhaps inevitable that the public should come to be invited to some performances on payment of a fixed price of admission. When this occurred, the liveried companies in effect took over a role which had long been exercised by unlicensed strolling players. The importance of James Burbage and the Earl of Leicester's Men is that they were able to establish public performance for money as a regular function of a liveried company of players, and that they did this in spite of the opposition not only of merchants and clergy, but also of such amateur actors as the companies of schoolboys and their masters who had long been entertaining at court and in great houses.

Leicester had players wearing his badge (of the staff and rugged bear) as early as 1559, when he wrote to the President of the North requesting that they be permitted to perform in Yorkshire. However, we know little of his troupe until 1572. As a result of the repressive act of that year, the six members of his company appealed to Leicester for protection, asking that he retain them as his servants, permit them to continue to wear his livery, and grant them a license which they might carry with them on their travels. Two years later, on May 10, 1574, the Queen's Privy Council, doubtless through Leicester's influence, issued a patent under the Great Seal of England permitting James Burbage, John Perkyn, John Laneham, William Johnson, Robert Wilson, and Thomas Clarke, the six members of the Earl of Leicester's Men, to perform plays within the city of London and in any other cities throughout England, in spite of local regulations, provided that their plays first be censored and approved and that no performances be put on during times of religious worship or when the plague was raging. Thus the power of the local authorities was undercut, and Leicester's Men were granted a virtual monopoly over theatrical performances, although the city fathers continued their repressive activities, and the monopoly could not long be maintained. By 1577 three other great companies had already come into being: the Lord Admiral's Men, Lord Pembroke's Men, and Lord Strange's Men. In 1583 a company of twelve players, including the great Richard Tarleton, was taken into the royal household and called the Queen's Men, giving the acting profession a new level of respectability. Actors moved from company to company, and new troupes were formed out of the remnants of those which were disbanded. When the Earl of Leicester died in 1588, the principal actors in his company joined the troupe already under the patronage of Ferdinando Stanley, Lord Strange.

Innyards

Although travelling companies of licensed players no doubt preferred to put on their shows in the halls of great houses, a convenient setting for outdoor public performances was furnished by the typical English innyard. There is good reason to believe that Leicester's Men and other troupes were performing at such hostelries well before 1572. The inn provided a rectangular courtyard with galleries all around it, and a single entrance from the road where a member of the company could be stationed to collect the price of admission. As a place where travellers congregated and with little opportunity for amusement, the inn provided a naturally receptive audience. The innkeeper, who was given a share of the takings, was no doubt eager to participate in the profits as well as to make his inn a more attractive place for visitors. After the main midday meal a scaffold could easily be erected at the end of the yard. The room behind it could be used as a tiring house, and the audience could be accommodated in the yard in front of the platform stage and on the gallery above. This provided essentially the same kind of viewing situation as the medieval tournament arena or the stands and wagons of medieval street pageants and mystery plays.

Sometimes a portable booth theatre, containing its own tiring house, could be brought into an inn yard; sometimes a pageant wagon could be used in the same manner. Inns no doubt had long been used by travelling players in the provinces, and they continued to be used throughout Shakespeare's career. The inns on the main highways approaching the city of London appear to have been the earliest put to use by the London companies. These included the Saracen's Head in Islington on the North Road, the

FIGURE 3   A performance in a sixteenth-century innyard, as drawn by Brooks McNamara.

Tabard in Southwark, and the Red Lion and Boar's Head in Whitechapel to the east of the city. Within the city itself, the Bell, the Bull, the Belsavage, and the Cross Keys were all famous by Shakespeare's time as inns where plays were regularly to be seen.

An obvious next step, as acting proved to be an increasingly lucrative activity, was for a company of players to take over an inn entirely and convert it into a theatre. The Red Lion and the Boar's Head seem to have been equipped with permanent stages and seating arrangements for spectators so that they could be devoted to more elaborate theatrical use than otherwise would be possible. John Brayne, the brother-in-law of James Burbage, was engaged in the construction of a stage and scaffolding for spectators at the Red Lion Inn in 1566. It was Brayne who ten years later was to finance Burbage in his construction of the first regular playhouse. The London city authorities had issued stringent regulations governing play performance, in order to counteract the royal patent of 1574. They had been in part successful, a fact which led to continued conflict between the players and the city fathers. Thus when Burbage on May 13, 1576, secured a lease of ground for his new playhouse, it was outside the city walls to the north, in Holywell in the parish of St. Leonard's, Shoreditch.

The Elizabethan Public Playhouse

James Burbage was a carpenter by trade, and he supervised the construction of his new playhouse which was completed in 1576 and named the Theatre. It was to serve as a main acting place, at first for Leicester's Men and then for various other London companies, until it was torn down in 1589 and its scaffolding transported across the Thames to be used in the construction of the Globe. Just as other licensed companies grew in prominence to rival and finally replace Leicester's Men, so other theatres came to be built. In 1577 the Curtain was constructed, probably by a syndicate of actors, close to the Theatre.

Other theatres followed. In 1587 Philip Henslowe, who had long been involved in money lending, bearbaiting, boat renting, and other enterprises, built the Rose Theatre on the Bankside in Southwark, an area which soon came to rival the northern suburbs as a theatrical centre. Here, in 1598, Francis Langley built the

Swan. On the Bankside in 1599 was erected the Globe, where all of Shakespeare's plays were to be performed until 1608 when his company acquired the indoor theatre at Blackfriars as well. In 1600 Henslowe and Alleyn offered competition to the Globe by constructing the Fortune in Finsbury Fields, to the north of the city, just west of the old Theatre and Curtain. In 1606 the Red Bull theatre was built in Clerkenwell. The Hope theatre, with a portable stage so that it could also be used for bull- and bearbaiting, was built on the Bankside in 1614. These were the principal playhouses of Elizabethan and Jacobean London, although there must have been other obscure and temporary places were performances also were given, and inn yards continued to be used, particularly during the winter months.

We do not know exactly what any of the Elizabethan theatres looked like. It is obvious that there must have been differences among them, for each construction must have made advances over its predecessors. Various indications of the theatres' general appearance have, however, come down to us. They make it clear that Burbage and his followers were building upon a long tradition of theatrical structure extending back to the tournaments and street theatres of the Middle Ages and drawing also upon the experience of theatrical production indoors in the halls of great houses. The builders' specifications for the Fortune and the Hope have survived in the contracts for their construction. Stage directions in plays also give us valuable hints. Probably our most important single piece of evidence, now in the university library at Utrecht in Holland, is a drawing of the Swan theatre made by a travelling Dutchman, Johannes de Witt, who had visited London in 1596. Although the sketch was probably made from memory after de Witt's return home, there is no reason to doubt the accuracy of its essential features.

The Swan drawing reveals certain details which we have good reason to believe were common to all Elizabethan playhouses. There is the circular, unroofed yard, such as is pictured also in several contemporary maps of Elizabethan London. Around the yard are galleries for spectators, and there is room also for them in front and to the sides of the uncurtained platform stage. A roof, or "shadow," is supported by two pillars. Above it is a struc-

FIGURE 4   A drawing of the Swan theatre by Johannes de Witt, now in the university library at Utrecht, Holland.

ture for the housing of stage machinery. Two doors at the rear provide access to the stage. Above and behind them is a space occupied by what appear to be spectators, but which obviously could be used as a playing space if required. Otherwise there is no inner stage and no upper stage. The players perform before an audience which surrounds them on three sides.

It is likely that the Theatre built by Burbage in 1576 resembled this general design. The Globe of 1599 must have been a somewhat more elaborate structure than the Swan, for all contemporary accounts attest to its magnificence. As to its actual appearance, there has been great and seemingly endless controversy, and there have been numerous reconstructions, on the details of which scholars have not been able to agree. The most celebrated of these reconstructions has been that of John C. Adams, developed in his book, *The Globe Playhouse,* a model of which is now in the Folger Library in Washington, D.C. Adams pictured the Globe as a multiple-staged theatre, with curtained "inner below" and "inner above" stages and with a music gallery on a third level which could also be used for a playing area.

Adams conceived of the Globe in terms of the half-timbered structure of Elizabethan dwellings and inns. Other scholars such as George R. Kernodle, *From Art to Theatre,* and C. Walter Hodges, *The Globe Restored,* have seen it more in terms of the ornate architecture of Renaissance Italy and as drawing more from the street pageants of medieval processions than from the traditional design of inn yards. Adams's reconstruction has, in fact, been under considerable attack in recent years. Leslie Hotson, in *Shakespeare's Wooden O,* has argued that the Globe was a theatre in the round which reflected the staging practices of the halls of great houses and which relied heavily upon such *mansions* as had been used in medieval staging. Other scholars, including Richard Hosley, have argued against the existence of inner and upper stages and have held that the Globe in its playing areas did not differ materially from what is depicted in the Swan drawing. Such a theatre as these scholars postulate is reflected in the drawing by Brooks McNamara.

Whether or not the Globe actually had curtained "inner below" and "inner above" stages (and the evidence for the "inner below" or "study" is especially tenuous), it is obvious that the platform stage

FIGURE 5   The stage of the Globe theatre as reconstructed by John C. Adams.

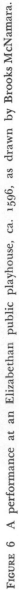

FIGURE 6 A performance at an Elizabethan public playhouse, ca. 1596, as drawn by Brooks McNamara.

extending into the pit and descended from the medieval *platea,* was its principal playing area. It is obvious also that certain scenes were staged "above," possibly upon some kind of upper stage or balcony or at a window. It seems fairly certain also that there was some space in the middle rear area, between the two entry doors, which could be curtained off at need and used for "discovery" scenes, whether or not this was an inner stage such as Adams supposes. Behind this space must have been the tiring room where actors changed their costumes, kept play-books and other equipment, and awaited their turns to appear on stage.

In the small houses or "huts" at the very top of the theatre structure was located whatever stage machinery the Globe contained, probably some kinds of pulleys or winches for raising and lowering equipment. Although we know that such machinery was used at an indoor theatre such as Blackfriars, there is actually no specific evidence for its existence at the Globe. On the platform stage there were trap doors, of uncertain number, providing access to the space beneath, which some scholars believe was open to the view of the audience. Adams supposes that there was one large central trap and one additional smaller trap at each of the four corners of the platform stage, and that there were two additional traps in the inner stage. There were two entrance doors at the rear of the stage. It was conventional for actors never to exit through the same door from which they had entered. Whether these were oblique doors, as Adams supposes, or flush doors, as in the Swan drawing, has never been determined, although most scholars today favour the latter supposition. The roof of the theatre, extending over the platform stage, was supported, as in the Swan drawing, by two pillars, and Adams believes that the ceiling was painted with stars and the signs of the zodiac, so that the entire structure could be imaginatively taken to be a model of the universe. Indeed the notion of the stage as representing the world is one of the commonest metaphors of Shakespeare's age.

Largely on the basis of the Fortune builders' contract, Adams has estimated the entire theatre to have been about eighty-three feet in diameter, and the stage to have been forty-one feet wide and twenty-nine feet deep, tapering towards the front and extending to about the middle of the yard. Most scholars accept these general dimensions as accurate, although it is now more widely believed that the stage was rectangular in shape. For spectators there was the pit and three galleries, each divided into boxes or "rooms." The highest gallery was the cheapest in price. On the lowest gallery, adjacent to the stage, were the "lords' rooms" where great nobles might sit. Although gallants might sit on the stage at private theatre performances, there is no evidence that they ever did so at the public playhouses. The entire structure, most scholars agree, was designed to accommodate an audience of about two thousand persons. It is important that we keep firmly in mind, however, that in spite of all our conjectures and hypotheses, and in spite of all the reconstructions of scholars, we do not really know what the Globe or any other Elizabethan theatre looked like. The danger inherent in the many models with which teachers for generations have edified their classes is that they may cause students to visualize as fact structures which can never be more than conjectural.

Various properties were used in performance, most notably beds, tables, chairs, trees, hedges, and objects behind which actors could be concealed. Heavier properties may have sometimes been hidden in the "discovery space" at the back of the stage until they were ready for use; others may have been placed on the stage before performance began; and we know that some were carried on and off by the actors themselves. Adams believes that the entire theatre was highly decorated. Other scholars prefer to regard it as having been relatively barren, the plays themselves being permitted to supply whatever imaginative colouring might be needed.

All contemporary accounts, however, attest to the magnificence of the Globe, and we know that large sums were spent on costumes for the actors — often more than was paid to dramatists for their plays. The Elizabethan public playhouse, like its medieval antecedents, was designed to accommodate a drama not limited by time or space. Its stage could stand for a specific locale, or it could represent the entire universe, and it could instantaneously shift from the one kind of representation to the other. Ghosts could move from one world to the next; they could disappear as easily as they appeared. Great periods of time could be encompassed in seconds as actors passed from one scene to the next, using every part of the structure, including sometimes even the pit, and attaining an intimate relation to the audience which few later theatres have been able to equal. At some theatres, notably the private ones, there were pauses in the action while music was played, but there is no evidence that this was ever done at the Globe. The dramatic illusion created by the opening words of a play probably remained unbroken until the final lines had been spoken.

When specific locations were called for, they were usually indicated in the lines of the play, although there is a likelihood that they were sometimes indicated by sign-boards. But much of the action of Elizabethan plays was deliberately vague in locale. While properties were used, they were not of crucial importance, for the essential element of an Elizabethan play was the spoken word, not setting or scenic representation. As an outdoor theatre without artificial lighting of any kind, the public playhouse was always subject to the vagaries of the weather, which the more fortunate players in private theatres could ignore.

The Children's Companies

The prominence of the public outdoor playhouse is a phenomenon of only the final quarter of the sixteenth century. The most significant theatrical activity of the first half of Queen Elizabeth's reign had been conducted indoors, in private theatres, in great houses, in schools, at the Inns of Court, and at the royal court itself. Sophisticated and courtly plays had been acted primarily by children, boy actors who had had their origins in the choir schools going back at least to the twelfth century. From the performance of religious plays and of Latin imitations of the classics, these children had progressed by Shakespeare's time to the performance of original plays in English by some of the finest dramatists of the age, and they had emerged as powerful and influential troupes which maintained a close rivalry with the adult professional companies.

In the early years of Elizabeth's reign, the choir boys had performed at court on special occasions while devoting most of their time to their religious duties. Only when the licensed adult companies began to gain in importance and to acquire theatres did the children become organized into what were in effect professional acting companies. They began to give performances before the public, at first in their own schools and chapels, and finally at specially adapted indoor theatres in London where they catered to a wealthier and more sophisticated audience than that at the outdoor playhouses. The companies had from eight to twelve boy members, and they were trained and managed by their school choir masters who became, in effect, professional theatre managers. The children seem to have attained a remarkable proficiency as actors.

While there were many children's companies throughout the Elizabethan and Jacobean period, two troupes were dominant: the Children of St. Paul's, who continued to act until 1606, and the Children of the Chapel Royal, who, under various names, continued to give performances until 1616. Although they performed at various places, the playhouses most notably associated with the boy actors were the two private theatres constructed successively in the old Dominican friary of Blackfriars. They were not really "private," of course, since the public was welcome to attend upon payment of a price of admission, albeit a much higher one than that at the Globe, but the term "private" was used to distinguish the indoor from the outdoor theatres until the closing of both in 1642. When the second Blackfriars theatre, built by James Burbage in 1596, passed into the hand of the King's Men in 1608, it provided a winter home for Shakespeare's company, which at that time, it has been observed, began to avail itself of theatrical techniques long associated with the boy actors and especially related to private indoor performance.

Production at Blackfriars

These techniques involved a more lavish use of masque scenes requiring more elaborate stage machinery than could have been available at the Globe, most notably the flying devices which we know that Blackfriars possessed. Music had always been a prominent feature of plays performed by choirboys, and music came now to play a larger role in Shakespeare's plays than ever before. Between the acts at Blackfriars there were intermissions during which there was music and often dancing as well. Perhaps more important, these final plays of Shakespeare's, performed indoors by candlelight before a more sophisticated audience than that at the Globe, reveal a refinement and elegance which such an audience might suggest.

Fine sentiment rather than extravagant passion became the keynote of the acting style at Blackfriars. It is nevertheless somewhat of an oversimplification to argue that Shakespeare around 1608 deliberately revised his dramatic technique so as to conform to the requirements of a new kind of theatre. Many influences combined to shape the nature of Shakespeare's final plays; that they were to be staged at Blackfriars may have been one, but no more, of these.

The plays which Shakespeare wrote after 1608 were probably performed at the Globe as well as at Blackfriars. There is no reason to believe that either these or Shakespeare's earlier plays were substantially altered for presentation in the indoor theatre. Indoor and outdoor performances were by the same actors working with the same play-books. Such performances may have had far more in common than they had differences, for Blackfriars, like the Globe, was the product of a long history of theatrical design going back to the Middle Ages, and one in which both theatres fully shared. Although we cannot know exactly how James Burbage designed the second Blackfriars theatre in 1596, we can safely surmise that he drew upon his own experiences in building the Theatre and upon the ideas to be incorporated in the Globe some two years later.

The most elaborate and ambitious attempt to reconstruct the second Blackfriars is by Irwin Smith in *Shakespeare's Blackfriars Playhouse: Its History and Design.* Drawing upon our knowledge of Dominican friary construction throughout England, of the many records of the London Blackfriars which have survived, of the contracts for the Fortune and Hope theatres, and of the stage directions and obvious requirements of some one hundred and thirty-three plays which we can ascertain to have been performed by the King's Men at Blackfriars, Smith emerges with a conception which in its essential features does not differ remarkably from Adams's reconstruction of the Globe. There are similar curtained "inner below" and "inner above" stages, with a music gallery above them, side windows, and oblique entry doors. The large platform stage, according to Smith, contained at least one trap, access to it being from the room below, and there was probably a trap with a similar means of access in the rear or inner stage, behind which was a room used for a tiring house. Elaborate stage machinery was housed in the "heavens" above. There were accommodations for spectators on benches before the stage, in boxes or "lords' rooms" along the side, and on two upper galleries, as well as on stools placed on either side of the stage itself, where gallants might display their finery without obstructing the action of the play. For this privilege they paid an additional sixpence. Smith estimates that Blackfriars was capable of accommodating five hundred and sixteen spectators.

Elizabethan Acting

We know the names of the great actors of Shakespeare's day — Richard Burbage and Edward Alleyn for tragedy; Richard Tarleton, Will Kempe, and Robert Armin for comedy — and we have abundant contemporary testimony to their magnificence and skill upon the stage, but just how they appeared to an Elizabethan audience we do not really know and never can hope to know. Indeed, that the stage performance of any actor in any period can adequately be described in words and made known to later generations is very unlikely. Like other ultimately unknowable subjects, the style of Elizabethan acting has accordingly been a subject of considerable controversy.

Most of the debate has centred about the question of whether Elizabethan acting was "natural" or "formal." The natural or realistic actor is one who attempts to impersonate a real character in a real situation, whose speech and manner are what the person he is portraying would naturally use in the situation in question. A formal actor, on the other hand, symbolizes action rather than represents it. His language is recitation rather than natural speech, and he uses all of the arts of formal rhetoric and oratory to convey what the play requires the audience to perceive. Most scholars have argued that Elizabethan acting was predominantly formal. They have pointed to the long tradition of rhetorical and oratorical training in Elizabethan schools, where conventional gestures had been prescribed to depict specific feelings and moods, and where the recitation of "set speeches" to illustrate particular emotions had long been a formal exercise. They have held that actors might have been expected to draw upon this training, and that thus the arts of oratory could not have been much different from those of acting.

Another group of scholars, however, have held that Elizabethan acting was natural, with little relation to oratory. They have argued

FIGURE 7 The second Blackfriars, as reconstructed by Irwin Smith in *Shakespeare's Blackfriars Playhouse: Its History and Design* (New York: New York University Press, 1964).

that it must have reflected the common Elizabethan critical notion that the drama was an imitation of life. While the evidence of formal style in the earlier plays is very strong, these scholars have maintained that whereas Elizabethan acting may have begun as formal oratorical exercise, it gradually changed until by Shakespeare's time a naturalistic style had come to predominate. A classic argument for the formal nature of Elizabethan acting is in Bertram Joseph, *Elizabethan Acting*. The naturalistic school is perhaps best represented by John Russell Brown, *Shakespeare's Plays in Performance*.

It is likely that there were many kinds of acting upon the Elizabethan stage, both natural and formal. The child actors, coming directly from the schools, may have been prone to a more formal oratorical style, but one tempered by the intimate atmosphere of the private playhouses where they acted. That tragic heroes were to portray passion had long been traditional, and it is likely that Burbage and Alleyn acted, especially in the public playhouses, in a highly formal style, replete with elaborate gestures and a good deal of rhetorical bombast. But we have no right to assume that they were incapable of more subtle realistic performance when the occasion demanded.

We must remember also that acting styles were changing throughout Shakespeare's lifetime, just as every other aspect of the theatre was undergoing evolution. The Middle Ages had left a tradition of boisterous and bumptious clowning as the stock-in-trade of the comic actor. We have reason to believe that this was the method of Will Kempe, as it had been also of Richard Tarleton, who died in 1590. Both were famous for their comic improvisation. Robert Armin, however, was a singer and a dancer who played comic roles less dependent upon primitive slapstick techniques, relying instead upon subtle word play and satire. The parts of Feste and Touchstone were written for Armin, just as that of Dogberry was written for Will Kempe. While we are fairly certain that Shakespeare created his dramatic characters with specific members of his own company in mind, we must not fall into the common error of regarding this company composition as a restrictive control upon Shakespeare's genius. To do so is to underestimate the skill of the actor and the virtually infinite potentialities of his art. There is no reason to suppose that Shakespeare ever refrained from challenging his actors to perform whatever he chose to write for them, or ever assumed their inability to portray whatever he considered essential to the total conception of whatever play he was writing. Like any great dramatist, he controlled his theatrical medium; he did not permit himself to be controlled by it.

Elizabethan acting was a difficult craft. Since companies were small, parts had to be doubled. Actors having to play several roles in a single play had little opportunity to develop any one of them fully. Because plays were given in repertory and the repertories of the major companies were large, an actor had to learn a great many roles. He had little opportunity to fix any single role firmly in his memory, for even the most popular play would not be given more than twice in a single week, and never on two days in succession. Players had to develop extraordinary powers of memory. It is estimated that a member of Shakespeare's company had to learn a new part every week. There was also very little time for rehearsal. The evidence is that new plays were mounted with a speed which would be unthinkable in the modern theatre. Since all female roles were played by boys, talented boy actors were especially prized, and since they could no longer act after their voices began to change at about the age of fourteen, they must have developed extraordinary skill in the space of very few years so as to perform credibly such roles as Ophelia and Cleopatra.

Shakespeare's Audience

There is an old notion, intrinsically absurd but nevertheless very slow in dying, that Shakespeare prostituted his genius by catering to the demands of a crude audience interested only in violence, sex, and the lower kinds of comedy. This idea was stated most prominently by the poet Robert Bridges in an essay called "On the Influence of the Audience," first published in 1904 in the Shakespeare Head edition of Shakespeare's works. It is based upon two cardinal misconceptions — one regarding the nature of any dramatist's relation to his audience, and the other regarding the specific audience for whom Shakespeare wrote. It is a gross perversion of the creative act to suppose that a dramatist of genius caters to the demands of an audience. The art of the dramatist lies rather in his ability to enthral a heterogeneous audience, without regard to its composition, and to make this audience accept whatever he chooses to give it. He is successful as an artist only to the extent that he can cause his viewers to suspend whatever prejudices, preconceptions, or ingrained attitudes they may have brought to the theatre with them and to accept at its face value the dramatic illusion which he offers them. In this art Shakespeare was as supremely successful in his own day as he continues to be today. His plays may be performed before audiences comprising the most learned and the most ignorant, the most naïve and the most critical, the most sensitive in nature and the most coarse and brutal of temperament, and every viewer will come away with at least some pleasure from what he has beheld. No great dramatic artist ever permits his artistry to be controlled by the audience — which the nature of his craft requires that he manipulate.

Bridges considered the audience at the Globe to have been a coarse and ignorant one, drawn from the lowest levels of Elizabethan society. Alfred Harbage has demonstrated in an important study, *Shakespeare's Audience,* that this simply was not so. The contemporary audiences of Shakespeare's plays encompassed a wide spectrum of Elizabethan society, from the queen herself at court, to the upper-class gentry at Blackfriars, to the many elements of the ordinary London population who came to the public playhouses. These elements included respectable persons of modest means, shopkeepers and artisans who paid their pennies to stand as groundlings in the pit. These were generally solid citizens who came to the theatre to be both entertained and edified and not to engage in riotous behaviour. Among the more numerous and regular attendants were the London apprentices who ranged in age from fourteen to twenty-four. These were not juvenile delinquents. They were the sons of respectable bourgeois merchant families, almost all of them with grammar-school educations equal to Shakespeare's own.

Occupying two- and three-penny seats in the galleries were court attendants of various kinds and visiting noblemen from the country. There were also twelve-penny rooms which could be occupied by the greatest and wealthiest men of the kingdom, for these were extremely expensive places by Elizabethan standards. Among the women in the audience were the wives and daughters of London merchants, and although prostitutes sometimes appeared, there is no ground for the supposition that the theatre was a place where they might ply their trade. That cutpurses worked among the groundlings in the pit is true, for such thieves always congregate wherever there are crowds. The very fact that they could operate successfully, however, demonstrates that the eyes of the groundlings must have been fixed firmly upon the stage and that they must have been fully absorbed in whatever play they were watching.

There is some reason to believe that Elizabethan audiences were somewhat more demonstrative than those in our present-day theatres. They seem to have wept openly at scenes of pathos, just as they laughed unrestrainedly at comedy and interrupted the action with applause whenever they felt moved to do so. It is clear also that they did not hesitate to show their displeasure with hisses and catcalls when a play displeased them. Otherwise, it is not likely that the audiences who watched Shakespeare's plays in the public theatres were much different in their understanding, responsiveness, and general probity of conduct from those at our better present-day theatres and movie houses.

The attacks upon the theatre as a centre of thievery, vice, and every other kind of iniquity, which appeared in the diatribes of the Puritans, did not accurately reflect theatre conditions. If anything, dramatists writing for the public playhouses at times may have exerted themselves excessively — as in the plays of Heywood and Dekker — to assert a conventional middle-class morality. Vice is almost never a subject for comedy in plays written for the public playhouses, although it often is in plays performed by the children. Attacks upon the stage, however, continued throughout Shakespeare's career, and they grew more virulent, if anything, as the players attained increasing social status. Actors were attacked as vagabonds, no better than whores or thieves in seeking to earn their livelihoods by what a Puritan morality could consider to be only idle frivolity rather than useful, manly labour. The theatres were reviled as institutions of perversion, where boys dressed as women, where every kind of improper conduct could be seen by the innocent and corruptible, and where sinners spent time they should have been devoting to work or to religious service. They were dens of iniquity whose sinful existence God would punish periodically by the visitation of the plague upon the entire city. During plague time the playhouses were duly closed. They were closed also when the theatre companies presented politically offensive works such as Jonson and Nashe's *Isle of Dogs* in 1597 or Chapman's *Byron* plays in 1608. When the Puritans at last came to political power, they closed the theatres entirely. These theatres were never to reopen, for in 1642 the great public drama of England effectively came to an end. The theatres which opened after the Restoration provided dramatic entertainment of a different kind.

6

The Publication of Shakespeare's Plays

◇◇◇◇◇ Shakespeare's plays, like those of his contemporary writers
◇◇◇◇◇ for the public stage, were written for performance, and
◇◇◇◇◇
once they were turned over by the author to a theatre company
they became the company's property in which the author had little
further right. They were, in fact, the most important property
which the company owned, and play-books were guarded zealously.
The actors had no particular desire, in most instances, to see the
plays in their repertory published, but they fought a losing battle,
for as the theatre became a more and more important part of
English life, and as at the same time the English reading public
rapidly expanded, the demand for printed copies of plays could
not be resisted. The theatre companies seem to have accepted the
situation and to have sought as best they could to insure that when
plays were printed it was with the least possible disadvantage to
their own interests. In this they were not always successful.

All of the advantage lay with the printers. None of the privileges
of copyright which we take for granted today were present in
Shakespeare's time. A printer could publish any manuscript which
he managed to get hold of, without consulting its author or the
theatre company to which it belonged, and without paying for
permission to print it. The publication of books was a closely
controlled monopoly in sixteenth- and seventeenth-century England. Control lay in the hands of the London Company of Stationers, to which all printers and booksellers belonged. The powers
of the Stationers' Company were authorized by the crown, and

the company performed the work of the crown in controlling propaganda and the dissemination of opinion of every kind. With the exception of several licensed university printers in Oxford and Cambridge who were controlled in other ways, the crown restricted all printing of books to the members of the London Stationers' Company, and gave vast powers to its wardens. The Stationers' Company conducted a court with power to destroy books, fine printers, and settle disputes between them. It restricted the number of presses which could operate, controlled the number of apprentices taken into the trade, and regulated the number of copies of particular books to be printed. Its powers over the publishing business were all-pervasive. In its regulations were the only form of copyright known to Elizabethans. The interests it protected were those of the printers, not those of authors or theatre companies. While it was to the advantage of printers of plays to retain cordial relations with the theatre companies, and many of them did so, legally such printers were restricted in their activities only by government censorship and by the rules of the Stationers' Company to which they belonged.

Censorship

Before they could be either performed or printed, Elizabethan plays were subject to censorship by civil and ecclesiastical authorities. What was considered either morally or politically offensive was to be suppressed, but in moral concerns censorship seems to have been rather lax, although there were attempts to restrict the use of oaths and religious blasphemy. Most subject to suppression was matter likely to promote political sedition and unrest and likely to cast doubt upon established religion. Political and religious issues were, in fact, so deeply intertwined in Shakespeare's England that it is difficult to make a clear distinction between the two. It was probably because of censorship that the deposition scene of *Richard II* was neither publicly staged nor printed during Elizabeth's lifetime.

Among the "Injunctions" issued by Queen Elizabeth in 1559, one year after she came to the throne, was a provision for the licensing of all books before they could be printed, as well as a requirement that mayors and justices of the peace in all the municipalities of England examine plays performed within their jurisdictions to see that they contained nothing objectionable in terms of religion or politics. This rule proved to be especially damaging to the dramatic companies of London, for the strong Puritan bent among the city fathers made almost any dramatic performance objectionable to them. Partly to help these companies, the Queen's Privy Council in 1581 transferred the duty of censoring plays to the Master of the Revels, an official of the queen's household who was responsible for the supervision of court entertainments. Violations of the rules against blasphemy and obscenity were extremely common, however, and as Puritan attacks upon the stage grew more and more intense Parliament passed an act in 1606 to restrain the abuses of players — an act which resulted particularly in the removal of oaths and the name of God from the texts of plays. In 1607 the Master of the Revels was given the additional authority to license all plays before they could be printed. During Shakespeare's career the position of Master of the Revels was held by only two persons, Sir Edmund Tilney, who was appointed to the post in 1579 and held it until his death in 1610, and his nephew, Sir George Buc, who was appointed Tilney's Deputy in 1597 and succeeded him in the post, to be succeeded himself by Sir Henry Herbert in 1622.

The licensing of all books before they could be printed had been established in England even before Queen Elizabeth's proclamation of 1559. Government concern with the publication of books began to be evident in England as early as 1518 when a book printed by Richard Pynson was given a special license by the crown. In a proclamation of November 16, 1538, King Henry VIII decreed that "no persone or persons in this realme, shall from hensforth print any boke in the englyshe tonge, onles vpon examination made by some of his gracis priuie counsayle, or other suche as his highnes shall appoynte." By Shakespeare's day the privilege of licensing books was vested in the Bishop of London, the Archbishop of Canterbury, the Lord Chamberlain, and members of the Privy Council. In practice, however, they delegated the authority to a panel of London clergymen called "correctors of the press," one of whom passed upon each manuscript under consideration. How stringent the censorship was we are not sure; from the evidence of what was printed in spite of censorship, it does not appear to have been extremely stringent. Probably the wardens of the Stationers'

Company themselves subjected the manuscripts submitted to them to close scrutiny for material likely to offend. They were not eager to approve the printing of any books which might disturb the authorities and thus bring down further restrictive regulations upon their trade.

The Stationers' Register

As soon as a manuscript was approved by the censor it was taken to Stationers' Hall where it was inspected by one or both of the wardens of the company. If he found no objections to its publication, the publisher's right to the work and his intention to print it were duly entered in the official record book of the company known as the Stationers' Register. A typical entry might be that made for Shakespeare's *A Midsummer Night's Dream* in 1600:

> 8 Octobris. Thomas Fyssher. Entred for his copie vnder the handes of master Rodes and the Wardens. A booke called A mydsommer nightes Dreame vj^d.

The entry indicates that on October 8, 1600, the stationer Thomas Fisher presented to the company a manuscript of *A Midsummer Night's Dream* as approved by Mr. Rhodes, one of the "correctors of the press" and by the wardens of the Stationers' Company and that for a fee of sixpence his permission to print the play was recorded in the register. Sometimes an entry will supply a good deal more information, as does that for *King Lear* in 1607:

> 26 Novembris. Nathanael Butter John Busby. Entred for their Copie under thandes of Sir George Buck knight and Thwardens A Booke called. Master William Shakespeare his historye of Kinge Lear, as yt was played before the Kinges maiestie at Whitehall vppon Sainct Stephens night at Christmas Last, by his maiesties servantes playinge vsually at the Globe on the Banksyde vj^d.

Here we have the name of the Master of the Revels who had licensed the play, the name of its author, the occasion of a recent performance, the company which performed it, and even the name of the theatre where that company usually was to be seen.

Sometimes a publisher, either for his own purposes or at the request of the theatre company, would enter in the Stationers' Register a play which he had no immediate intention of publishing. The purpose of such entry was usually to prevent publication by another publisher. Under the date of August 4, 1600, for instance, Shakespeare's *As You Like It, Henry V,* and *Much Ado About Nothing* were entered in the register with the notation "to be staied." Separate entries were later made for *Much Ado* and *Henry V* when they were printed in 1600, but *As You Like It* was not printed until it appeared in the folio of 1623.

Not all books printed in the sixteenth and seventeenth centuries were entered in the Stationers' Register, but about seventy per cent of them were. The register is thus one of the most important sources of information about the plays of Shakespeare and his contemporaries that we have. *A Transcript of the Registers of the Company of Stationers of London: 1554–1640,* edited by Edward Arber, was printed in London in five volumes between 1875 and 1877. It has been recently reprinted. A slightly more accurate transcription of all those entries which relate to plays is included in W. W. Greg's *A Bibliography of the English Printed Drama to the Restoration.*

Dramatic Manuscripts

While many kinds of books were presented to printers by the authors themselves, thus providing copy which the authors presumably had polished and corrected with care, this was rarely done with plays. Since these belonged, legally as well as morally, to the theatre companies rather than to their authors, it was usually the companies which arranged for their printing. They did so when it was to their financial advantage, usually when a play was no longer sufficiently popular to be retained in the repertory and when the fee to be derived from a printer might be greater than could be expected from the play's continued production. Sometimes a dramatic company went bankrupt, as happened to Lord Pembroke's Men after its disastrous provincial tour of 1593–1594, and then it might be forced to raise money by selling its play-books to printers as well as to other dramatic companies. A dramatist might, of course, sell a copy of his play to a printer in spite of whatever arrangements he had made with a theatre company. We know that this was sometimes done, but there is no sign that it was ever done by William Shakespeare.

Playwrights could cooperate closely with printers in the publication of their plays, and in some instances we know that they did. Some of the plays written for the childrens' companies seem to have been presented to printers by the playwrights themselves. Plays belonging to the adult professional companies were sometimes provided by their authors with prefaces after they had passed into the hands of printers, and these dramatists may even have had some part in seeing their plays through the press. We know that Ben Jonson did these things whenever his plays were printed, but since Jonson's practices seem to have been unlike those of other writers for the stage, he provides the unique instance and not the rule. Often authors may have cooperated with printers to assure satisfactory editions of plays secured without their authorization. We are virtually certain, however, that Shakespeare had no part whatever in the publication of the eighteen of his plays which were printed in quarto during his lifetime. This is made abundantly clear by the quartos themselves, their lack of adequate stage directions, *dramatis personæ,* and of all the other elements important to readers of plays but not customarily found in the manuscripts employed by theatre companies.

Whatever dramatic manuscripts were likely to come into the possession of a printer were limited in number, for no theatre company would want needless proliferation of manuscripts of plays still in its active repertory, thus increasing the danger that a popular play might fall into the hands either of a rival company or of a printer who would have no scruples about publishing it without authorization. Paper, moreover, was expensive, and copying was a tedious task which would not be undertaken without clear necessity. Whatever manuscripts were in existence would have been prepared to serve the needs of the theatre company and not of the printer, although transcriptions of theatre manuscripts were sometimes made specifically for the use of printers. The kind of manuscript copy from which a printer worked would determine in large part the kind of text he printed and so have considerable bearing upon the question of the closeness of this text to what the dramatist actually wrote. Thus it is important that we understand the various manuscript forms a play might take before it reached the hands of a printer and the extent to which these forms were influenced by the special conditions and problems of theatre production.

We can never know the exact conditions under which Shakespeare or any of his contemporaries composed their plays, the number of drafts which were written out before the author was satisfied with his work, or the extent to which particular passages were deleted or rewritten. There are some Elizabethan statements to the effect that Shakespeare wrote with extraordinary ease, never altering a line after he had set it down, the best known being Ben Jonson's statement in his *Timber, or Discoveries,* published in 1641: "I remember, the Players have often mentioned it as an honour to Shakespeare, that in his writing, (whatsoever he penn'd) hee never blotted out line." Whether Jonson was accurate in this or not, we know that at some point in his labours Shakespeare would have completed a draft of the play he was working on which he considered sufficiently finished to present to the theatre company. This copy, in his own handwriting, we call his "foul papers." It would have various recognizable features. Entrances and exits might not always be exact (on the assumption that these matters could be worked out by the actors in rehearsal); stage directions would tend to be descriptive indications of what the author intended rather than specific imperative directions to actors. It might contain deleted passages and substitutions of others for them. Sometimes passages intended for deletion found their way into a text printed from such copy, as occurred in several places in the 1598 quarto of *Romeo and Juliet.*

If these foul papers were clear and legible they would be presented to the Master of the Revels for his approval. If they were not, a clean copy would be made from them, probably by a playhouse scribe. We refer to such copy as "fair papers." The Master of the Revels might request certain changes and deletions before he would grant his approval, but when this had been secured, the next step would be to prepare a prompt-copy or play-book. This was the copy of the play to be used in performance. It was prepared under the direction of the theatre prompter with the specific requirements of stage performance in view. In the work of an experienced theatre man such as Shakespeare, probably there would not be need for a great deal of alteration, but speech-prefixes would be regularized, stage directions would be made specific, stage noises would be called for in the proper places, and necessary cuts would be made. It is axiomatic that an author's foul papers will present a version of the play closer to the author's original intention than a prompt-book prepared from them. After some years of use in the theatre a prompt-book might acquire an accretion of addition and interpolation arising out of stage production for which the author was in no way responsible. A prompt-book might sometimes substitute the names of actors for those of the characters they were to portray. Sometimes special prompt-books were prepared for provincial tours when a smaller company performed the play and thus extensive cuts had to be made. This may have happened to the copy from which *Macbeth* was printed in 1623.

When the prompt-book was completed, parts would be copied from it and distributed to the individual actors for their use. In addition, a "plot" was usually prepared. This was a brief summary of the play's action, with indication of the various roles and of the stage properties necessary for performance. It was pinned up in back of the stage as a quick guide during production, and, if the play-book was lost, it could be used as a guide in preparing a new play-book from actors' parts. Several such plots have survived, including one for a lost play about Troilus and Cressida, probably by Thomas Dekker and Henry Chettle, which is extant in British Museum MS. Add. 10449.

It used to be supposed that most of Shakespeare's plays were printed from prompt-book copies, but we are now fairly certain that this was not widely done. More of Shakespeare's plays appear to have been printed from his foul papers, for which there was little use after the prompt-book had been prepared, or from fair copies of them. Theatre companies were not eager to entrust their valuable prompt-books to printers who might lose or mutilate them. One play, *Timon of Athens,* probably was printed from an unfinished draft which represents a stage of composition earlier than that of the usual foul papers. *Hamlet,* which provides one of the most interesting and puzzling of textual problems, was printed in the quarto of 1604 [Q²] from Shakespeare's foul papers. For the version in the folio of 1623 [F¹] the printers used as their copy a prompt-book which had been employed in the theatre for some time and had accumulated many changes and additions in the course of theatre production. There is thus considerable divergence between the two texts. Although plays could be printed from assembled actors' parts, there is no clear certainty that any of Shakespeare's plays was printed in this way. It used to be believed that the texts of *The Two Gentlemen of Verona* and *The Winter's Tale* in the folio of 1623 derived from such a source, but it is now more generally believed that they were printed from transcripts of the prompt-books made by Ralph Crane, a professional scrivener employed by the King's Men after 1619.

Bad Quartos

Inevitably certain popular plays were stolen from the theatre companies and issued in forms so corrupt that they bore little real relation to what their authors had written. Such texts, which could have been printed neither from a theatre prompt-book nor an author's foul papers, nor from any authorized transcription of either of these, we call "bad quartos." In their "Address to the Great Variety of Readers," prefixed to the Shakespeare folio of 1623, Heminges and Condell referred to such versions of Shakespeare's plays as "stolne, and surreptitious copies, maimed, and deformed by the frauds and stealthes of injurious imposters." Thomas Heywood in a preface to his *The Rape of Lucrece* (1608) complained about the pirating of his plays:

> Yet since some of my plaies haue (vnknowen to me, and without any of my direction) accidentally come into the Printers handes, and therefore so corrupt and mangled, (coppied onely by the eare) that I haue bene as vnable to know them, as ashamde to challenge them.

In his *Pleasant Dialogues and Dramas* (1637) Heywood complained that his play *If You Know Not Me You Know Nobody* had been pirated some years earlier by means of a stenographic report. It was so popular, he claimed, that the audience

> Did throng the Seates, the Boxes, and the Stage
> So much; that some by Stenography drew
> The plot: put it in print: (scarce one word trew).

Just how the copy for bad quartos was derived by their printers has been a matter for much conjecture, and we still are uncertain. Largely on the basis of Heywood's complaint, it has been supposed that stenography was one method. But if this was used at all, it cannot have been used very widely. Although it was possible for a stenographer sitting in the theatre gallery to take down a play as it was being performed, even with so primitive a stenographic system as Timothy Bright's *Characterie,* published in 1588, or John Willis' *Stenography,* a more sophisticated system published in 1602 (too late for most of Shakespeare's bad quartos), it would have been extremely difficult to do so. Also, a stenographer attempting the task probably would have attracted the attention of the actors who hardly would have allowed him to leave the theatre with his notes.

It is now widely believed that bad quartos resulted in most instances from a process of "memorial reconstruction." An actor, perhaps one out of favour with the company for some reason, or a group of actors working together, might recite a play from memory, often with the help of one or two actors' parts, while a printer's scribe wrote down what they recited. A text of a play printed from copy derived in this manner might have certain obvious characteristics: the story line would be generally accurate, but individual speeches would be misplaced and assigned to the wrong speakers; speeches other than those of the pirate actor or actors would be garbled, with evidence of attempts to create crude blank verse out of obvious prose or to restore blank verse which the pirate could only partly remember; there might be fanciful additions to the play reflecting the pirate's own taste and predilections. One value of such a text is that its stage directions would be likely to be clearer and more frequent than in a text printed from an author's foul papers, for the pirated text would be based closely upon recollection of the details of actual stage performance by actors observant of many of these details.

Of Shakespeare's plays which were printed in bad quartos, *Romeo and Juliet* (1597) [Q^1] appears to have been assembled from memory with the help of some manuscript material, especially in the part of the Nurse, which is printed in italics; *Henry V* (1600) [Q^1] and *The Merry Wives of Windsor* (1602) [Q^1] were probably pirated in similar ways. *Hamlet* (1603) [Q¹] is probably the most interesting of Shakespeare's bad quartos. Not only does it show signs of memorial reconstruction, probably by more than one actor, but it seems also to have been influenced by the old pre-Shakespearian *Hamlet* which was being staged before 1589. It has been suggested that the pirate or pirates had acted in this old play as well as in Shakespeare's and confused the two works in the process of recollection. Some scholars have argued, on the other hand, that this text is a memorial reconstruction of an early Shakespearian version of *Hamlet,* later revised by Shakespeare to give us our authorized text.

While the bad quarto of *Hamlet* contains some features, such as the sequence of scenes, which are more dramatically effective than their counterparts in the authorized text, the text itself is very badly mangled. Hamlet's "To be, or not to be" soliloquy (III.i. 56–90), for instance, appears in the bad quarto of the play in the following form:

> To be, or not to be, I there's the point,
> To Die, to sleepe, is that all? I all:
> No, to sleepe, to dreame, I mary there it goes,
> For in that dreame of death, when wee awake,
> And borne before an euerlasting Iudge,
> From whence no passenger euer returnd,
> The vndiscouered country, at whose sight
> The happy smile, and the accursed damn'd.
> But for this, the ioyfull hope of this,
> Whol'd beare the scornes and flattery of the world,
> Scorned by the right rich, the rich curssed of the poore?
> The widow being oppressed, the orphan wrong'd,
> The taste of hunger or a tirants raigne,
> And thousand more calamities besides,
> To grunt and sweate vnder this weary life,
> When that he may his full *Quietus* make,
> With a bare bodkin, who would this indure,
> But for a hope of something after death?
> Which pusles the braine, and doth counfound the sence,
> Which makes vs rather beare those euilles we haue,

Than flie to others that we know not of.
I that, O this conscience makes cowardes of vs all,
Lady in thy orizons, be all my sinnes remembred.

In these lines may be found virtually every kind of distortion characteristic of a memorial reconstruction.

Other plays printed during Shakespeare's lifetime appear to be bad quartos, but are not usually classified among them because they are different in nature from those which can be ascribed more certainly to memorial reconstruction. One of these is the "pied bull" quarto of *King Lear* (1608) [Q¹], which is some kind of derivative text, although scholars have never been able to agree about just what kind. Some have suggested that it was reconstructed from memory by a whole company of actors working together in order to replace a lost prompt-book. This kind of communal effort of memory may well have been behind the text of *Richard III* (1597) [Q¹], a corrupt version of the play much briefer than that in the folio of 1623. It is likely that *Pericles* (1609) [Q¹], a badly printed text which confuses poetry and prose and reduces some speeches to virtual nonsense, was printed from a text obtained in some surreptitious way. There is reason to believe that a bad quarto of *Love's Labour's Lost* was printed in 1596, but no copy of it has survived.

Other plays which for a long time were regarded as source plays revised by Shakespeare have in recent times been added to our list of bad quartos. These include *The First Part of the Contention* (1594) and *The True Tragedy of Richard Duke of York* (1595) which are now generally recognized to be bad quartos of Shakespeare's *Part II* and *Part III* of *Henry VI*, derived almost certainly by memorial reconstruction. A special instance is provided by *The Taming of A Shrew* (1594), long regarded as a source of Shakespeare's *The Taming of the Shrew*, first printed in the folio of 1623, but now generally considered to be a bad quarto of that play. But if it is a bad quarto, it is one of a unique kind, not a memorial reconstruction by an actor, but an imitation of Shakespeare's play by a hack dramatist attempting to capture its salient features and at the same time to improve upon it.

Good Quartos

Most of the plays published during Shakespeare's lifetime, however, were printed from authorized copy, presumably with the consent of the theatre company and possibly with that of Shakespeare himself. Such texts we call "good quartos." In some instances where a bad quarto had been published, Shakespeare's company seems to have felt the need to replace it with a text which more accurately represented their play. A good quarto of *Romeo and Juliet* [Q²], for instance, appeared in 1599. The printer this time had access to Shakespeare's foul papers, but it is clear that he made some use also of the 1597 bad quarto of the play. He may have relied upon the bad quarto where the foul papers were defective, but it is just as likely that he printed from a copy of the bad quarto which had been marginally corrected by reference to the foul papers. Corrected quartos were often used in the printing house. An authorized version of *Hamlet* [Q²] was printed directly from Shakespeare's foul papers in 1604 (some extant copies bear the date of 1605). The words "Newly corrected and augmented" on the title page of the 1598 quarto of *Love's Labour's Lost* would indicate that this authorized edition was issued to replace the bad quarto which has not survived. It was printed from foul papers.

In other instances there seems to have been no attempt to replace the bad quarto with a more reliable text. Five quartos followed the bad quarto of *Richard III,* each based closely upon its immediate predecessor, and it was not until Q⁶ of 1622 was corrected against an independent manuscript (probably Shakespeare's foul papers or a transcript of them) that an acceptable version could appear in the folio of 1623. A second quarto of *King Lear* was printed in 1619 (with a false title page bearing the date of 1608), but it was based closely upon the bad quarto. The corrupt first quarto of *Henry V* [Q¹] was simply printed without essential alteration in 1602 [Q²] and again in 1619 [Q³], and it was not until the folio of 1623 that a satisfactory text of this play was printed, this time directly from Shakespeare's foul papers. *The Merry Wives of Windsor* was not reprinted before the folio of 1623 included a version set up from a transcript of either Shakespeare's foul papers or a prompt-copy. The corrupt text of *Pericles* was reprinted three times by 1619, and the play was not included in the First Folio at all.

Shakespeare's foul papers or transcripts of them, sometimes with playhouse additions and annotations, served as copy for eight plays which were printed for the first time in good quarto editions. *Titus Andronicus* appeared in 1594, without Shakespeare's name on the title page, and this quarto was reprinted in 1600 and 1611. *Richard II* was printed in 1597 without the deposition scene in the fourth act. Four more quartos, each reprinting its immediate predecessor, had appeared by 1615, only the last two of these containing an imperfect version of the deposition scene. Our earliest edition of *Henry IV, Part I* is dated 1598, but it was reprinted from an earlier quarto, only four pages of which have accidentally survived. By 1613 four additional quartos had appeared, each printed from the one before it. In 1600 appeared *Henry IV, Part II, A Midsummer Night's Dream, Much Ado About Nothing*, and *The Merchant of Venice*. This play was reprinted in 1619 [Q²] with a false title page bearing the date of 1600. *Troilus and Cressida* was printed in 1609, probably from a transcript of Shakespeare's foul papers made especially for the use of the lawyers of one of the Inns of Court. Only one play appeared in quarto for the first time after Shakespeare's death, and this one does not seem to have been printed from foul papers. It is *Othello*, which was printed in 1622, probably from a transcript of a shortened version of the play prepared for performance in the provinces.

None of Shakespeare's quartos, good or bad, was divided into acts or scenes except for *Othello* (1622), which was divided into acts only. There was really no need to divide a dramatic manuscript into scenes, because on the Elizabethan stage, in contrast with the classical practice, a new scene occurred whenever there was a blank stage, and this was made obvious by the exits and entrances. Act division was entirely conventional and had no bearing upon stage presentation in the public theatres, although it is likely that Shakespeare, following classical precedent, conceived of his plays in terms of a five-act structure. Act division was of some importance in private theatre productions where music was played between the acts. We do not find act and scene division becoming a regular part of printed dramatic texts until the second decade of the seventeenth century.

It should be noted that quartos of individual Shakespeare plays continued to be printed throughout the seventeenth century. Editions of *Hamlet,* for instance, appeared in 1676, 1683, 1695, and 1703; of *Othello* in 1655, 1681, 1687, 1695, and 1705. The texts were often altered to reflect changing theatrical conditions and they sometimes bore on their title pages the revealing words "as it is now acted," but in the main they were printed either from the early quartos or from one of the four great folio collections which had appeared in the meantime.

The First Folio

When Ben Jonson in 1616 produced an edition of his *Works* in folio, he raised the stature of the playwright to a level it had never known before, for this was the first time that the plays of any English dramatist had been gathered together and published in a single volume. It may have been the appearance of this book and the death of William Shakespeare in that same year which led two leading members of the King's Men, John Heminges and Henry Condell, to begin their planning of what was to emerge in 1623 as the handsome volume containing thirty-six of Shakespeare's plays — which we call the First Folio [F¹]. Actually, however, we know little about the origins of the project. It is possible that Heminges and Condell were approached by a publisher or publishers. It is possible that Shakespeare himself may have had some interest in the plan before his death, for he must have known as early as 1613 that the Ben Jonson folio was in prospect.

So large a volume was a considerable enterprise for any one publisher to undertake. Although the printing was all done in the shop of William Jaggard and his son, Isaac, the stationers Edward Blount, John Smethwicke, and William Aspley were also partners in the project. Isaac Jaggard was apparently the leading spirit in the affair; William Jaggard, who died in 1623, may have had very little to do with it. The Jaggards had already contemplated some kind of collection of Shakespeare's plays some years earlier, for in 1619 they had printed ten Shakespearian and pseudo-

Shakespearian plays in conjunction with Thomas Pavier, all ten apparently to be issued in a single volume. We do not know the details of this affair, but we do know that the project was for some reason hastily abandoned, perhaps because it had been without the authorization of the King's Men and because the King's Men had intervened with the Lord Chamberlain to stop it. The ten plays printed were sold separately, as single quartos, some of them with falsely dated title pages to obscure the facts of their publication. One copy of the ten plays bound in a single volume, the only one extant, is now in the Folger Library. Why Heminges and Condell should have chosen the Jaggards, after their abortive effort, as printers for the First Folio is unknown, although there has been considerable speculation.

On the title page of the folio appeared the engraving of Shakespeare by Martin Droeshout which, with the Stratford monument, is the only unquestioned likeness of Shakespeare we possess. It was preceded by a preliminary page containing a poem by Ben Jonson which calls attention to the portrait:

To the Reader.

This Figure, that thou here seest put,
It was for gentle Shakespeare cut;
Wherein the Grauer had a strife
With Nature, to out-doo the life;
O, could he but haue drawne his wit
As well in brasse, as he hath hit
His face; the Print would then surpasse
All, that was euer writ in brasse.
But, since he cannot, Reader, looke
Not on his Picture, but his Booke.
B.I.

Following the title page appeared a dedication of the volume to William Herbert, third Earl of Pembroke, and his brother Philip Herbert, third Earl of Montgomery. There is a suggestion in it of past relations of these earls to Shakespeare which has lent support to those who have argued that William Herbert was the "fair youth" to whom Shakespeare's sonnets were written:

But since your L. L. haue beene pleas'd to thinke these trifles some-thing, heeretofore; and haue prosequuted both them, and their Author liuing, with so much favour: we hope, that (they out-liuing him, and he not hauing the fate, common with some, to be exequutor to his owne writings) you will vse the like indulgence toward them, you haue done vnto their parent.

Heminges and Condell further assert their purpose as "onely to keepe the memory of so worthy a Friend, & Fellow aliue, as was our *Shakespeare,* by humble offer of his playes, to your most noble patronage."

This dedication is followed by an epistle "To the Great Variety of Readers," part of the second paragraph of which is important both as evidence as to Shakespeare's working habits and as an indication of how Heminges and Condell conceived of their edito-rial task:

It had bene a thing, we confesse, worthie to haue bene wished, that the Author himselfe had liu'd to haue set forth, and ouerseen his owne writings; But since it hath bin ordain'd otherwise, and he by death departed from that right, we pray you do not envie his Friends, the office of their care, and paine, to haue collected & publish'd them; and so to haue publish'd them, as where (before) you were abus'd with diuerse stolne, and surreptitious copies, maimed, and deformed by the frauds and stealthes of iniurious imposters, that expos'd them; euen those, are now offer'd to your view cur'd and perfect of their limbes; and all the rest, absolute in their numbers, as he conceived them. Who, as he was a happie imitator of Nature, was a most gentle expresser of it. His mind and hand went together: And what he thought, he vttered with that easinesse, that wee haue scarce receiued from him a blot in his papers. But it is not our prouince, who onely gather his works, and giue them you, to praise him. It is yours that reade him.

The folio editors thus claimed to be presenting Shakespeare's plays in more accurate versions than had been available before to the public, and they claimed to be presenting all of the plays that Shakespeare had ever written.

This important epistle is followed by four poems: Ben Jonson's tribute "To the Memory of My Beloued, the Author Mr. Wil-liam Shakespeare: and what he hath left us," and shorter poetic trib-utes by Hugh Holland, Leonard Digges, and "I.M." who has been generally identified as James Mabbe, although John Marston and Jasper Mayne have also been proposed. Then followed a list of "The Names of the Principall Actors in all these Playes," a roster of all those who had acted in the company known variously as the Earl of Derby's Men, Lord Hunsdon's Men, the Lord Chamberlain's Men, and finally the King's Men.

The plays themselves were printed in double columns in three separately paginated sections, devoted respectively to comedies, histories, and tragedies. *Troilus and Cressida,* originally designed to occupy a place among the tragedies between *Romeo and Juliet* and *Julius Cæsar,* was withdrawn, probably for copyright reasons, after the type for three pages had been set, and *Timon of Athens* was put in its place. When the difficulties were resolved, *Troilus and Cressida* was inserted without pagination between the histories and the tragedies. There was no attempt to arrange the plays in any logical order within the three sections, except that the histories were arranged chronologically. *Cymbeline* was placed among the tragedies.

In writing of "stolne, and surreptitious copies," Hemminges and Condell were apparently referring to the bad quartos. In almost every instance where a good quarto of a play existed it was used by them as copy for the folio. The only likely exceptions were *Hamlet,* which was probably set from a theatre prompt-book (although some scholars still maintain that the good quarto [Q²] was in fact used), and *Henry IV, Part II,* which may have been set from an edited prompt-copy without regard to the 1600 quarto. In most instances, the folio editors seem to have checked their good quarto copy against either a prompt-book or foul papers. The bad quartos of *Hamlet, Romeo and Juliet, Henry VI, Parts II and III, The Taming of the Shrew, Henry V,* and *The Merry Wives of Windsor* seem to have been entirely ignored by the folio editors. The 1608 quarto of *King Lear* [Q¹] and the 1622 quarto of *Richard III* [Q⁶] were used as copy for the folio, but in each case only after extensive correction by reference to a playhouse manuscript or foul papers.

For their texts of the plays not previously published, either Shakespeare's foul papers or transcripts of them were most likely used for *Henry VI, Part I, The Comedy of Errors, King John, All's*

Well That Ends Well, Antony and Cleopatra, Coriolanus, and *Henry VIII. Timon of Athens* was set from an unfinished draft. Prompt-books or transcripts of them were probably used for the texts of *The Two Gentlemen of Verona, Julius Cæsar, As You Like It, Twelfth Night, Measure for Measure, Macbeth, Cymbeline, The Winter's Tale,* and *The Tempest.* Eighteen of the plays in the folio were divided into acts and scenes; *Hamlet* was divided only through the second act; eleven plays were divided into acts only; and six were printed without divisions of any kind. To what extent these divisions reflect the intent of the author or the conditions of playhouse production, it is never possible to be sure; some of them are obviously in error. Seven of the plays had *dramatis personæ* lists.

Work on the printing of the First Folio appears to have continued over a period from April of 1621 to December of 1623, with interruptions from time to time for various reasons — often so that disputes over the ownership of various plays to be included could be resolved. Two compositors, who are known as "Compositor A" and "Compositor B," were responsible for setting the type. They have been identified by certain distinctive characteristics of spelling and punctuation and by the general appearance of the pages set by each. Of the two, Compositor A was by far the more careful workman, Compositor B having a tendency to carry more words in his head than he could memorize and thus frequently to omit words and lines and to make unauthorized substitutions. This fact is important to the modern editor, for if he can identify the compositor of a page with which he is working, he can estimate better the kinds of errors in the text which he is likely to find. The two compositors appear to have worked alternately rather than simultaneously.

Printing was by one sheet at a time. Each sheet consisted of four pages, two on each side. Gatherings of three sheets were then sewn together to make a quire of twelve pages. When printing was completed, all of the quires were bound together to make the finished book. Each side of a sheet, including two pages, made up one "form." Sufficient copy was allowed a compositor ("cast off") for him to set up two forms ("inner" and "outer") to be printed on a single sheet. When composition was completed, the sheet was printed on the hand press, and when a sufficient number had come from the press the forms were broken and the type redistributed. Type was not plentiful in the shops of seventeenth-century printers, and thus to leave forms set up in type for future use was hardly possible. As the sheets were coming from the press, they were read for errors. For many books of the period this was done by the author or his representative, but Shakespeare was dead when the First Folio was printed, and we do not know who was responsible for proofreading it. Corrections in the forms were made whenever errors were found, but sheets continued to be printed while the proofreader worked, and sheets containing errors were bound along with corrected ones in the finished book. This practice was used in the printing of virtually all books in the sixteenth and seventeenth centuries, and thus different copies of the Shakespeare quartos as well as of the First Folio contain variant readings which must be taken into consideration by the modern editor. Part of his task must be to collate all available specimens of any edition with which he is working and determine which readings represent corrected and which uncorrected states. Although Jaggard's workmen have sometimes been censured for sloppiness, we now know that they were careful and proficient by the standards of their age and that Heminges and Condell were concerned with producing the most accurate possible copy of Shakespeare's plays. The very printing conditions under which they worked, however, made it inevitable that the First Folio should contain a considerable number of errors.

The Later Folios

When we consider that about twelve hundred copies of the First Folio were printed and that these were sold at the very high price of about one pound per volume, it is not surprising that it took nine years for the stock printed by the Jaggards to be exhausted. In fact, the time was rather short for so expensive a book. A Second Folio [F^2] was printed in 1632, this time by Thomas Cotes, who had taken over the business of the Jaggards upon the death of Isaac Jaggard in 1627. It was basically a reprint of F^1, although it was carefully corrected by someone who seems to have relied entirely upon his own taste and judgment. An average of two changes per page were made. While F² carried over a great many of the errors of F¹, and made new errors of its own, it supplied about eight hundred corrections which have generally been accepted by modern editors. Much of the preliminary matter of F¹ was reprinted, including the "Address" by Heminges and Condell and the poems by Jonson, Digges, Holland, and I.M. To them was added a poem of tribute by John Milton and a magnificent long poem, followed by the cryptic initials "I.M.S.," whose authorship has never been determined, although it is clearly the work of one of the master poets of the age.

The Second Folio served as copy for a Third Folio [F³] printed in 1663 and then reprinted in 1664 with the addition of seven plays: *Pericles Prince of Tyre, The London Prodigal, Thomas Lord Cromwell, Sir John Oldcastle, The Puritan, A Yorkshire Tragedy,* and *Locrine.* Of these plays only *Pericles* is now generally accepted as by Shakespeare. *Sir John Oldcastle* was a collaborative effort by Anthony Munday, Michael Drayton, Robert Wilson, and Richard Hathaway, and written as a kind of reply to Shakespeare's portrait of Falstaff in the *Henry IV* plays. *Locrine* is generally attributed to Robert Greene. The authorship of the other plays remains a matter for dispute. The Third Folio, while it made some corrections now accepted, compounded the errors of F¹ and F² and made new errors of its own.

All of the additional plays were included in a Fourth Folio [F⁴] which appeared in 1685. It was printed directly from F³, with a great deal of correction and modernization designed obviously to make the plays easier to read. Its changes, together with the compounded errors it carried over from its three predecessors, resulted in texts of the plays considerably removed from what Shakespeare actually had written. The only plays in which Shakespeare may have had a share which were not printed in any of the four seventeenth-century folios were *Sir Thomas More, The Two Noble Kinsmen,* on which he probably worked with John Fletcher, and the anonymous *Edward III,* for which more and more scholars are coming to believe that Shakespeare was in part responsible. None of the folio editors apparently regarded any of these plays as sufficiently Shakespearian to be included.

The Eighteenth Century Editors

The Fourth Folio, with all of its errors, was used by Nicholas Rowe, an important poet and dramatist, as the basis for his edition of Shakespeare which appeared in six volumes in 1709 and was reprinted in nine volumes in 1714 in order to include the poems. Indeed, the edition appears to have been conceived of by its publisher, Jacob Tonson, as a revision of the Fourth Folio, the rights to which he had purchased. What Rowe produced is the first critical edition of Shakespeare designed for a popular audience. It included many features which have become conventional in editions of our own time. Although Rowe did not consult either the First Folio or any of the quartos, he made a great many emendations so as to eliminate textual cruces, and he modernized spelling, punctuation, and grammar so as to make reading of the plays more easy. Often he substituted modern forms of words for Shakespeare's older forms. He divided the plays into acts and scenes more carefully than they had been divided in any of the folios, paying more attention to this matter as his edition progressed; while there is little division of the comedies among his texts, those of the tragedies are fairly well divided. Whereas the folios gave indications of place locales in only two instances (in *The Tempest* and in *Measure for Measure*) Rowe began the practice of localizing scenes, although he did not do so in all the plays. He carefully marked exits and entrances and provided each play with a *dramatis personæ*, correcting the seven such lists in F⁴ and making up new ones for the other plays.

In all of these matters Rowe was aided by his own considerable experience as a dramatist. His edition of Shakespeare was more readable than any of the folios, but it was even further removed from what Shakespeare had written, having acquired at Rowe's hands features which were a part of eighteenth-century, rather than Elizabethan, taste and theatrical practice.

The attempt to adapt Shakespeare to current tastes was carried much further by Alexander Pope, who used Rowe's edition as a basis for his own, published also by Jacob Tonson, in six volumes in 1725, and reissued in 1728. Unlike Rowe, Pope did consult the First Folio, and he listed twenty-nine quartos which he claimed to have consulted. He did not, however, make proper use of them. He did not seem to conceive of Shakespeare's text as having an independent validity which it was his duty as an editor to uphold. He was more concerned with vindicating Shakespeare's greatness by making him conform to eighteenth-century poetic and dramatic ideals. Pope replaced whole passages with lines of his own composition and rejected other passages as unworthy of Shakespeare in any form. He made many verbal changes so as to regularize Shakespeare's metre and so as to remove anachronisms, substituting "caps" for "hats," for instance, in the Roman plays.

Pope's edition was set up by the printers from pages of Rowe's edition which Pope had annotated. He carried on the process of modernization begun by Rowe, dividing the plays more fully into acts and scenes than Rowe had done, but using the classical system of indicating a new scene whenever a major character entered or left the stage, so that the result was a far greater number of scenes than we find in modern editions. He continued Rowe's practice of localizing the scenes, providing a place designation for every single one of them, a practice which has continued to our own day, but which has little relation to Elizabethan theatrical practice.

Pope's edition was criticized by Lewis Theobald in his *Shakespeare Restored* of 1726. Pope took over some of Theobald's suggestions in his 1728 edition, but never forgave him his adverse comments, and in his 1728 edition of *The Dunciad* he made Theobald the King of Dullness. Theobald's own edition in seven volumes came out in 1733. It was reissued in 1740, 1752, 1772, and 1773. A learned scholar, trained in the use of classical manuscripts, Theobald was the first eighteenth-century editor to go to the First Folio and the quartos for readings which were obviously more correct than those in the Fourth Folio. He also made brilliant emendations, many of which survive in present-day editions, and which he supported by citing evidence of Shakespeare's parallel usage in other places, a method no previous editor had employed, but a standard device of every modern editor. Theobald was also the first Shakespeare scholar to pay any attention to Shakespeare's sources.

Strangely enough, however, Theobald based his edition of Shakespeare on the one he had most severely criticized, that of Alexander

Pope. He took over Pope's stage directions and scene locations, and although he improved upon Pope in many places by the substitution of quarto and First Folio readings, he also took over a great many of Pope's faulty emendations, even when better readings were available in the early quartos which he claimed to have collated. Although he recognized the importance of the quartos, he did not know how to use them. His great error was that he did not set up his text from the quartos or the First Folio, but merely consulted them for alternate readings with which to correct Pope when he seemed to require correction. He was thus, in spite of his knowledge, perpetuating the errors of the Fourth Folio as they had been compounded by Rowe and Pope before him. Theobald was followed by a steady stream of editors, most of whom took advantage of his work, made emendations of their own, and at the same time compounded the errors which had steadily accumulated as each editor took the text of his immediate predecessor as the basis for his own. Among the more important later eighteenth-century editions were those of Robert Walker (1734–1735), Sir Thomas Hanmer (1744), Bishop William Warburton (1747), Samuel Johnson (1765), Edward Capell (1768), George Steevens (1773), and Edmund Malone (1790).

Of these editors Warburton probably did the greatest disservice to Shakespeare scholarship. Not only was his edition based on that of Pope and were his emendations, with a few exceptions, generally infelicitous, but he owned a large collection of Elizabethan quartos and manuscripts which were inadvertently burned by his cook, who used them to line pie pans. Hanmer ignored the work of his contemporaries as well as the early editions and contributed very little to scholarship. Samuel Johnson recognized the fact that the First Folio was superior to any of its successors and that any departures from it in the later folios must be the work of printers, and he was more conservative than his predecessors in his reluctance to emend the text. He made few textual advances in his edition, however, because it was printed from that of Warburton, and the folio was merely used as a check upon Warburton's readings. Thus, he perpetuated the errors of his predecessors more often than he was able to correct them. His edition is notable not for its text but for the Preface, which permanently establishes

Samuel Johnson among the greatest of Shakespeare critics, and for the elaborate commentary with which he accompanied his text, some of which is still as perceptive as anything ever written.

The editor most scorned by his contemporaries was Edward Capell, whose edition went through the press at the same time as the great Dr. Johnson's. It was published without notes because he refused to mar his pages with unsightly footnotes. When his notes were later published separately, his contemporaries professed not to understand them. Capell recognized the importance of the quartos, and he gathered together a collection of some sixty-nine of them. Unlike any editor before him, Capell made an independent transcript of the text of each play, instead of relying like Johnson and the others upon a previous editor and thus carrying on errors. He collated the early editions of each play and worked from what he considered the "best" of them, that one closest to the author's own manuscript. In many cases his decision as to what was the "best" is endorsed by modern editors. He was thus the first editor to base texts of plays upon independent transcripts of the quartos and the First Folio, and he anticipated modern scholars by contending that the quartos were based upon Shakespeare's own manuscripts rather than upon prompt-books corrupted in the playhouse or upon patched-together actors' parts, as Pope and others had supposed. Unfortunately he did not possess copies of all the quartos containing substantive texts, and he was fairly free in his emendations, often relying on little more than his own taste and judgment. He was an eclectic editor whose text is one of the greatest produced in the eighteenth century. Editorial practice of our own time owes much to the principles he established.

In revising Samuel Johnson's edition in 1773, George Steevens drew heavily upon Capell, without acknowledging his indebtedness. Steevens thus improved Johnson's text, and added to Johnson's commentary. Edmund Malone collaborated with Steevens on his second edition of 1778 and his third edition of 1780, and in 1790 Malone issued his own edition in eleven volumes. Steevens, who had now become Malone's rival, followed this with a fourth edition in fifteen volumes in 1793. At the time of his death in 1812 Malone was working on an extensive revision of his edition. It passed into the hands of James Boswell, son of the biographer, and was issued by him in 1821. It was a variorum edition, containing Boswell's as well as Malone's notes and recording textual variants. It is usually called the "Third Variorum" because it was preceded in 1803 by the First Variorum edition of Isaac Reed, which included the notes of Johnson and Steevens as well as his own. This became the Second Variorum when it was reprinted in 1813. No other variorum edition of Shakespeare was attempted until 1871 when H. H. Furness issued the first volume of his New Variorum Edition in Philadelphia.

Of all the eighteenth-century editors, Malone had read most widely in Elizabethan literature. Following the methods of Capell, he collated the quartos and the earlier folios. Thus his judgments were based upon a wide knowledge and range of experience, and many of them today still remain as basic premises in Shakespeare study. Upon his death, his great collection of Elizabethan quartos went to the Bodleian library at Oxford, where it still provides a rich quarry for Elizabethan scholars.

We should remember, lest we criticize the eighteenth-century editors too severely, that their editions were not generally designed for scholars. They sought only to make Shakespeare available to a public which had learned to love his plays in the theatre, and they gave that public exactly what it wanted: intelligible editions, without confusions of language or grammar; and all of the help in the way of stage directions and other aids needed to visualize the plays as they might be performed upon an eighteenth-century stage. Many modern editions of Shakespeare have sprung from not dissimilar motives. Yet at the same time men such as Capell and Malone established working principles which had to be developed before textual scholarship could make further progress.

Early nineteenth-century editors drew heavily upon the work of their predecessors, particularly Capell, Steevens, and Malone. A great many editions at various prices enabled Shakespeare to reach every segment of the reading public. Among the more notable editions of the early nineteenth century were those of William Harness (1825), S. W. Singer (1826 and 1856), John Payne Collier (1841–1844), Charles Knight (1838–1842), Alexander Dyce (1857), Howard Staunton (1868–1870), Nicholaus Delius (1854–1861), H. N. Hudson (1851–1856), J. O. Halliwell-Phillips (1853–1861), and

Richard Grant White (1857–1865). Other editions were published both in England and America, often accompanied by extensive critical commentary. The Rev. Thomas Bowdler's expurgated *Family Shakespeare,* designed for family reading, first appeared in 1804 in four volumes, containing twenty-four plays, and then in ten volumes in 1818. Bowdler used the text of George Steevens, cutting from it anything which might "raise a blush on the cheek of modesty." His work continued to be reprinted regularly throughout the nineteenth century. The effect of this "bowdlerized" edition on the popularization of Shakespeare should not be underestimated.

The Globe Text

Between 1863 and 1866 appeared the most notable edition of Shakespeare in the nineteenth century, and one which continues to influence strongly the editions of our own time. It was called the "Cambridge Shakespeare," was issued in nine volumes, and was under the editorship of W. G. Clark, J. Glover, and W. A. Wright. All of the long progress in the study of texts, from the time of Capell and Malone, found its culmination in their work. They went to the First Folio for their text, and they collated this with the great collection of quartos left to Trinity College, Cambridge, by Edward Capell, to whose methods they were much indebted. They used the quartos primarily, however, to correct what seemed to them to be errors in the First Folio. In 1864 their text was reissued in a one-volume edition — the Globe text. This rapidly became the standard edition of Shakespeare's plays. Its act and scene division was taken over by succeeding editors, and its line numbering was followed not only in most works of criticism, but also in the reference works which began to appear around the turn of the twentieth century. The Globe text is still probably the most widely reprinted of editions of Shakespeare. It forms the basis for most texts printed for use in the schools, including such popular textbook editions as those of G. B. Harrison (1948) and Hardin Craig (1951).

Later nineteenth-century editions include those of W. J. Rolfe (1871–1896), Sir Israel Gollancz (1894–1895), Appleton Morgan (1888), W. J. Craig (1894), and C. H. Herford (1899). In 1906 the first important edition of Shakespeare to be prepared in America under the influence of the Globe text was issued by W. A. Neilson. In 1936 was published the most influential and widely used of all American editions of Shakespeare, that of George Lyman Kittredge. Like the Cambridge editors, Kittredge allowed great authority to the First Folio and was even more conservative in his reluctance to depart from it. Most later American editions have drawn heavily upon the Kittredge edition, some being printed from annotated pages of it.

The variorum edition begun by H. H. Furness in 1871, with the encouragement of the Shakespeare Society of Philadelphia, sought to include, in a single volume devoted to each play, everything that anyone had ever written about Shakespeare, as well as every textual variant, and at the same time to reproduce the sources of the plays. It was probably the most ambitious Shakespeare project ever attempted in England or America. In his later years Furness was joined in the project by his son, H. H. Furness, Jr., who took it over entirely following the death of his father in 1912 and continued with it until his own death in 1930. In 1936 the project was taken over by the Modern Language Association of America and, supervised by a committee of eminent American Shakespeare scholars, it is still in progress. The volumes, however, take so long to complete, and Shakespeare commentary continues to be written at so rapid a pace, that they are often obsolete by the time they are printed.

Bibliographical Method

While the Globe text of Shakespeare and its successors provided better texts of the plays than had ever been known before, the work of restoration had only just begun. The editing, not only of Shakespeare, but of his contemporary dramatists as well, was revolutionized in the first decade of the twentieth century by a group of scholars which included A. W. Pollard, R. B. Mc-Kerrow, W. W. Greg, E. K. Chambers, and J. Dover Wilson. These men, later to be joined by such scholars as F. P. Wilson and Peter Alexander, became the nucleus of the Malone Society, an organization devoted to the scholarly reprinting of Elizabethan plays and theatrical documents. The society was reactivated in

1906, although it had been first organized by McKerrow at Cambridge in 1896. Appropriately enough, it took its name from that of one of the greatest of eighteenth-century Elizabethan scholars. These men applied to the study of Shakespeare's texts a body of knowledge about the details of book production which had begun to be developed by librarians in the late nineteenth century.

The assumptions about the Shakespeare quarto and folio texts which had been held by editors since the eighteenth century were, in effect, rendered obsolete by the publication of A. W. Pollard's *Shakespeare's Folios and Quartos* in 1909. In this work bibliographical techniques were used to reveal the false dates on the title pages of the quartos printed by Jaggard in 1619, and the important distinction was made between good and bad quartos, with all of its implications for understanding the practice of the editors of the First Folio. The honesty of Heminges and Condell was vindicated, for it was seen that in referring to "stolne, and surreptitious copies" they were referring only to the bad quartos, which they had indeed scorned to use, and not to the good quartos which, as had long been known, they had themselves used as copy for the texts they claimed to be "cur'd and perfect of their limbes." As a result of Pollard's work, editors could begin for the first time to understand the nature of Shakespeare's earliest texts.

The editorial principles of the group were to be employed in a great, new, old-spelling edition of Shakespeare to be edited by R. B. McKerrow for the Clarendon Press. McKerrow did not live to begin the project, but his *Prolegomena for the Oxford Shakespeare: A Study of Textual Problems* admirably explains the principles which would have governed his work, and which, with modifications, are now governing the work of Alice Walker, who has taken over the project. The bibliographical method, like that of the Cambridge editors, begins with identification of the substantive text closest to the author's hypothetical final manuscript version of the play. This text is identified by careful collation of all the early texts to determine their relation to one another, and with the principle enunciated by Johnson and Capell that no text of a play can be more accurate than the copy from which it was printed. Bibliographical scholars go beyond the Cambridge editors, however, in attempting to identify the kind of manuscript from which the earliest substantive text was printed, and then, by applying all that is known about manuscript transmission and about the techniques of the Elizabethan printing house, in trying to determine the changes the manuscript underwent in the course of its transmission and final appearance in print.

In their study of dramatic manuscripts, bibliographical scholars were greatly aided by the identification of Shakespeare's handwriting in the manuscript *Booke of Sir Thomas More*. With a knowledge of how Shakespeare made his letters, they could determine how they were likely to be misread in the movement both from manuscript to manuscript and from manuscript to print. Much effort has gone into the study of Elizabethan spelling and punctuation, and Shakespeare's practice has been evaluated in terms of that of his contemporaries. The distinctive characteristics of different kinds of dramatic manuscripts have been extensively explored, for obviously a quarto printed from prompt-copy would have errors quite different from one printed from an author's foul papers.

Even more attention has been paid to the mechanics of book production in the sixteenth and seventeenth centuries. Elizabethan printing presses have been reconstructed. Thanks to the bibliographical scholars, we know how type was set, how forms were set up and locked, how sheets were printed, how proof was read. There have been studies of paper making, watermarks, techniques of cancellation, printers' ornaments. The characteristics of individual printers have been examined, together with a thousand and one other little details of book production which enable us to follow the transmission of a play from the author's pen to the printed page and to identify the accidents of distortion which might accompany it on the way. W. W. Greg in his important British Academy lecture for 1928, *Principles of Emendation in Shakespeare,* stated as a primary requirement for emending the text that the editor be able to explain by bibliographical means just how the error he is replacing came into being.

While earlier editors, like those of the Cambridge Shakespeare, had collated the quartos thoroughly with the folio texts, they had no clear understanding of the origins and natures of these texts and thus could never be entirely sure of just how to use them. It is this knowledge which bibliographical scholarship has tried to supply. Only when we know the complete history of a substantive text and are aware of all of the elements which have helped to make it what it is, can we really know to what extent and in what respects it can be relied upon. The goals which men like McKerrow and Greg set have not been attained, for bibliographical investigation of Shakespeare's texts after half a century is still virtually in its infancy. New knowledge continues to appear, often published in *The Library,* the journal of the British Bibliographical Society, and in the *Studies in Bibliography* of the University of Virginia, under the editorship of Fredson Bowers, probably America's leading exponent of the bibliographical school. We still do not know enough to construct a text entirely by bibliographical means, and we may never see the day when that is possible. As the best bibliographically oriented editors all agree, there is still no absolute substitute for an editor's taste and judgment, although that judgment must rest on whatever scientific knowledge is available.

The most important edition of Shakespeare designed to embody the principles of the bibliographical method was the New Cambridge Shakespeare, begun in 1921 under the joint editorship of Sir Arthur Quiller-Couch and John Dover Wilson, and devoting a single volume to each play. Following the death of Quiller-Couch in 1944, Wilson assumed sole responsibility for the edition, completed in 1969 with the publication of *The Two Noble Kinsmen.* For the later volumes Wilson has enlisted the aid of younger scholars. The Arden Shakespeare under the general editorship of W. J. Craig from 1899 to 1906 and of R. H. Case from 1909 to 1924, although it was primarily notable for its extensive critical commentary, was influenced by the bibliographical method, particularly in its later volumes, depending largely upon the attitudes of the editors responsible for the individual plays. Bibliographical method has played a much larger role in the revision of this edition now in progress. It was begun under the general editorship of Una M. Ellis-Fermor in 1951, and, following her death in 1958, taken over by the present editors, Harold Jenkins and Harold

F. Brooks. Other editions strongly influenced by the new bibliography are those of Peter Alexander (1951) and C. J. Sisson (1954). The new knowledge assembled by the bibliographical scholars has been applied as fully as possible to the revision of the edition of George Lyman Kittredge.

7

Shakespeare Criticism

◇◇◇◇◇ The evaluation of Shakespeare's achievement as a dra-
◇◇◇◇◇ matic artist began during his own lifetime. It has con-
◇◇◇◇◇ tinued at an ever increasing rate up to our own time. The bulk
of Shakespeare commentary is now so vast that it is virtually impossible for any one person to read all of it. Fortunately, it is
unnecessary for anyone to make the attempt, for, like all criticism,
a large part of it is ephemeral and inconsequential, the product of
passing and irrelevant preoccupations. Like most literary criticism,
that of Shakespeare mirrors the interests and prejudices of the
times in which it was written, so that its study not only throws light
on Shakespeare but also provides one kind of insight into the
changing intellectual climate of the last four centuries. All that
can be attempted in these pages is a brief survey of the general
directions which such criticism has tended to take, with particular
emphasis upon the directions of the last half century, for it is in
the terms of twentieth-century criticism that Shakespeare is most
alive and meaningful to us today, although twentieth-century
criticism cannot really be understood without some awareness of
the foundations upon which it is based.

When Francis Meres, in his *Palladis Tamia* of 1598, declared
that Shakespeare was comparable in his artistry to the poets of
classical antiquity, he was praising him in the highest terms of
which Renaissance literary criticism could conceive; at the same
time he was foreshadowing in this earliest of tributes the kind of
comparison to which Shakespeare's work was to be subjected for
the next two centuries. Ben Jonson, in his great poetic tribute
prefixed to the First Folio, named Shakespeare the "soul of the
age" because of all contemporary English poets, he alone belonged

in the company of "thund'ring Æschylus, Euripedes, and Sophocles." At the same time it was Jonson's own sense of classical precision and decorum which led him to censure Shakespeare, as he frequently did. Jonson seems to have had a special disdain for Shakespeare's final romances, a dramatic genre quite removed from the cold intellectual comedy which Jonson himself admired, and particularly prone to sacrifice logical consistency in a way that Jonson could not tolerate. In his conversations with William Drummond of Hawthornden in the winter of 1618–1619 Jonson declared that Shakespeare "wanted art" largely because "Shakespeare in a play brought in a number of men saying they had suffered shipwreck in Bohemia, where there is no sea near by some one hundred miles." He was referring, of course, to *The Winter's Tale.*

In a celebrated passage in *Timber, or Discoveries,* a set of notes which Jonson prepared for his lectures at Gresham College, not published until 1641, we may find an epitome of Jonson's attitude towards Shakespeare:

> I *remember,* the Players have often mentioned it as an honour to *Shakespeare,* that in his writing, (whatsoever he penn'd) hee never blotted out a line. My answer hath beene, would he had blotted a thousand. Which they thought a malevolent speech. I had not told posterity this, but for their ignorance, who choose that circumstance to commend their friend by, wherein he most faulted. And to justifie mine owne candor, (for I lov'd the man, and doe honour his memory (on this side Idolatry) as much as any.) Hee was (indeed) honest, and of an open, and free nature: had an excellent *Phantsie;* brave notions, and gentle expressions: wherein hee flow'd with that facility, that sometime it was necessary he should be stop'd; *Sufflaminandus erat;* as *Augustus* said of *Haterius.* His wit was in his owne power; would the rule of it had beene so too. Many times hee fell into those things, could not escape laughter: As when hee said in the person of *Caesar,* one speaking to him; *Caesar thou dost me wrong.* Hee replyed: *Caesar did never wrong, but with just cause* and such like: which were ridiculous. But hee redeemed his vices, with his vertues. There was ever more in him to be praysed, then to be pardoned.

That the logical lapse in *Julius Cæsar* does not, in fact, appear in the text of that play, first published in 1623, may suggest that if Jonson actually made the comment to Shakespeare while he lived, the play may have been revised in the light of it. The passage reveals Jonson's great admiration for Shakespeare both as man and artist, his appreciation of Shakespeare's great ease in writing and natural facility of wit — attested to also by the editors of the First Folio — but also his regret that that wit was not sufficiently restrained and directed by the rules of art. This attitude, expressed in various ways, tended to dominate Shakespeare criticism until almost the beginning of the nineteenth century.

The Neo-Classical Critics

It has sometimes been argued that Jonson's own reputation was greater than Shakespeare's in the late seventeenth and early eighteenth centuries. However, the cumulative body of evidence — in critical comment, editions, and stage performance — reveals that this was not so. No writer in English was more revered than Shakespeare in the very age when criticism was upholding as the canons of art those classical rules which Shakespeare most flagrantly violated. While English neo-classical critics, familiar with the criticism of Aristotle, Horace, and Boileau, and admiring the classically inspired drama of seventeenth-century France, censured Shakespeare for what we today recognize as the romantic qualities of his artistry, they rarely ceased to affirm his greatness in spite of these apparent shortcomings. The most important critic of his age was John Dryden, whose love and admiration for Shakespeare are everywhere evident in his own writings. In the many prefaces he wrote throughout his career he refers again and again to Shakespeare, never hesitating to censure him, but still affirming his greatness. A characteristic and memorable statement of Dryden's position appears in his *Essay on Dramatick Poesie* (1668):

> He was the man who of all modern, and perhaps ancient poets, had the largest and most comprehensive soul. All the images of nature were still present to him, and he drew them, not laboriously, but luckily; when he describes anything, you may see it, and feel it too. Those who accuse him to have wanted learning, give him the greater commendation; he was naturally learned; he needed not the spectacles of books to read nature; he looked inwards, and found her there.

To Dryden and his contemporaries, the Elizabethan age was a barbaric era, and Shakespeare was censured by them for qualities which they saw as springing from a general lack of refinement and taste: general sloppiness of plot construction, particularly in the history plays; failure to observe the neo-classical conception of the unities of time, place, and action; mingling of tragedy and comedy; improbable and unconvincing characterization; lack of decorum in the speech and behaviour of characters; failure to observe poetic justice, allowing the good to suffer along with the evil; catering, in general to the tastes of a benighted age which delighted in ridiculous stories, such as *The Winter's Tale* and *Measure for Measure,* and which demanded magical and supernatural events rather than looking for rational and logical answers to questions of human behaviour. Shakespeare's language, moreover, was seen as coarse and ungrammatical, having not yet experienced the purification which neo-classical artists were to give it. While Dryden objected to all of these things, he nevertheless regarded Shakespeare as a natural genius, able to transcend the limitations of his own age and to achieve greatness in spite of faults which could not be countenanced in other writers. With only "nature" to guide him, Shakespeare could create characters of amazing fidelity to life. Dryden found in Shakespeare's plays an honest strength which he could not find in the work of Restoration dramatists, including, as he admitted, even his own.

Dryden's general attitude of almost idolatrous appreciation combined with minute criticism was carried on in the work of such followers as Charles Gildon in his *Miscellaneous Letters and Essays on Several Subjects* (1694) and John Dennis in his *Impartial Critic* of 1693 and his *On the Genius and Writings of Shakespeare* of 1712. Of Shakespeare, Dennis wrote:

His imaginations were often as just as they were bold and strong. He had a natural discretion which never could have been taught him, and his judgment was strong and penetrating. He seems to have wanted nothing but time and leisure to have found out those rules of which he appears ignorant. His expression is in many places good and pure after a hundred years; simple tho' elevated, graceful tho' bold, and easy tho' strong. He seems to have been the original of our English tragical harmony.

In this Dennis is echoing the judgment of Dryden. Both he and Gildon wrote their defences of Shakespeare in answer to Thomas

Rymer, a more consistent neo-classical critic than Dryden or his followers, whom later ages — perhaps unjustly — have subjected to ridicule for his uncompromising derogation of Shakespeare's achievement.

Thomas Rymer was an extremely learned antiquarian and an unsuccessful writer of tragedy. So dominated was he by his love of the ancients that he could see nothing in Elizabethan literature that was not debased and barbaric, a proposition which he argued in *The Tragedies of the Last Age consider'd and Examin'ed by the Practice of the Ancients, and by the Common sense of all Ages,* published in 1678. He had little to say about Shakespeare here, although he derogated him cursorily in his Preface. His extensive attack upon Shakespeare appeared in his *Short View of Tragedy* of 1693, in which he singled out *Othello* for special opprobrium for the improbability of its characterization and for a dwelling upon events beneath the dignity of tragedy. It was here that he dismissed this play as "plainly none other than a Bloody Farce without salt or savour" whose only "moral" might be "a warning to all good Wives, that they look well to their Linnen." He subjected *Julius Cæsar* also to special ridicule for its falsity to and general debasement of history. In his emphasis upon the need for tragedy to present a consistent moral and to observe poetic justice, and in his censure of Shakespeare for his violation of decorum in characterization, Rymer merely reflected the common neo-classical notions of his age, much as they were reflected in Dryden. Unlike Dryden, however, he was able to see in Shakespeare nothing more than an obvious and blatant failure to achieve what neo-classical critics considered the obvious ends of literary artistry. His position is actually more logically consistent than Dryden's, and he had some followers, such as Edward Taylor, who in his *Cursory Remarks on Tragedy* (1774) could find equally little of value in Shakespeare. Dryden's position, however, was by far the more influential one, and to it all the great critics of the eighteenth century were indebted. The idea of Shakespeare as the higher kind of genius who could achieve greatness without the discipline of the rules of art upon which the lesser kind of genius must depend was notably expressed by Joseph Addison, who in *The Spectator* (Number 160), included Shakespeare among "the prodigies of mankind" who "by the mere strength of natural parts, and without any assistance of art or learning, have produced works that were the delight of their own times and the wonder of posterity."

While this praise of Shakespeare as a natural genius who stood above the rules was carried on in England by Nicholas Rowe, Lewis Theobald, and Alexander Pope, whose Preface to his edition of 1725 is one of the monuments of eighteenth-century Shakespeare criticism, Shakespeare was being introduced to French readers by Voltaire. Although Voltaire had an understanding of Shakespeare's greatness which reflected the influence of Dryden — and for which he is not usually given credit by English readers — he did criticize Shakespeare severely for his violation of the classical rules, and it was to his fault-finding that eighteenth-century Englishmen most vehemently objected, virtually ignoring all that he had to say in Shakespeare's praise. Much of the Shakespeare criticism of the later half of the eighteenth century consists of defence of Shakespeare against the strictures of Voltaire. Among these answers must be included Lady Elizabeth Montague's *Essays on the Writings and Genius of Shakespeare*, published in 1769, and, most notably, the great Preface which Samuel Johnson wrote to accompany his edition of 1765.

Samuel Johnson

Johnson's Preface, together with the lucid notes with which he accompanied his edition, is among the major achievements of Shakespeare commentary. It is a summary and evaluation of the principal issues in Shakespeare criticism with which his eighteenth-century contemporaries had been concerned, and at the same time is amazingly modern in its foreshadowing of attitudes which were to become commonplace in our own century. While in some respects Johnson's criticism is an affirmation of distinctively neo-classical positions and thus very much a reflection of his own age, it is more generally a refutation of the strictures of more rigidly narrow commentators. Behind it lies the conviction, carried on from Dryden, that no matter what his faults Shakespeare is still the greatest of English writers, and that many of the faults attributed to him, when examined closely, are found to be no faults at all. Johnson was criticized by some nineteenth-century romantic idolators of Shakespeare for his daring to criticize Shakespeare, but Johnson was not a blind idolator of any poet, and the faults he found in Shakespeare are never viewed by him as more than slight human imperfections which could not lessen the sense of awe and admiration with which the greatest of poets must be viewed. Johnson's criticism is as honest as it is dominated by common sense.

Johnson found evidence for Shakespeare's greatness in the fact that his plays had withstood the test of time, providing an accurate mirror of human life as meaningful to eighteenth-century men as it had been to Elizabethans. He praised Shakespeare for his ability to portray basic human emotion and to create characters recognizable as common types:

> Shakespeare is above all writers, at least above all modern writers, the poet of nature: the poet that holds up to his readers a faithful mirror of manners and life. His characters are not modified by the customs of particular places, unpractised by the rest of the world; by the peculiarities of studies or professions, which can operate but upon small numbers; or by the accidents of transient fashions or temporary opinions: they are the genuine progeny of common humanity, such as the world will always supply, and observation will always find. His persons act and speak by the influence of those general passions and principles by which all minds are agitated, and the whole system of life is continued in motion. In the writings of other poets a character is too often an individual; in those of Shakespeare it is commonly a species.

He praised Shakespeare rather than censured him for his neglect of the traditional rules, for his ability to violate decorum when a play required that he do so. He defended Shakespeare's mixture of comedy and tragedy in terms of the larger dramatic effect, and he found no particular virtue in observation of the unities. Those very things to which Voltaire most objected, he found to be among the surest evidences of Shakespeare's artistic greatness.

But there were elements in Shakespeare which Johnson did not like: the loose construction of his plots, failure to distinguish time and place of action, improper endings, jokes which were unnecessarily coarse, effusiveness of passion in the tragedies, obscurity of much of the poetry, and too great a tendency to employ elaborate conceits and to indulge in puns. Johnson found puns a form of humour which was especially distasteful, failing to recognize the power of word play to enhance the intellectual complexity of poetic metaphor. But Johnson's most important criticism was a development of the general eighteenth-century tendency to censure Shakespeare for his failure to observe poetic justice. Johnson found Shakespeare sometimes inadequately moral in his point of view, as in his ending of *King Lear*. An important function of any artist, for Samuel Johnson, was to make clear his moral purpose, to instruct while he delighted. Thus he wrote of Shakespeare:

> His first defect is that to which may be imputed most of the evil in books or in men. He sacrifices virtue to convenience, and is so much more careful to please than to instruct, that he seems to write without any moral purpose. From his writings indeed a system of social duty may be selected, for he that thinks reasonably must think morally, but his precepts and axioms drop casually from him; he makes no just distribution of good or evil, nor is always careful to shew in the virtuous a disapprobation of the wicked; he carries his persons indifferently through right and wrong, and at the close dismisses them without further care, and leaves their examples to operate by chance. This fault, the barbarity of his age cannot extenuate, for it is always a writer's duty to make the world better, and justice is a virtue independent of time or place.

In this conception of the moral purpose of art Johnson may have been influenced by Henry Home, Lord Kames, whose *Elements of Criticism*, published in 1762, subjected Shakespeare to the same kind of censure. For Kames the misfortunes which befall a character could not be depicted as mere chance; they must spring from obvious defects in his own personality, for tragedy must be shown as the product of moral delinquency.

Character Criticism

Lord Kames may have been in part responsible for the preoccupation with vice and virtue through close analysis of Shakespeare's dramatic characters (often divorced from their dramatic contexts) which comes to share largely in Shakespeare criticism of the later eighteenth century. But character analysis had begun to be a concern of Shakespeare critics even before Kames wrote. Falstaff appears to have been the first to be singled out for special attention, for Corbyn Morris had appended a detailed study of him to his *Essay towards Fixing the True Standards of Wit, Humor, Raillery, Satire, and Ridicule,* published in 1744. Johnson included a memorable description of Falstaff as one whose "licentiousness is not so offensive but that it may be borne for his mirth" among his notes to the plays, and in 1777 Falstaff became the subject of one of the most important and influential of all character studies, Maurice Morgann's *Essay on the Dramatic Character of Sir John Falstaff.* By a study of all aspects of Falstaff's personality, Morgann tried to vindicate him from the charge of cowardice. To do so Morgann had to ignore the problem of the function of Falstaff within the total scheme of the *Henry IV* plays, but it was not the whole play which interested him. Nor was his concern really with Falstaff; he used him merely to show that Shakespeare's plays could be read for the insight they offered into "the principles of human nature itself." With Morgann we have, in effect, the beginning of a kind of criticism whose end is not the understanding of Shakespeare, but the understanding of philosophical and psychological issues into which Shakespeare was believed to provide a more profound insight than could be furnished by lesser men. It was this philosophical approach to Shakespeare which was to dominate the criticism of the nineteenth century and which is still important today.

Another influential character critic was Thomas Whately, whose *Remarks on Some of the Characters of Shakespeare* was written around 1770 and published posthumously in 1785. Whately treated Shakespeare's characters as though they were actual human beings, speculating about what they would have done in situations other than in the plays in which they appear. He treated only Macbeth and Richard III in detail, seeing each as a completely individual creation placed in the same dramatic situation as the other, but reacting to it according to his own nature. Whately intended to treat other characters in the same manner, but his work was cut off by his death. Even more influential was the work of William Richardson, professor of humanities at the University of Glasgow, a philosopher and moralist for whom the primary purpose of literature was moral instruction:

> Moralists of all ages have recommended poetry as an art no less instructive than amusing; tending at once to improve the heart and

entertain the fancy. The genuine and original Poet, peculiarly favoured by nature, and intimately acquainted with the constitution of the human mind, not by a long train of metaphysical deductions, but, as it were, by immediate intuition, displays the workings of every affection, detects the origin of every passion, traces its progress, and delineates its character. Thus, he teaches us to know ourselves, inspires us with magnanimous sentiments, animates our love of virtue, and confirms our hatred of vice. Moved by his striking pictures of the instability of human enjoyments, we moderate the vehemence of our desires, fortify our minds, and are enabled to sustain adversity.

This classic statement appears at the beginning of his *Essay on Some of Shakespeare's Dramatic Characters,* published in 1784, in which he probed the characters of Richard III, Lear, and Timon and found the source of destruction in the sinfulness of each. He had already applied this technique to Macbeth, Hamlet, Jaques, and Imogen in his *Philosophical Analysis and Illustration of Some of Shakespeare's Remarkable Characters* (1774), drawing from his analysis of each character an appropriate moral lesson. He also wrote essays on John Falstaff and on Shakespeare's female characters. All of his writings on Shakespeare were published in a single volume in 1787. With Richardson we have come to a point in the evolution of Shakespeare criticism where the plays are only important as illustrations of philosophical principles, the critics' real concern, and character is regarded as the most significant element of drama for the illustration of these principles.

A somewhat unusual character critic for his age was William Jackson, whose *Thirty Letters on Various Subjects* was published in 1782 and reprinted in 1784 and 1795. Jackson, who was almost idolatrous in his praise of Shakespeare, saw his characters not as realistic portraits from life who could afford a universally valid insight into human behaviour, but rather as characters heightened and distorted from reality for the sake of dramatic effectiveness. Had Shakespeare's characters been natural, he writes:

> they would not be sufficiently marked for stage effect. A strong proof of this is in the portrait of Lear, who is "fourscore and upward." Were the character natural, Lear would be best acted by an old man: but every one must instantly perceive that the strength as well as the abilities of the vigour of life are required for its due performance. So

that we commend plays for being natural, we mean dramatically so
— but there is a great difference between heightening a situation or
character which may exist, or have its foundation in nature, and that
want of nature and foundation we perceive in most of the old writers.

Here then we have a view of Shakespeare as the artist who dramatically heightens nature, rather than merely depicts it as in a mirror.
Jackson's view, like Richardson's, was to have a profound effect
upon later criticism.

Samuel Taylor Coleridge

The early nineteenth century is the most enthusiastic of all
eras in its response to Shakespeare. Its criticism is marked by a
bardolatry which leaves little room for fault finding, and which
exalts the dramatist as the supreme philosopher and moral teacher.
In this critics were following the direction of pre-romantic character criticism, but were influenced also by the new idealistic criticism
of Germany, which rebelled against any notion of classical authority
in art and held that fidelity to nature was the only standard against
which a play could be judged. They regarded Shakespeare as the
artist in whom the laws of nature were most profoundly and perfectly reflected. Writers such as Lessing, Herder, Goethe, and
Schlegel went beyond the simple moralizing of Whately and Richardson and examined Shakespeare's characters for a profound insight
into the eternal mysteries of human life. The influence of such
philosophical critics was carried into England largely by Samuel
Taylor Coleridge whose criticism of Shakespeare, fragmentary and
ill-preserved as it is, dominates that of his own times and continues
to influence us strongly today.

Coleridge published only two brief essays on Shakespeare during
his own lifetime. The great bulk of his commentary was delivered
as lectures to public audiences in Bristol and London between
1808 and 1819. Fragments of his own notes and reports of what he
said from the platform have come down to us from various sources,
but they were not put into really usable form until 1930, when
T. M. Raysor published his *Coleridge's Shakespearean Criticism*.
Coleridge's most important contribution to Shakespeare criticism is
not as an analyst of dramatic character, although commentators
have stressed this aspect of his work sometimes unduly, and perhaps

understandably, because in this area he has had few equals. His great comment on Iago's soliloquy as "the motive-hunting of motiveless malignity" is justly celebrated, as is his view of Hamlet, which probably more than any view has established that character in the popular consciousness:

> we see a great, an almost enormous, intellectual activity, and a proportionate aversion to real action consequent upon it, with all its symptoms and accompanying qualities. This character Shakespeare places in circumstances, under which it is obliged to act on the spur of the moment. — Hamlet is brave and careless of death; but he vacillates from sensibility, and procrastinates from thought, and loses the power of action in the energy of resolve.

This vision of Hamlet as a character incapable of attaining the proper balance between the active and the contemplative faculties owes much to the Hegelian view of tragedy by which Coleridge was profoundly influenced. In general Coleridge's character criticism is philosophical rather than psychological; he is not primarily interested in the personality disorders which intrigued later critics, but rather in the universal principles of philosophy which he saw character as capable of illustrating. Shakespeare's dramatic characters revealed to him a larger vision of human potentiality than could be found in any other place.

Coleridge did not — as has sometimes been charged — divorce Shakespeare's characters from their dramatic contexts. For him to have done so would have been to ignore his own principle of the organic unity of the work of art, a principle whose application to Shakespeare, in fact, may be Coleridge's most important contribution. The most basic function of art, as he explained in the *Biographia Literaria* is one of synthesis, the creation of balance and unity out of seemingly discordant elements, this new unity being its own justification, responsible to no criteria outside of itself. To the organic unity of the Shakespeare play, all of its parts, character included, must be subordinate. Once the play is viewed in this manner as a self-contained unity to which all external canons of artistic propriety are irrelevant, unless evoked by the work itself, the shortcomings for which eighteenth-century critics had censured Shakespeare cease to have any bearing upon his work.

Coleridge thus could defend such supposed Shakespearian faults as his mixture of tragedy and comedy in terms of the larger unity which is the play. The truth of the imagination was the only truth relevant to dramatic poetry, as he explained in a memorable passage on *The Tempest,* which he recognized as a romantic play and characterized as

> a drama, the interests of which are independent of all historical facts and associations, and arise from their fitness to that faculty of our nature, the imagination I mean, which owes no allegiance to time and place, a species of drama, therefore, in which errors in chronology and geography, no mortal sins in any species, are venial, or count for nothing.

In this manner he disposed of the ancient objections to Shakespeare's anachronisms, his looseness of plotting, and incredibility of action, particularly in the comedies. In arguing that the work of art was something separate from reality and never to be simply identified with it, Coleridge countered that entire school of eighteenth-century criticism which praised Shakespeare as the mirror of actual life. Drama for Coleridge was a kind of illusion, and dramatic illusion need be faithful only to the imagination of its creator; its power to move an audience rested only in the ability of the artist: "if only the poet have such power of exciting our internal emotions as to make us present to the scene in imagination chiefly, he requires the right and privilege of using time and space as they exist in the imagination, obedient only to the laws which the imagination acts by." The appreciation of drama calls, on the part of the audience, for "that willing suspension of disbelief for the moment which constitutes poetic faith."

In Coleridge's criticism those elements for which Shakespeare had been condemned in the age of Pope were cast aside, and those for which he had been praised were regarded, for the most part, as equally irrelevant. He judged Shakespeare as a creative artist in terms he defined as applicable to all art, and at the same time, although he did no historical research himself, he recognized the importance of an understanding of Shakespeare's own age and suggested what were to be the methods of modern historical criticism. Few commentators who have written since the time of Coleridge have failed to show his influence in some way.

Philosophical Criticism

William Hazlitt, Charles Lamb, and Thomas De Quincey all celebrated the perfection of Shakespeare's genius and the unity of whatever he created. They were sometimes almost religious in their conception of Shakespeare as a transcendant spirit whose greatness lesser men must acknowledge while they strive with all their beings to comprehend it. De Quincey in his essay, *On the Knocking at the Gate in Macbeth*, published in 1823, wrote of the plays as works "which are to be studied with entire submission of our own faculties, and in the perfect faith that in them there can be no too much or too little, nothing useless or inert — but that, the farther we press in our discoveries, the more we shall see proofs of design, and self-supporting arrangement where the careless eye had seen nothing but accident."

Coleridge's interest in Shakespeare as a philosophical poet was carried on in Germany, where in the middle nineteenth century we begin to find comprehensive attempts to evaluate Shakespeare's total growth and development as a philosophic artist, an enterprise aided by developments in scholarship which had made considerable progress in fixing the chronology of the plays. Among the most important of these attempts was Hermann Ulrici's *Über Shakespeares Dramatische Kunst*, published in 1839 and translated into English as *Shakespeare's Dramatic Art* in 1846. Ulrici imitated Coleridge in his concentration on the unity of design and the philosophical implications of character. A very similar work was that of Georg Gottfried Gervinus, whose *Shakespeare*, published in four volumes between 1849 and 1852, was translated into English as *Shakespeare Commentaries* in 1863. Gervinus's methods are very close to those of Ulrici, and like his, owe much to Coleridge, but Gervinus is also the first of the critics to divide Shakespeare's plays into distinct periods. He made this division on the basis of verse tests, a method of study which was widely imitated, although it today has fallen into disrepute. By arranging Shakespeare's plays in chronological order, such critics attempted to study the growth of his soul and to determine his evolving attitudes towards every concern of human life. Their conclusions on these matters inevitably tended to reflect their own personal predilections. Inevitably also, biographical considerations began to intrude, for Shakespeare the man was seen as inseparable from Shakespeare the artist and philosopher. His life was reconstructed from the plays, and this hypothetical biography was used in turn to illuminate the plays.

Victorian England and America are both marked by comprehensive interpretations of Shakespeare's "life and art." Probably the most influential to be published in America was Henry Norman Hudson's *Lectures on Shakespeare* of 1848 and his later *Shakespeare, His Life, Art and Character* of 1872. Among the most curious was that of the neo-Hegelian Denton J. Snider, whose *System of Shakespeare's Dramas* was published in St. Louis, Missouri, in 1877 and whose *The Shakespearean Drama* followed in 1887. For Snider, Shakespeare's plays must be read in the light of Hegelian philosophy, which they in turn served to illuminate. Among the many volumes published in England, Walter Bagehot's *Shakespeare the Man* (1853) and A. C. Swinburne's *A Study of Shakespeare* (1880) are worthy of notice, Bagehot's for its biographical method and Swinburne's as the first critical study of Shakespeare by a poet of genius since Coleridge. The culminating work of Victorian criticism, however, was Edward Dowden's *Shakespeare: A Critical Study of His Mind and Art*. It was first published in 1875, destined to go through innumerable printings, and comprised the first comprehensive critical biography of Shakespeare — carrying on the tradition inaugurated by Coleridge, but embodying also specific attitudes of his Victorian contemporaries.

The Great Victorians

Dowden is only one of a group of scholars whose work may be said to dominate Shakespeare criticism in the closing years of the nineteenth century and early years of the twentieth and who, by the specific directions which they pursued, have to a large extent shaped the course of what has been written about Shakespeare since their own time. Generally our twentieth-century Shakespeare critics have seen themselves — and have been seen by others — as writing in reaction to the great Victorian critics; such reaction, of course, was inevitable. There has, however, been a continuing influence, which may be more important than any reaction. Of the Victorian and Edwardian writers who have most significantly shaped the direction of modern Shakespeare criticism, the most important, in addition to Dowden, have been A. C. Bradley, whose *Shakespearean Tragedy* appeared in 1904; Richard Moulton, whose *Shakespeare as a Dramatic Artist* appeared in 1885, to be followed by *Shakespeare as a Dramatic Thinker* in 1907; Walter Raleigh who, after a long career at Oxford contributed his slim volume, *Shakespeare,* to the English Men of Letters series in 1907; and Robert Bridges, whose influential essay, "The Influence of the Audience on Shakespeare's Drama," was first published in the Shakespeare Head edition of the plays in 1907 and reprinted in Bridges's *Collected Essays* of 1927.

Dowden's work may represent the highest achievement of the philosophical-biographical approach to Shakespeare. He went beyond Gervinus in dividing the plays into four distinct periods, each of which reflected a time of joy or sorrow in Shakespeare's life. The plays themselves provided biography, and this biography, in turn, was used to illuminate the plays. Dowden thus could explain the disparity between such plays as *As You Like It* and *Measure for Measure* as a reflection of times when Shakespeare was joyfully "on the heights" or despondently "in the depths." Dowden's biographical assumptions were attacked by C. J. Sisson in a British Academy lecture for 1934 called "The Mythical Sorrows of Shakespeare," and today biographical criticism is no longer very highly esteemed. The belief that Shakespeare's life may be seen through his plays nevertheless survives. We may find it in so recent a book as Edward G. McCurdy's *The Personality of Shakespeare* (1953), where the author attempts by means of a body of Freudian theory unknown in Dowden's time to delineate Shakespeare's personality by examining the fantasies in his plays.

Such "psychological" criticism is of relatively slight importance — although a considerable bibliography could be compiled of the articles on Shakespeare's complexes and compulsions which appear in the psychoanalytic journals — but Dowden's assumptions have survived in our own time in a much more important form. Caroline F. E. Spurgeon's analysis of imagery, which may have had more influence than any other critical method of the last half century, began with Dowden's assumption that Shakespeare the man could be discovered in his plays. She was no more successful in this discovery than Dowden had been, but her method was a new one with wide implications, and a whole school of contemporary critics, with little interest in Shakespeare's personality, has used imagery as an index to Shakespeare's themes and as the key to the poetic texture of his plays. Dowden's influence has led, through a strange metamorphosis, from a futile study of Shakespeare the man to a very fruitful study of Shakespeare the poet.

Bradley and Moulton

Bradley, following the path of Coleridge, saw Shakespeare as a philosophical artist. In his lectures on the great tragedies, he attempted to define the moral world of Shakespeare. He followed Hegel in his view of the tragic hero as one incapable of attaining a proper balance between the extremes of his personality, displaying "a fatal tendency to identify the whole being with one interest, object, passion, or habit of mind." Tragedy he saw as a probing of the mystery of human life in a way that was fundamentally moral. The world of Shakespeare was one in which good and evil are equally destroyed by an indefinable, mysterious power, but in which, while there is a terrible sense of waste, there is also one of restitution and reconciliation at the end, so that the audience never leaves the theatre with a sense of despair. For Bradley, evil is always an aberration in nature, never its natural condition.

Like Dowden, Bradley approached Shakespeare's plays through intensive analysis of character, and although at times he seemed to be taking characters out of their dramatic contexts and asking questions about them whose answers Shakespeare did not supply, he never really lost sight of the fact that he was dealing with plays and not with life. Bradley carried character analysis probably as far as it could be carried. L. C. Knights's important 1933 essay, "How Many Children had Lady Macbeth?" published in *Explorations* (1946), was effective in demonstrating some of the fallacies inherent in his method. Works of character criticism nevertheless continue to appear. One of the most interesting has been J. I. M. Stewart's *Character and Motive in Shakespeare* (1949), which uses modern psychology (largely Freudian) and anthropology to argue a naturalistic fidelity to life in Shakespeare's characters more subtle than even Bradley had imagined.

The greatest influence of Bradley may have been in his attempt to define a moral order in Shakespeare's plays. It has been argued that he did not succeed in doing so, for a world in which a Romeo or Hamlet must suffer through lack of balance as fully as a Macbeth or Othello is a world in which it is difficult to find the kind of reconciliation and the sense of the naturalness of good which Bradley felt to be essential ingredients of tragedy. Many succeeding critics have accepted Bradley's view of tragedy's necessary philosophical dimension and inherent morality, and they have tried to find in Shakespeare a moral order more meaningful than that which Bradley could find. There are few who have not shown his influence.

R. G. Moulton, who was convinced that Shakespeare was a supreme moral teacher, attempted to approach the dramatist's moral substance more systematically than it had ever been approached before. He tried to apply what he called an inductive method to Shakespeare criticism, that is to approach each play without consideration of the other plays, but with a sympathetic appreciation which might enable him to comprehend each play fully and, independently of external fixed standards, judge it as a unique totality. He thus applied Coleridge's principle of the self-sufficiency and organic unity of the work of art, and he avoided the biographical assumptions of his contemporaries. He differed from Coleridge and Bradley in placing his major emphasis upon plot. Although he made use of character analysis, it was primarily in the elements of story that he found Shakespeare's moral themes implicit.

Moulton thus came close to a modern mythographic view of Shakespeare, in which story, as the embodiment of idea, assumes a large symbolic function. Moulton, moreover, tried to systematize the moral philosophy of Shakespeare in a way that neither Coleridge nor Bradley would ever attempt. He found through plot analysis certain root ideas to which Shakespeare again and again returns: the relation of heroism and morality, of sin and retribution, of wrong and restoration, the antithesis between man's relation to himself and his relation to society. Moulton's readings of the plays in terms of these central ideas are often rigid, but this was perhaps an inevitable aspect of his method — and an objection which has been levelled often at more recent critics who have employed similar techniques.

Historical Criticism

Although Walter Raleigh and Robert Bridges wrote very little about Shakespeare, they are important in that they laid the basis for the kind of historical criticism which has dominated Shakespeare study in our own time. Raleigh carried on some of the attitudes of Dowden, believing that the plays might be an index to the mind and personality of their author. Yet he is the only important critic of his time who stressed that Shakespeare's plays are a product of the theatre and thus governed by the requirements and physical conditions of the Elizabethan stage. Raleigh, moreover, stands apart from Coleridge, Bradley, and Moulton in denying a philosophical dimension to Shakespeare's art. He saw the artistry of the plays in their power to make an immediate emotional impression upon an audience in a theatre. He criticized the great concern with character analysis among his contemporary critics, holding that such concentration obscured other elements in a play, which must be viewed as a total stage artifact. He censured those critics who would discuss character details outside of a play's context, and he argued for the influence upon Shakespeare of the tastes of his audience, holding that Shakespeare's greatness lay in his ability to cater to these tastes and at the same time triumph over the restraints and limitations they imposed upon him. Raleigh's anti-romantic approach to Shakespeare was carried further by George Lyman Kittredge in his notes to sixteen of the plays and in his *Shakespeare: An Address* (1916) in which he expounded his credo that the end of Shakespeare criticism was to discover what Shakespeare meant to his own audience in his own time. All other kinds of interpretation, Kittredge held, were subjective and unverifiable impressions, with no lasting validity. This is the essential principle of historical criticism. Kittredge especially attacked the attempt to derive Shakespeare's biography from his plays.

Robert Bridges also saw Shakespeare's plays as governed by the conditions under which they were produced, but for this sensitive

Victorian poet, Shakespeare was a great potential genius who had prostituted his talent by catering to the crude, low tastes of a degenerate audience — interested only in sex, violence, and coarse buffoonery. That Bridges' conception of Shakespeare's audience was based upon lamentable misinformation has been demonstrated long since, but his greatest shortcoming was that his historicism was misapplied, for he had no real conception of what any dramatist's relation to his audience must be in any age.

His views, however, attracted wide attention. They may have been particularly influential upon E. E. Stoll, a student of Kittredge's, and perhaps the strongest exponent of historical criticism in our century. To Bridges, Stoll probably owed the notion that the principal effect of Shakespeare's tragedies lay in their power to shock by what he called "steep tragic contrast," revealing a hero performing an act of which the author has conditioned the audience to believe him incapable, such as Macbeth's murder of Duncan or Othello's of Desdemona. The audience, Bridges had argued, demanded such shock, in defiance of logic, credibility, and morality, and Shakespeare sacrificed his art in order to give it to them. For Stoll, however, it was in Shakespeare's very ability to hold an audience by such means that his true greatness as an artist lay.

Probably the most important of the many books in which Stoll argued his principles are his *Shakespeare Studies* (1927) and his *Art and Artifice in Shakespeare* (1933). He went back to Longinus in his belief that the dramatist's mission is to "enthral" by means of the imagination and to Aristotle in his belief in the primacy of plot. He broke with the nineteenth-century followers of Coleridge in denying both a philosophical dimension and realistic characterization in Shakespeare (Bradley), a moral content in the plays (Moulton), and the possibility that the plays might have any relation at all to the life of their author (Dowden). Stoll stressed the conventional nature of drama, relating Shakespeare to the physical factors of the Elizabethan stage. He argued that drama was essentially artificial and that it needed to distort physical reality in order to exist and therefore could never hold a faithful mirror up to nature. He explained Hamlet's failure to kill Claudius before the end of the play as merely the result of a need to extend the play for five acts, and Othello's belief in Iago on the basis of a stage convention which required that the calumniator always be credited. Stoll has had many followers who have begun with his basic premises and have extended his influence in various directions.

Stoll's work gave impetus to an important critical movement which would reassert the essence of the plays as drama and which would place Shakespeare specifically in the theatrical milieu of his own London. This was a movement already underway when he began to write, and evident in the work of Walter Raleigh. It was further developed in books such as George Pierce Baker's *The Development of Shakespeare as a Dramatist* (1907) and Brander Matthews' *Shakespeare as a Playwright* (1913), both of which treated Shakespeare as a writer for the stage, generally ignoring, like Stoll, that he was a poet as well. Probably the greatest theatre-oriented critic of our time has been Harley Granville-Barker, who approached the plays in his *Prefaces to Shakespeare* (1927–1937) with his own rich theatre experience to draw upon. Stoll may have exerted a great influence upon S. L. Bethell's *Shakespeare and the Popular Dramatic Tradition* (1944), which has tried to see Shakespeare in terms of the requirements of popular drama, drawing often upon our modern cinema for analogies. Bethell, however, has gone far beyond Stoll in emphasizing the moral and religious elements of popular drama and the symbolism which Shakespeare's art carried on from the Middle Ages. He has countered the naturalistic psychological critics in his contention that Shakespeare's chief interest lay in mankind rather than in the peculiarities of individual men.

Recent years have seen a great many books which begin by placing Shakespeare firmly in the Elizabethan theatre. Notable among them are Peter Alexander's *Hamlet, Father and Son* (1955), Bertrand Evans' *Shakespeare's Comedies* (1960), and William Rosen's *Shakespeare and the Craft of Tragedy* (1960). There is a wide difference, however, between a book such as G. E. Bentley's *Shakespeare and His Theatre* (1964) and one such as Nevill Coghill's *Shakespeare's Professional Skills* (1964). The first severely limits Shakespeare's genius by refusing to see in his work anything which cannot be explained by the requirements of popular entertainment. The second draws upon a rich knowledge of the Elizabethan theatre to illuminate subtleties in Shakespeare's plays which might not otherwise be perceived — without denying that Shakespeare was a poet as well as a dramatist and that the poet is capable of expressing meanings beyond the capabilities of any actor. Similarly excellent is John Russell Brown's *Shakespeare's Plays in Performance* (1967), which examines how actual performance of the plays may reveal layers of meaning not readily to be gleaned from the printed text.

Closely allied to Stoll's was the work of Levin Schücking, whose books include *Character Problems in Shakespeare's Plays* (1922) and *The Meaning of Hamlet* (1937). He too was concerned with Elizabethan stage conditions, and to him we owe the concept of "episodic intensification," the notion that Shakespeare developed individual scenes for immediate effect, often sacrificing the structure, coherence, and logic of his total play in order to do so. Schücking was interested also in primitive survivals in Shakespeare, and he explained *Hamlet* in terms of the brutal revenge story at its source. He may be Stoll's most important follower, although he does not reveal much further development of Stoll's premises, and he is even more narrow than Stoll in their application.

The History of Ideas

The historical method had far-reaching results when it was extended beyond considerations of the stage to an examination of the entire social, political, and intellectual milieu in which Shakespeare worked. This movement was carried on in the middle years of the twentieth century by an important group of writers which included Hardin Craig, Lily B. Campbell, Walter Clyde Curry, W. W. Lawrence, Theodore Spencer, Willard Farnham, and E. M. W. Tillyard. All of these critics share the premise of Kittredge and Stoll that Shakespeare must be seen as a product of his own age, and they tend to see the English Renaissance as tied more closely to the Middle Ages than earlier writers had recognized. Unlike Stoll, these critics have been concerned with Shakespeare's intellectual content, and they have tried to study Shakespeare's ideas in the light of what they found to be the general beliefs of Elizabethans.

Probably the most comprehensive argument for the continuity of Shakespeare's theatre with its medieval forerunners has been Willard Farnham's *The Medieval Heritage of Elizabethan Tragedy*

(1936), which stressed the evolving morality play and *de casibus* story as the sources of Elizabethan tragedy. In the same year appeared Theodore Spencer's *Death and Elizabethan Tragedy* which stressed the medieval gothic quality of Shakespeare's tragedies. Howard Baker, in *Introduction to Tragedy* (1939), went beyond Farnham in denying the Senecan influence in Elizabethan tragedy and stressed instead the influence of the morality play. W. W. Lawrence, in *Shakespeare's Problem Comedies* (1931), already had tried to relate Shakespeare's long-debated problem comedies to the conventions of medieval romance and story. W. C. Curry, in *Shakespeare's Philosophical Patterns* (1937), applied medieval and Renaissance philosophy and demonology to a study of *Macbeth* and *The Tempest*.

O. J. Campbell, in *Shakespeare's Satire* (1943), has tried to relate some of Shakespeare's plays to Jacobean notions of satire. E. C. Pettet, in *Shakespeare and the Romance Tradition* (1949), has tried to do for Shakespeare's romantic comedies what Lawrence did for his more sombre ones, relating them to the traditions of romance as they had developed among such earlier dramatists as John Lyly and Robert Greene. M. C. Bradbrook, in *Shakespeare and Elizabethan Poetry* (1951), has treated Shakespeare's plays in relation to the non-dramatic poetry of his age, thus countering the distortions of stage-oriented critics who had neglected the fact that Shakespeare was a poet as well as a dramatist.

Hardin Craig and E. M. W. Tillyard have argued that Shakespeare's plays must be seen in terms of Elizabethan Christian humanism, with its religiously oriented conception of order and degree in a regulated universe. Craig's *The Enchanted Glass* (1936) was a pioneer work in the exploration of Elizabethan cosmology, and it was followed by Tillyard's influential *The Elizabethan World Picture* (1943). Douglas Bush, although not primarily concerned with Shakespeare, has argued along similar lines in *The Renaissance and English Humanism* (1939). Theodore Spencer, in *Shakespeare and the Nature of Man* (1942), saw Shakespeare's tragedies as reflecting the conflict in Shakespeare's age between the settled values which Christian humanism carried over from the Middle Ages and the new skepticism which was challenging them. Tillyard, in his *Shakespeare's History Plays* (1946), examined the English histories in terms of the Tudor doctrines of order and the Tudor conception of how earlier history reflected a divine plan for England's destiny.

Craig's *Enchanted Glass* attempted to explicate the "Elizabethan mind," to probe the ways of viewing things which belonged to a pre-Cartesian world. This book was the culmination of many years of work already reflected in the writings of Craig's students and other "history of ideas" critics who applied common Elizabethan ideas to the understanding of Shakespeare's plays. Ruth L. Anderson examined them in the light of popular treatises on psychology and moral philosophy in her *Elizabethan Psychology and Shakespeare's Plays* (1927). She was followed in this by Lily B. Campbell, whose *Shakespeare's Tragic Heroes: Slaves of Passion* (1930), examined each of Shakespeare's major tragic heroes in terms of contemporary treatises on the passions.

There have been many other such studies. J. E. Phillips, in *The State in Shakespeare's Greek and Roman Plays* (1940), examined these plays in terms of Elizabethan theories of statecraft and attitudes towards Roman history. Paul A. Jorgensen, in *Shakespeare's Military World* (1956), used Elizabethan military treatises for a similar purpose. C. B. Watson's *Shakespeare and the Renaissance Concept of Honor* (1960) has examined the tragedies in the light of what he conceives to be Renaissance concepts of honour derived from classical sources. Alfred B. Harbage, in *As They Liked It* (1947), has related the moral content of the plays to the tastes and expectations of the Elizabethan popular theatre audience, and, in *Shakespeare and the Rival Traditions* (1952), he has differentiated between the morality of the public theatres and the more sophisticated views of the private theatre audiences. There has also been a considerable interest in Shakespeare's language. Sister Miriam Joseph, in *Shakespeare's Use of the Arts of Language* (1947), has tried to relate Shakespeare's poetic usage to traditional rhetorical forms. Paul A. Jorgensen, in *Redeeming Shakespeare's Words* (1962), has examined certain specific words in terms of the connotations with which they had been associated historically.

Imagery

Works of historical criticism continue to appear, but by the second quarter of the twentieth century a reaction against such criticism became evident, and, as might be expected, tended to emphasize what historical critics were most neglecting — the fact that Shakespeare was a poet. This reaction was given impetus by the publication of Caroline Spurgeon's *Shakespeare's Iterative Imagery* (1931) and *Shakespeare's Imagery and What It Tells Us* (1935), which along with some brilliant analyses of Shakespeare's poetic technique, provided a classification of Shakespeare's poetic images upon which other critics could build. Once the poetry of Shakespeare came under intensive study, he began to be seen not so much as a dramatist subject to the influences of his own age and the requirements of a relatively unsophisticated theatre, but rather as the author of "dramatic poems" which shared the universality of all poetry.

Analysis of imagery, of course, did not begin with Caroline Spurgeon. As far back as 1794, a Cambridge scholar, Walter Whiter, had published *A Specimen of a Commentary on Shakespeare* (reprinted in 1967) which attempted to apply to Shakespeare John Locke's doctrine of the association of ideas and did so by demonstrating the groupings and close imaginative associations of images in Shakespeare's plays. Whiter pointed out image clusters, such as the constant association of dogs and candy with flattery, which was to be rediscovered by Spurgeon, and he suggested the presence of iterative imagery in the plays. Whiter's book is amazingly modern for its time, but it seems to have remained virtually unknown until very recently.

Analysis of imagery had been a basic element in the study of lyric poetry since at least the turn of the century, and it was inevitable that techniques developed in the study of the metaphysical poets should be applied to Shakespeare. George W. Rylands's *Words and Poetry* (1928) and Elizabeth Holmes's *Aspects of Elizabethan Imagery* (1929) were important studies which appeared while Spurgeon's work was in progress. There were other books and articles as well. Since 1930 the study of Shakespeare's poetic imagery has developed in many directions. Wolfgang H. Clemen, in *The Development of Shakespeare's Imagery* (1951), more than any of his predecessors, related Shakespeare's imagery to the immediate dramatic context in which it occurs and tried to demonstrate Shakespeare's growth in power to use poetic imagery for dramatic purposes. Another book which has kept its study of imagery within a dramatic context is Maurice Charney's *Shakespeare's Roman Plays* (1961). A somewhat different kind of work was done by John E. Hankins in *Shakespeare's Derived Imagery* (1953), which is concerned with the traditional connotations of Shakespeare's images. Somewhat similar has been Russell A. Fraser's *Shakespeare's Poetics* (1962), which is concerned with the iconographic origins of Shakespeare's imagery and thus with the traditional meanings associated with it. The iconographic study of Shakespeare has only just begun; it promises to yield fruitful results.

While Spurgeon was developing her technique, G. Wilson Knight was evolving the critical method he was to illustrate in *The Wheel of Fire* (1930). In the introduction to this volume, which has gone through many editions and amplifications, Knight explained his method of "poetic interpretation" as opposed to criticism, with its distinction between the spatial and temporal aspects of drama. In that volume, in *The Imperial Theme* (1931), and in others, he has applied his method to specific plays. Although Knight recognizes the temporal aspects — the logical progression of event from scene to scene — as important, he is concerned with the spatial, by which he means the total impression created by all aspects of the play's language operating upon the reader without regard to the temporal relations within the play. It is a play's total mood, impression, or "music" which he seeks to identify, and he holds that this essential quality cannot be perceived by the critic who concentrates on character or plot (mere temporal matters) or who allows extraneous historical fact to interfere with his total sympathetic absorption in the poetry. To hear the "music" of the plays is to experience Shakespeare's philosophic sensibility and become aware of his unique poetic conception of the universe. It is Shakespeare the poet of comprehensive philosophic vision, rather than the man of the theatre, in whom Knight is interested. And he has linked his own work to the philosophical critical tradition of Coleridge and Bradley, a tradition from which he believes the stage-oriented criticism of Harley Granville-Barker must be excluded.

Knight has sought to arrive at a total imaginative perception of each of Shakespeare's plays, which only the critic of the most heightened sensibility may hope to achieve. His principal instruments of analysis have been poetic imagery and symbolism, by means of which he has tried to approach the integrating themes of Shakespeare's plays and to define the pattern by which each play is unified. These themes Knight often has found to be conveyed by conventional Christian symbols. He has contributed more than any other critic of this century to an awareness of Shakespeare's symbolism and of the relation of his plays to Christian tradition and belief, although he has never claimed that Shakespeare was interested in expressing Christian doctrine or that the poet's personal beliefs may be discovered in his artistic creations. Perhaps most important, Knight has broken down the distinction between drama and poetry implicit in Bradley as well as in Stoll, and he has stated the most basic truth of all recent Shakespeare criticism: the most important of the conventions which Shakespeare employed was the poetic. His poetry is not a mere ornamentation, but the essential feature of his plays, which includes within it every other one of their aspects.

Myth and Ritual

One of G. Wilson Knight's concerns has been with the embodiment in Shakespeare's plays of some of the primal myths of the human race, most notably that of the death and resurrection of Christ. The concern with myth and ritual has been important in recent Shakespeare criticism. It has taken various forms. Northrop Frye, in many books and essays, including *A Natural Perspective* (1965), has seen the enjoyment of Shakespeare's plays as resulting from our natural human desire to participate in traditional mythic patterns which are implicit in them. John Holloway, in *The Story of the Night* (1961), a work most concerned with refuting critics who find moral themes in Shakespeare, concludes, like Frye, that the basic substance of the plays is primal myth which must be experienced for its own sake. C. L. Barber, in *Shakespeare's Festive Comedy* (1959), a more historically oriented study, has traced the relation of Shakespeare's comedies to primitive fertility rites and May games.

This kind of criticism, which is concerned with archetypal patterns in the plays, owes much to Jungian anthropology and psychology, and sees the greatest appeal of Shakespeare as directed to the "collective unconscious" of the human race. One of the pioneer studies of this kind was Gilbert Murray's *Hamlet and Orestes* (1914), which traced a common source and common themes in these two stories of parental murder and filial revenge. Mythic criticism is still in its infancy, and its partisans are far from unified in their approach — the basic unanswered question being the exact relation of the primal myth or ritual to the finished work of art. The method and its implications, with special reference to Shakespeare, have been most fully examined by Herbert Weisinger in *The Agony and the Triumph: Papers on the Use and Abuse of Myth* (1964).

The Scrutiny Group and the "New Critics"

The influence of Knight has been most marked in the work of contributors to *Scrutiny* magazine in England and among the so-called "new critics" in the United States. These men have shared Knight's assumptions about the unity of the work of art and the importance of poetic imagery to its understanding. They have worked by methods of close textual analysis and they have tended for the most part to ignore historical considerations.

Of the *Scrutiny* group, dominated by the views of F. R. Leavis, the most important Shakespearian critics have been L. C. Knights and Derek Traversi. Leavis's own criticism has involved a search for value, cultural and moral, since an age's culture and its morality are closely related aspects of its ordering and perception of experience. He has regarded this search as imperative in our century, in which traditional aristocratic channels of culture are no longer operative and many traditional values are no longer pertinent. Leavis has been a moralist essentially in the tradition of Matthew Arnold, who believed that literature must reflect the best of which man is capable, that the perception of literature is a moral activity, and that the critic must make the moral value of literature pervade society. Leavis has thus opposed historical critics who would confine their understanding of Shakespeare to the meaning he may have had for his own time. He holds that the kind of ordering of experience which is in poetry is a universal process and not limited to one age; that if Shakespeare's moral vision has any validity, it must have it for our own time; and that therefore the critic must study what poetry means today. Indeed, for Leavis, the great body of criticism stemming from E. E. Stoll and his followers is essentially beside the point.

Leavis himself has written little on Shakespeare, although his essays on *Measure for Measure* and *Othello* in *The Common Pursuit* (1952) are classics. His views have been applied to Shakespeare best by L. C. Knights in books such as *Explorations* (1946), *Some Shakespearean Themes* (1959), *An Approach to Hamlet* (1960), and *Further Explorations* (1965). To understand the poetry of Shakespeare, Knights has used a method of close textual analysis, concentrating upon image and symbol — a method which owes much to those of G. Wilson Knight, of I. A. Richards, and of William Empson, who has been concerned with the ambiguities and connotations of language. Knights has been in the tradition of Coleridge and Bradley in that he has seen Shakespeare's plays as embodying an evolving view of life. Like G. Wilson Knight, he has sought the integrating pattern of each play. Like T. S. Eliot, he has held that no single play of Shakespeare's can be perceived fully without an awareness of the dramatist's total artistic development. Knights has argued strongly against the historical critics, denying that any specific historical setting controls the universal and self-contained truth of poetry.

Derek Traversi, like Knights, has argued the importance of growth and development in the total body of Shakespeare's work. In *An Approach to Shakespeare* (1938), he explained his method, and he has presented a view of Shakespeare's artistic growth in subsequent volumes: *Shakespeare: The Last Phase* (1955), which shows the influence of the mythic approach in treatment of the final romances; *Shakespeare: From Richard II to Henry V* (1957); and *Shakespeare: The Roman Plays* (1963). More than Knights, Traversi has tended to emphasize plot as an instrument of poetry. He has been concerned with the symbolism of action and with a conception of the play, or "dramatic poem" as he calls it, as one large extended metaphor.

The "new critics" have not differed widely from Knights and Traversi in their general assumptions and method, but thus far they have not concerned themselves with Shakespeare to a large extent. Cleanth Brooks's essay, "The Naked Babe and the Cloak of Manliness" in *The Well Wrought Urn* (1947), is a classic essay on the imagery of *Macbeth*. But, of the "new critics," only Robert B. Heilman has devoted himself to Shakespeare in any extensive way, treating *King Lear* in *This Great Stage* (1948) and *Othello* in *Magic in the Web* (1956). Heilman has tried to determine the central moral themes which give unity to these plays. He has sought these themes by close analysis of poetic imagery, action, and character in relation to one another. He has dwelled upon image patterns — clothes and blindness in *King Lear*, for instance — by which Shakespeare poses paradoxes and creates tension between opposing systems of value. Heilman's criticism moves always towards the definition of a comprehensive vision by which all of the parts of the play are united, and the vision of the tragedies which Heilman finds is not unlike Bradley's: Shakespeare embodies a faith in the naturalness of good and sees evil as never more than a corruption in nature. From among the many other critics who have sought Shakespeare's themes through his imagery, we might mention Brents Sterling in *Unity in Shakespearean Tragedy* (New York: 1956) and John Russell Brown in *Shakespeare and His Comedies* (1957).

Moral and Christian Criticism

Heilman, like the *Scrutiny* critics, has been concerned with the moral value of Shakespeare's art. The ability of Shakespearian drama — and tragedy in particular — to translate a moral vision into dramatic terms has been an important concern of much recent criticism, and the problem has been approached in various ways. Some have seen the plays only in secular terms, holding that Christianity and tragedy are essentially incompatible. Others have argued that Shakespeare wrote with the assumptions of the Christian Renaissance about man's relation to God, and that thus we cannot ignore the religious dimension of his work.

One of the best studies of Shakespeare's moral ideas has been Donald Stauffer's *Shakespeare's World of Images* (1949), which uses all of the elements of drama — plot, character, and language — to arrive at Shakespeare's view of experience, believing that all great literature must reflect the ideas of its creator and that, although these may be expressed in a form which transcends logical discourse, they may be discovered by analysis of the dramatist's "choice of subject, his shaping of sources, the judgments implicit or stated in the outcome of his plots, his ventriloquism when characters speak out of key, his undramatic set speeches, his repetitive ideas, his recurrent images, and his choric or touchstone figures." Stauffer, we can see, has been very eclectic in his methods, drawing upon the historical critics as well as upon those who have written in opposition to them.

Two important books concerned with Shakespeare's moral content and both committed to the thesis that tragedy and Christianity are incompatible appeared in 1951, *The Dream of Learning* by D. G. James, and *Character and Society in Shakespeare* by Arthur Sewell. James and Sewell, each in his own way, argued that tragedy constitutes a unique way of knowing, distinct both from the religious and the scientific, that Shakespeare's plays are unified structures which, by means of poetry, translate a moral vision into drama. This vision they define in terms of a terrible pessimism alien to Christian belief, with man the prey of demonic forces against which his struggles are always in vain. That tragedy and Christianity are incompatible has been argued also by Clifford Leech in *Shakespeare's Tragedies and Other Studies in Seventeenth Century Drama* (1950).

Other critics, for instance S. L. Bethell, have argued that Shakespearian popular drama, as it emerged from the moral plays of the Middle Ages, was always Christian in its moral argument, and that the metaphysical and ethical assumptions of Shakespeare's tragedies were rooted in the common Christian belief he shared with his audience. J. F. Danby, in *Shakespeare's Doctrine of Nature* (1949), has examined *King Lear* in terms of the conflicting Renaissance ideas of nature revealed by historical critics such as Craig and Tillyard, and he has concluded that Shakespeare is consistently Christian in his ethical and religious point of view. G. R. Elliott in *Scourge and Minister* (1951), *Flaming Minister* (1953), and *Dramatic Providence in Macbeth* (1958, revised 1960), by intensive scene-by-scene analyses of *Hamlet, Othello,* and *Macbeth,* has argued that Shakespeare deliberately made use of Christian principles to create dramatic conflict and tension, affirming always an orthodox Anglican religious position. The religious orthodoxy of Shakespearian tragedy has been argued also by Roy Walker in *The Time Is Out of Joint* (1948) and *The Time is Free* (1949), studies of *Hamlet* and *Macbeth* respectively; by Robert Speaight in *Nature in Shakesperian Tragedy* (1955); and by Eleanor Prosser in *Hamlet and Revenge* (1967).

Sometimes the recognition of a religious dimension in Shakespeare has been carried to extremes, as perhaps in the books of John Vyvyan, *The Shakespearean Ethic* (1959), *Shakespeare and the Rose of Love* (1960), and *Shakespeare and Platonic Beauty* (1961), which often see little in the plays other than elaborate religious allegories, in which Shakespeare proclaims a consistent and rigidly orthodox Christian moral philosophy. J. A. Bryant in *Hyppolita's View* (1961) sees the plays in terms of medieval typology as biblical analogues whose central theme is always the story of Christ.

R. M. Frye, in *Shakespeare and Christian Doctrine* (1963), has tried to destroy all Christian readings of Shakespeare by arguing that the authors are deficient in their own knowledge of theology. Unfortunately Frye distorts and misrepresents the arguments of those he is attempting to refute — calling them "The School of Knight" and attributing to G. Wilson Knight attitudes he has never espoused. Also, Frye does not seem to realize that for a critic to discover Christian symbol or analogy in a play is not for him to argue that that play was written as Christian polemic. Frye's conclusion is that, although Shakespeare is generally orthodox in his Christianity, he wrote secular plays which are not Christian propaganda — a proposition with which the antagonists Frye chooses for himself will certainly agree. And he concluded that the plays have no implications beyond man's secular life, their ethical content being entirely in temporal terms — a proposition with which few will agree.

A strong reaction to all criticism which would find order or meaning in Shakespeare's world appears in Jan Kott's *Shakespeare: Our Contemporary* (1964), originally written in Polish, but soon translated into most of the languages of Europe. Kott sees Shakespeare's plays as grotesque in their vision of a discordant and chaotic world such as might be seen by the inmates of a Nazi concentration camp. Shakespeare's only response to traditional values is to hold them up to derision, and he can assert no new values. Such a Shakespeare, whose plays closely resemble modern comedy of the absurd, Kott sees as more meaningful to our contemporary world than any other. In Kott's work we have a denial both of the romantic criticism which exalted Shakespeare for his philosophical insight and moral vision, and of the historical criticism which has seen him as the product of a specific era. Kott has tried to render Shakespeare meaningful to our own century, but, it must be recognized, only in terms of a limited and partial conception of our century. Every age, as we have seen, has read Shakespeare in the light of its own assumptions, and there can be no doubt that this process will continue. That every age has been able to find new meaning in Shakespeare may be our surest evidence that he transcends the limited perspective of any period of human history, including our own.

Shakespeare in the Theatre, 1642-1968

◇◇◇◇◇
◇◇◇◇◇   On the stage, Shakespeare's plays have been subjected to
◇◇◇◇◇   another kind of analysis and evaluation. Whenever one of
his works is performed, it acquires a life which it can never have on
the printed page. Every great performance is an act of the most
intensive kind of critical interpretation, for it can reveal new
truths beyond the experience of the mere reader, just as intensive
poetic analysis can in its own way reveal facets of Shakespeare's
artistry which can never easily be made evident in stage performance. The history of Shakespeare's plays in the theatre, no less
than that of literary criticism, may provide an index to the changing tastes and attitudes of the last three and a half centuries, just as
they furnish an epitome of the progress of the English theatre in
the same period.

In spite of the critical attacks upon them throughout the seventeenth century, Shakespeare's plays continued to be among the most
popular of all plays to be staged. When the theatres opened again
after the Restoration, Shakespeare was among the first of the earlier
dramatists to be revived, although his plays were staged in terms of
a theatre tradition somewhat different from that for which the
works had been written.

In spite of the fact that the acting of plays was prohibited during the period from the closing of the theatres in September of
1642 to their opening upon the return of Charles II to the throne
in 1660, play acting did not entirely cease. There were secret
performances, usually in private houses, throughout the period.

Since brevity was very important under such circumstances, one common device was to prepare short skits based upon scenes in Elizabethan plays. These were called "drolls," and frequently drew upon the plays of Shakespeare. Scenes from *The Taming of the Shrew, A Midsummer Night's Dream, Henry IV, Part I, Hamlet,* and other plays are among those which appear in adapted form in the texts of drolls which have come down to us. Scenes involving such colourful characters as Petruchio, Bottom, and Falstaff seem to have been among the most popular.

The Restoration Revival

The first of Shakespeare's plays to have been staged after the Restoration evidently was *Pericles.* It was performed at the Phoenix or Cockpit in Drury Lane by a company headed by John Rhodes, a bookseller who had been a wardrobe keeper at Blackfriars. By the summer of 1660 two theatre companies were giving regular performances, one at the Red Bull Theatre in Clerkenwell and the other at Salisbury Court, Whitefriars. The actors must have been drawn largely from those surviving from the time of Charles I. In August of 1660, King Charles II granted royal licenses to Sir William Davenant and Thomas Killigrew, allowing them to form two new companies to which were granted a monopoly over play production in London. Davenant and Killigrew drew their actors from the existing companies. The first of these was the Duke of York's company under Davenant, which began to perform at Salisbury Court, moved to a new theatre in Lincoln's Inn Fields, and finally settled in a theatre in Dorset Garden. The other company, under Killigrew, began in makeshift quarters on an old tennis court, moved to the Theatre Royal in Covent Garden, and when that was destroyed by fire, to a new Theatre Royal in Drury Lane, built by Sir Christopher Wren. In November of 1682 these two companies combined into one and acted at the Drury Lane theatre.

Since the new theatres were all indoor structures, the traditions of staging which they revived were those of such Jacobean private playhouses as Blackfriars, and they drew heavily upon such techniques as had been developed in the Jacobean and Caroline court masques. A proscenium, for instance, was used so as to frame pictures representing specific locales. A localization of scenes such as had been unknown in Shakespeare's own day now began to be a feature of the English stage. Scenes were changed while the actors remained on stage in full view of the audience. Scenery and spectacle soon came to be cultivated for their own sake, whereas earlier they had been used only sparingly in a drama one of whose features was an absence of localization. The theatres now catered to a sophisticated coterie audience closely connected with the court. Each of the two companies performed Shakespeare's plays, but when they did so they altered them so as to conform to the tastes of an age which considered the Elizabethans to have been a barbarous people, and which, while it recognized the native genius of Shakespeare in spite of his time, saw his plays as badly in need of refinement.

The history of Shakespeare upon the Restoration stage is thus one of unrestrained adaptation, with even the names of the plays undergoing alteration and parts of one play often being placed within another. Davenant placed Beatrice and Benedick into *Measure for Measure* and produced a new concoction which he called *The Law Against Lovers*. Charles Gildon transformed the same play into a work called *Measure for Measure, or Beauty the Best Advocate*, adding to it features which had been developed in the newly introduced art form of opera. Petruchio's Grumio became a Scottish servant in an adaptation of *The Taming of the Shrew*, and the name of the play was changed to *Sauny the Scot*. In George Granville's adaptation of *The Merchant of Venice*, renamed *The Jew of Venice* to suit a new emphasis, Shylock was made an utterly grotesque comic character who became the central interest of the play. *Cymbeline* was transformed by Thomas D'Urfey into *The Injured Princess, or the Fatal Wager*. *Twelfth Night* was adapted by Charles Burnaby as *Love Betray'd, or the Agreeable Disappointment*. Thomas Otway's *Caius Marius*, in 1679–1680, placed the story of *Romeo and Juliet* in ancient Rome.

Scarcely a play of Shakespeare's escaped such treatment. The most notable transformation, perhaps, was that of *King Lear*, acted at Dorset Garden in 1681 as revised by Nahum Tate, Poet Laureate of England. Into the most sombre of Shakespeare's tragedies, Tate introduced a love affair between Cordelia and Edgar, and he caused the play to end happily, with Lear restored to his throne. The aged king at the end gives the reign to Cordelia and Edgar and retires with Gloucester and Kent to a peaceful cell where the three aged men propose to pass their remaining lives in philosophical reflection. The play closes with a speech by Edgar to point the moral of the whole:

> Divine Cordelia, all the Gods can witness
> How much thy love to Empire I prefer!
> Thy bright example shall convince the World
> (Whatever storms of Fortune are decreed)
> That Truth and Virtue shall at last succeed.

That this moralistic and prosaic piece of work should have supplanted Shakespeare's play upon the stage for a century and a half and have won the approval of both John Dryden and Samuel Johnson indicates the kind of tastes to which the Restoration made Shakespeare conform and how closely these tastes were related to the canons of neo-classical criticism.

In general the Restoration adapters sacrificed Shakespeare for the sake of symmetry, balance, perfect clarity of action and dialogue, explicit moral lessons, the observation of poetic justice, and romantic love interests — all of which, wherever possible, were developed beyond anything in the Shakespearian originals. These ends are achieved in Tate's *King Lear*. His adaptation of *Richard II* was not so successful, and his version of *Coriolanus,* which he called *The Ingratitude of a Commonwealth, or the Fall of Caius Martius Coriolanus* was an utter failure upon the stage. The greatest of Restoration actors was Thomas Betterton (ca. 1635–1710), but he performed only in such adaptations. The female parts in these plays were now played by women, for the age of the boy actor had come to an end with the closing of the theatres.

The Restoration adaptations of Shakespeare continued to hold the stage until past the middle of the eighteenth century, and new adaptations continued to appear, the plays often being made to focus directly upon contemporary political problems. For this purpose *Coriolanus* was a favourite, as in John Dennis's 1719 version called *The Invader of His Country, or the Fatal Resentment.* Versions closer to Shakespeare came only slowly to replace them, perhaps under the influence of the editions of Shakespeare by Nicholas

Rowe and his eighteenth-century successors. Theatres multiplied in eighteenth-century London, and began to appear also in such fashionable resorts as Bath and Cheltenham. As this occurred the court influence declined, and the stage came more and more to respond to the tastes of a prosperous middle class.

Accordingly, great names of the stage multiplied and all played Shakespearian roles. Robert Wilks (ca. 1665–1732) played Hamlet, Othello, Macduff, and Prince Hal, while serving also as an important theatre manager. Colley Cibber (1671–1757), manager of the theatre in Drury Lane and Poet Laureate of England as well, played Jaques, Shallow, Wolsey, Richard III, and Iago. His son, Theophilus Cibber (1703–1758) was famous for his Ancient Pistol. James Quin (1693–1766), an Irish actor, excelled in comedy as well as tragedy and was especially famous for his Coriolanus and his Falstaff. One of the most important of the eighteenth century actors was Charles Macklin (1697–1797), a tempestuous Irishman (his real name was McLoughlin), who was involved in numerous brawls. With Macklin, the movement away from Restoration adaptations became marked. His greatest triumph was as Shylock in a version of the play which removed much of the extraneous comedy added by Restoration revisionists. In 1740–1741 he acted in a version of *Macbeth* very close to Shakespeare's, but with a Highland setting and Scottish kilts, which gave testimony to the realistic tastes coming to prominence. In 1737 *Richard II* and *Henry V* had already been played at Covent Garden in versions close to the Shakespearian originals.

David Garrick

The greatest and most important Shakespearian actor of his time was David Garrick (1717–1779), the pupil and friend of Samuel Johnson. As manager and chief actor of Drury Lane, Garrick probably did more than any other single person to shape the theatre of the later eighteenth century. He took it upon himself to defend Shakespeare's genius against the strictures of Voltaire, and, because of his influence, the return to Shakespeare's original texts was greatly accelerated, although Garrick himself, particularly in his later years, did not hesitate to improve upon Shakespeare when he felt so inclined. In 1772 he altered *Hamlet* more drastically than had ever been attempted before — for this was a play with which even Dryden and Davenant had hesitated to tamper. He increased the central role so as to fatten his own part. But it must be noted that at the same time he restored about six hundred lines which had not been heard on the English stage for more than a century. In 1759 Garrick had been responsible for the first performance of *Antony and Cleopatra* since Shakespeare's own time.

Garrick took London by storm when he opened there in 1742 in the part of Richard III in an unlicensed and unfashionable theatre in Goodman's Fields, and from that moment his rise was meteoric. He was particularly noted for his natural style of acting, which was quite at variance with the formal rhetorical style of a man such as James Quin, to which London audiences had become accustomed. An anonymous reviewer thus described Garrick's performance as Richard III:

> His voice is clear and piercing, perfectly sweet and harmonious, without monotony, drawling, or affectation; it is capable of all the various passions which the heart of man is agitated with, and the Genius of Shakespeare can describe; it is neither whining, bellowing or grumbling, but in whatever character he assimilates perfectly easy in transition, natural in its cadence, and beautiful in its elocution. He is not less happy in his mien and gait, in which he is neither strutting nor mincing, neither stiff nor slouching. When three or four are on the stage with him he is attentive to whatever is spoke and never drops his character when he has finished a speech, by either looking contemptibly on an inferior performer, unnecessary spitting, or suffering his eyes to wander through the whole circle of spectators. His action corresponds with his voice, and both with the character he is to play.

In this praise there is a valuable indication of the methods of some of the contemporary actors to whom Garrick provided a welcome contrast. His acting, in effect, came to represent upon the stage the view of pre-romantic critics that Shakespeare's plays were perfect mirrors of ordinary human life.

Garrick himself was small in stature, but he seems to have been of strong and persuasive personality. As manager of Drury Lane from 1747 to 1776, he shaped the theatre according to his own image. While he remained its star attraction, he insisted upon having excellent actors in his company, and he did not hesitate to take minor roles himself when he felt that major parts should be played by other members of the troupe. He seems to have regarded the production of a play as an experience in which every member of the cast played an important role, rather than as a vehicle for the display of a single star. Under his direction, twenty-four of Shakespeare's plays were produced at Drury Lane, increasing the vogue for Shakespeare and providing a reading public for the great new editions of the later eighteenth century. One of the greatest of the editors, George Steevens, acknowledged his own indebtedness to Garrick in a letter which he wrote in 1767 to accompany a gift of his edition:

> I am contented with the spirit of the author you first taught me to admire, and when I found you could do so much for him I was naturally curious to know the value of the materials he had supplied you with; and often when I have taken my pen in hand to try to illustrate a passage I have thrown it down again with discontent when I remembered how able you were to clear that difficulty by a single look, or a particular modulation of voice, which a long and laboured paraphrase was insufficient to explain half so well.

It would be difficult for any editor to acknowledge more distinctly the role of the actor as interpreter and critic. At Garrick's death his friend Edmund Burke declared that Garrick had raised the status of acting to that of a liberal art. This may have been a tribute to his genius which sums up all of its attributes.

The leading ladies with whom Garrick played at Drury Lane were the greatest actresses of the day. They included Hannah Pritchard (1711–1768), famous for her portrayal of Lady Macbeth; and Peg Woffington (ca. 1714–1760), who excelled in parts which called for male disguise, such as Portia, Rosalind, Viola and Imogen. A notable Cordelia was played by Susanna Cibber (1714–1766), the divorced wife of Theophilus, and she was remarkable also as Constance in *King John*, a role coveted by all of the great actresses of the time. Mary Ann Yates (1728–1787) was famous for such tragic roles as Desdemona, Cordelia, and Cleopatra. Other actresses who starred with Garrick included Anne Bellamy (1731–1788), Elizabeth Pope (ca. 1744–1797), Elizabeth Hartley (1751–1824), and Elizabeth Farren (1759–1829). Among the male actors who rivalled Garrick in his time were Spranger Barry (1719–1777), a Dublin silversmith turned actor, who was famous as a handsome stage lover and who excelled as Romeo, Hamlet, Macbeth, Othello, and Lear; and John Henderson (1747–1785), known as "the Bath Roscius," who apparently aroused Garrick's jealousy by his excellence in such roles as Falstaff, Shylock, and Hamlet.

In October of 1768 the mayor and corporation of Stratford-on-Avon made Garrick an honourary freeman of the borough and suggested that he might be willing to donate a statue or picture of Shakespeare for display in the new town hall. Garrick promised to do so and suggested that the occasion of his presentation of the gift might be made into a jubilee celebration which would do honour to Shakespeare. In May of 1769 Garrick was presented by the corporation with the gift of a box made from the wood of a mulberry tree supposedly planted by Shakespeare, and on September 6 the first great Shakespeare jubilee opened. It consisted of three days of festivities involving fireworks, cannon firing, parades, and masquerade balls — all unfortunately marred by constant rainy weather. The high point of the celebration was a recitation by Garrick, in a rotunda especially built for the occasion, of an *Ode Upon Dedicating the Town Hall, and Erecting a Statue to Shakespeare,* supposedly of his own composition. During the entire three days of celebration, not a single word of Shakespeare's was spoken, but the great crowds of visitors seem to have enjoyed themselves and to have permanently established Stratford as a centre for tourists.

The Romantic Tradition

The romantic cult of the individual, with its glorification of Shakespeare as the dramatist best able to reveal the essential truth of human character, had already begun to find expression upon the stage in the acting style of David Garrick. The Stratford jubilee had given evidence of the Shakespeare idolatry which was to be so marked a phenomenon in romantic literary criticism. This idolatry was carried further by the lavish productions of Shakespeare by Garrick's successor as manager of Drury Lane, John Phillip Kemble (1767–1823). He himself played twenty-seven distinct Shakespeare roles, scoring his greatest triumphs as Macbeth and Coriolanus. He made his London debut in 1783 in the role of Hamlet, and it was in his power to evoke the poetry of Shakespeare's lines that he was most impressive. A contemporary reviewer of this first performance wrote of him:

> his recitation is evidently his great talent, and here, in our mind, he has no equal. His tones are beautifully modulated, his emphasis critical and instructive, and he so accurately possesses and conveys the meanings of the Poet, that it is a feast to hear him.

Kemble was admired by Walter Scott, Charles Lamb, and William Hazlitt, and it was his rendition of Shakespeare which often furnished the impetus for romantic criticism.

Charles Kemble (1775–1854), his younger brother, excelled in comic roles, while his sister, the celebrated Sarah Siddons (1753–1831), was by far the greatest actress of her age. She was a small and gentle woman, famous for her renditions of Ophelia, Desdemona, and Rosalind, but capable also of naturalistic portrayals quite alien to her own nature. The most notable of these was her Lady Macbeth, in which she appeared for the first time in February of 1785, and which some stage historians still consider to have been the greatest portrayal of Lady Macbeth of all time. Her acting, according to contemporary accounts, was so lifelike that audiences could feel the horror of *Macbeth* as it had never been felt before.

Under the management of John Phillip Kemble, Drury Lane was rebuilt, and Covent Garden, which he managed from 1802 to 1817, underwent extensive renovation. Both were now large proscenium theatres, holding audiences of about three thousand persons, and far removed from the playhouses for which Shakespeare's plays had been written. Kemble added to the lavishness of scenery and spectacle in his productions, moving Shakespeare further away from the originals than the productions of David Garrick. Kemble restored to *King Lear,* for instance, many of Tate's additions which Garrick had dropped, and almost all of the plays he produced were in versions altered by writers later than Shakespeare. Inspired by the antiquarian interests of romantic critics, he provided his actors with historically accurate contemporary costumes, although in the interests of spectacular display many of his plays were performed also in costumes which would have been as foreign to Shakespeare's age as to the periods in which the plays had their settings.

Romantic individualism as it affected stage performance may have been reflected most perfectly in the acting style of Edmund Kean (1787–1833), one of Kemble's most important successors. Kean was a virtuoso performer, concerned always with his own display of a central character for whom all the other members of a cast were mere background supporters. He was even smaller than Garrick in stature, and his voice, unlike Kemble's, was noted for its harshness, but when he assumed a role such as Othello he appeared to rise to heroic proportions. Few actors have equalled his ability to portray passion on the stage. Hazlitt has left a memorable report of Kean's ability:

> His face is the running comment on his acting, which reconciles the audience to it. Without that index to his mind, you are not prepared for the vehemence and suddenness of his gestures; his pauses are long, abrupt and unaccountable, if not filled up by the expression; it is in the working of his face that you see the writhing and coiling up of the passions before they make their serpent-spring; the lightning of his eye precedes the hoarse burst of thunder from his voice.

One of Kean's greatest roles was that of Shylock which he for the first time played as the wronged villain of intense and savage passion.

William Charles Macready (1793–1873) managed Covent Garden from 1837 to 1839 and Drury Lane from 1841 to 1843, but he was ill-suited to the task of theatre management, and neither playhouse prospered under his guidance. He exceeded Kemble in the magnificence of his scenery and costuming, but his great contribution was that he abandoned the Restoration and eighteenth-century adaptations and restored Shakespeare's own texts to the stage. His return in 1838 to Shakespeare's own text of *King Lear,* for the first time since before the Restoration, marks a significant point in the history of Shakespeare's fortunes on the stage.

Macready in his early days played opposite Sarah Siddons and with John Phillip Kemble, and during his acting career of some forty years there were few male Shakespearian roles which he did not perform. He rivalled Edmund Kean as Richard III and in other tragic parts. In 1826 and 1827 he made the first of several tours of the United States, performing Macbeth in New York and probably beginning his long enmity with the American actor,

Edwin Forrest (1806–1872), who was playing in New York at the same time and whose acting Macready apparently disparaged. In 1828 Macready acted the parts of Macbeth, Hamlet, and Othello in Paris.

Although he made several trips to America, Macready disliked the country and made no secret of the fact. He aroused considerable animosity, for most of which he blamed Edwin Forrest, and it is true that both in England and America the two actors went to extraordinary lengths to discredit the performances of each other. Macready is said to have hired persons to disrupt Forrest's performances when he toured England in 1845. In May of 1849 Macready's rendition of *Macbeth* at the Astor Place Opera House in New York was stormed by a crowd of some twenty thousand persons, many of them Irish immigrants resentful of the English enemy whom they considered to have insulted America. The ensuing "Astor Place riots" left some twenty-nine persons dead, and Macready, who apparently went through the entire play in spite of the disturbance outside, was forced to escape from the theatre in disguise and flee to Boston, whence he returned to England.

By Macready's time there were a great many theatres in London and in other cities as well. In 1843 the royal patents which had officially given a monopoly to Drury Lane and Covent Garden were formally terminated, and a free theatre existed in England. After 1843 the Sadler's Wells theatre, in what had been a fairly disreputable resort some distance from London, became an important playhouse under its actor-manager, Samuel Phelps (1804–1878), who produced thirty-four of Shakespeare's plays, along with plays by the lesser-known Jacobean dramatists. At the Princess theatre in London Shakespeare was produced and acted by Charles Kean (1811–1868), the son of Edmund, who carried historical accuracy in costumes and setting almost to the point of absurdity, and who filled his programs with historical notes which were ridiculed by his contemporaries. Kean's wife, Ellen Tree (1805–1880), was his principal supporting actress.

The last of the great nineteenth-century Shakespearian actor-managers was Henry Irving (1838–1905), who managed the Lyceum theatre in London from 1878 to 1902, where he staged lavish and spectacular productions of Shakespeare, starring himself in all of the major roles, and often playing opposite Ellen Terry (1848–1928). Irving (whose real name was John Henry Brodribb) acted the Shakespeare of Victorian philosophical critics deeply concerned with human character. Thus the tragedies were his special forte. He strove to make of each play a unified production. Probably his greatest role was that of Shylock in which he first appeared in 1879 and which he was to repeat many times — with a memorable performance before Queen Victoria in 1889. Irving's Shylock became a sentimentalized tragic hero who dominated the play, although Ellen Terry was always a memorable Portia as well. In 1895 Irving was knighted by Queen Victoria, the first actor in history so to be honoured. Like David Garrick, he was buried in Westminster Abbey.

Shakespeare in America

Henry Irving visited America many times, as Kean, Macready, and other great British performers had done before him. Although play acting was long banned in the New England colonies, it thrived in various cities along the Atlantic seaboard and was carried westward by pioneers crossing the Alleghenies. The first native American to play Hamlet was John Howard Payne (1791–1852) who opened in the play in New York in 1809. Edwin Forrest, who began by playing under Edmund Kean on that actor's American tours, went on to achieve a reputation in England as well as America, the first American actor to be celebrated abroad. Forrest's greatest American successor was Edwin Booth (1833–1893) son of the actor, Junius Brutus Booth (1796–1852), himself a Shakespearian performer who had been born in London of Jewish ancestry and who had played Shylock with a Jewish accent. Edwin began his career in 1849 with a *Richard III* in New York, toured England where he was not very enthusiastically received, and then settled in New York at the Winter Garden, where he began in 1863 to mount brilliant productions of Shakespeare with his brothers, Junius Brutus Jr., and the unfortunate John Wilkes, often in supporting roles. Following his brother's assassination of Lincoln, Edwin Booth retired briefly from the stage, but public demand caused him to return, and when the Winter Garden was destroyed by fire in 1867, he built his own theatre where he continued to stage Shakespeare until the costly lavishness of his productions sent him into bankruptcy in 1874. His performance as Othello in London in 1880, with Henry Irving as Iago and Ellen Terry as Desdemona, was one of the great triumphs of his career. One week after the opening performance Booth and Irving exchanged roles in the play.

Another important producer of Shakespeare in nineteenth-century America was Augustin Daly (1838–1899), who did not act himself, but who was important as a dramatist as well as a producer. Among the great American actors who toured widely, satisfying the demand for Shakespeare in the south and on the western frontier, were Lawrence Barrett (1839–1891), Robert Mantell (1854–1928), Richard Mansfield (1857–1907), and E. H. Sothern (1859–1933). Among the great American actresses of the nineteenth century who were famous for their Shakesperian roles were Fanny Davenport (1850–1898), Adelaide Neilson (1846–1880), Ada Rehan (1860–1916), and Julia Marlowe (1866–1950), who came from England to the United States at the age of five.

In our own century American Shakespearian actors of distinction have included John Barrymore (1882–1942), who acted in Colley Cibber's version of *Richard III* in 1920, and won wide acclaim for his performance as Hamlet which he gave for the first time in 1922. David Warfield was a famous Shylock in the same year. In the years just prior to World War II and during the war years themselves Shakespeare production on the New York stage was dominated by Margaret Webster. She featured elaborate sets, imaginative use of lighting, and star performers, usually from England, at the head of brilliant casts. Her *Richard II* in 1937 starred Maurice Evans. In the following years she staged an uncut version of *Hamlet* in which Evans starred along with Mady Christians as Gertrude. Her *Henry IV, Part I* of 1939 used Evans as Falstaff, and in her *Twelfth Night* of 1940 he played Malvolio, while Helen Hayes acted the part of Viola. In 1941 she directed Evans in *Macbeth,* with Judith Anderson as Lady Macbeth. One of her best New York productions was her *Othello* of 1943, with Paul Robeson as the Moor, José Ferrer as Iago, and Uta Hagen as Desdemona. There have been many other Broadway productions, one of the best of which was an *Antony and Cleopatra* directed by Guthrie McClintic in 1947, with

Katharine Cornell as Cleopatra, Godfrey Tearle as Antony, and Kent Smith as Enobarbas. But America has made its most important contribution to Shakespeare production in the last two decades not upon Broadway, but rather in the various Shakespeare festivals which have sprung up throughout the United States.

William Poel and the Elizabethan Revival

In England Henry Irving had had his great successors, such as Johnston Forbes-Robertson (1853–1937) and Herbert Beerbohm Tree (1853–1917), actor-producers who staged lavish and spectacular performances with such leading ladies as Mrs. Patrick Campbell (1867–1940), the Polish Helen Modjeska (1840–1909), and the American Mary Anderson (1859–1940) in supporting roles. In their productions, the unity of the play was frequently lost in the spectacle of stage setting, which often changed from scene to scene, and most other considerations were made to yield to the brilliant elocution of the star performer. But by the turn of the twentieth century this tradition of stellar scenic performance, while it continued both in England and America, was beginning to fail.

One result of the taste for a simpler kind of Shakespeare was the formation of repertory companies which performed as cohesive units, with emphasis upon the text of Shakespeare in simple stage settings, rather than upon scenic backgrounds and the performance of stars. The first of these companies was formed in 1883 by Frank Benson (1858–1939). It toured widely in the English provinces and in America, performing every one of Shakespeare's plays. An annual Shakespeare festival had been established at Stratford-on-Avon in 1879, and, aside from performances in 1889 and 1890 by a company under Osmond Tearle, and one in 1895 under Ben Greet, Frank Benson's company performed at Stratford every year from 1886 to 1913. In the spring of 1906 his company staged at Stratford all of Shakespeare's history plays in chronological sequence, apparently the first time that this was ever attempted.

Another closely related reaction against the older romantic tradition of Shakespeare production was represented by William Poel (1852–1934) and his productions for the Elizabethan Stage Society which he founded in 1895. The goal of the society was to recapture the simplicity of the Elizabethan stage itself. They tried to do so by studying the conditions of Shakespeare's own staging, by reconstructing models of Elizabethan theatres, and by producing Shakespeare's plays under conditions approximating those of the Globe. Their work was given impetus by the study of Elizabethan texts by scholars such as W. W. Greg and F. C. Furnivall. They represent an early counterpart in stage production to the historical criticism of Shakespeare which stemmed from Kittredge and his students in the early years of this century.

In the spring of 1881, on a specially constructed stage designed to resemble the Elizabethan, young William Poel put on a performance before a private audience of the 1603 bad quarto version of *Hamlet,* a version which was to be performed frequently in later years by the Ben Greet players. Poel followed this performance with productions of other Elizabethan plays. He used uncut texts of the plays and had them acted continuously, without scenery, and with casts of relatively unknown actors. In June of 1895 the Elizabethan Stage Society did an Elizabethan *Twelfth Night,* and in December of the same year it attempted to repeat the original performance of *The Comedy of Errors* by staging it in the great hall of Gray's Inn. In 1898 *The Merchant of Venice* was produced, with Shylock as a broad comic character, quite at variance with the passionate villain of Edmund Kean or the long-suffering tragic figure established by Henry Irving. Poel's greatest triumph was probably a production of *Everyman* in 1901 in which he tried to recapture the essence of the medieval stage.

Although never popular with Edwardian audiences and critics, except in rarified academic circles and with the notable exception of George Bernard Shaw, who enthusiastically defended Poel's productions, the movement has had a profound effect upon subsequent staging of Shakespeare. In 1921 the Maddermarket theatre was constructed out of a dilapidated eighteenth-century house in Norwich upon the model of the Fortune theatre so that it could be used for Elizabethan-style performances. In September of 1921 it opened with such a production of *As You Like It,* and it has been in continuous use by the Norwich players since that time. In spite of Poel's failure to capture the imagination of his contemporaries, his movement was effective in making clear how far removed from Shakespeare the performances of such actors as Forbes-Robertson and Beerbohm Tree had become. One important result of the Elizabethan revival was in the productions of Shakespeare by Harley Granville-Barker, who had been one of Poel's earliest supporters, at the Savoy theatre in London between 1912 and 1914.

Granville-Barker, while he objected to the lavish picture-frame settings of Forbes-Robertson and Beerbohm Tree, felt also that the barrenness of Poel's staging went to an opposite extreme and did not sufficiently realize the possibilities of modern stage techniques. He sought for a middle ground which would adapt Elizabethan stagecraft to a modern theatre. For his production of *The Winter's Tale* in September of 1912, he used three acting areas: a small space at the back of the stage for which a false proscenium was built; a larger area, some steps lower, which covered the front of the stage and was spanned by the proscenium arch; and a twelve-foot apron stage built out into the orchestra pit of the Savoy theatre. From this apron the actors could speak directly to the audience in the Elizabethan manner, and Granville-Barker emphasized rapidity and continuity in their delivery. He captured the rapid movement of Elizabethan staging by eliminating breaks between scenes, some of which — as in the productions of Beerbohm Tree — had become interminably long as stagehands rearranged furniture for each spectacular picture scene. For his scenic backgrounds Granville-Barker used symbolically painted curtains, and he illuminated the stage with clear white lights.

He went further in his costuming and settings in *Twelfth Night*, performed in November of 1912, eliminating the scenic extravagances which had become fashionable in productions of this play, but adding such lights and colours as would serve the needs of the total play and contribute to its tone of romance. One did not need to be an Elizabethan scholar to appreciate his productions. They permitted Shakespeare to speak for himself. Their settings aimed at suggestion rather than literal interpretation, and they depended upon the use of subtle lighting techniques, of symbolic rather than literal forms, and of different planes for the presentation of action. Although Granville-Barker's productions were not widely acclaimed by his contemporary critics, in historical perspective they may be seen to have marked the beginning of a new era. The age of the great spectacular actor-managers was coming to an end. The play rather than the star performer was establishing itself as the central concern of Shakespeare production, and although the old methods still continued to linger, modified Elizabethan staging, with symbolic rather than literal settings, was to be an important factor in the production of Shakespeare's plays in the ensuing years.

Shakespeare Festivals

Although Shakespeare has always been and continues to be performed regularly in the theatres of London's West End and New York's Broadway, the last half century has seen the spectacular rise, both in England and America, of professional Shakespeare companies performing regularly at Shakespeare festivals. What Frank Benson helped to establish at Stratford-on-Avon has grown stronger with each passing year. The first Memorial theatre in Shakespeare's birthplace had been opened on April 23, 1879, and when that structure was destroyed by fire in 1926 temporary quarters were used until funds could be raised for a new theatre. On April 23, 1932, the present structure on the banks of the Avon was finally opened. Frank Benson had been succeeded as manager in 1920 by W. Bridges-Adams, and he in turn was succeeded in 1934 by Ben Iden Payne. Under the successive managements of Anthony Quayle, Glen Byam Shaw, and Peter Hall, the Stratford theatre has continued to flourish. In 1961 it was renamed the Royal Shakespeare theatre, and its company now performs Shakespeare's plays in the Aldwych theatre in London as well as at Stratford.

The company has always fought for cohesive productions which emphasize the unity of the total play, although its styles have varied with the years and with the proclivities of individual directors. England's greatest actors have been among its performers. These have included Godfrey Tearle, Michael Redgrave, Ralph Richardson, Anthony Quayle, Laurence Olivier, John Gielgud, Emlyn Williams, Charles Laughton, Richard Burton, Paul Scofield, Christopher Plummer, Peter O'Toole, Ian Holm, and David Warner. Among the actresses who have appeared with frequency have been Edith Evans, Diana Wynyard, Peggy Ashcroft, Margaret Leighton, Vanessa Redgrave, and Diana Rigg. Among its outstanding directors have been Peter Brook, Michael Benthall, Nugent Monck, Frank McMullen, Tyrone Guthrie, Anthony Quayle, Michael Langham, Tony Richardson, and Franco Zeffirelli.

Under the management of Peter Hall, who assumed the post in 1960, the Stratford productions, no matter who the individual director, have attained a remarkable unity of style which in itself attests to the submergence of the individual performer to the unity of the total production — an ideal since Frank Benson's time. Generally they are marked by a precision of language which makes it certain that each actor understands the meaning of every word he speaks and by a psychological realism in presentation. Stage settings are generally simple, more often symbolic than realistic, although both kinds have been used, and a revolving stage introduced by Hall is now frequently employed. Strong, dominant colours are generally used in the costumes and sets, in keeping with the mood of the particular play. Sometimes there is a good deal of realistic stage business, as in the series of history plays produced in 1965 and 1966, when battle scenes were simulated with a realism that filled the stage with gunsmoke.

In his interpretation of the plays — and each play is unified by a central conception — Peter Hall tends to emphasize those elements in them which relate most immediately to the problems of our modern world. The Hamlet acted by David Warner in 1965 and 1966, for instance, was recognizable as the apathetic and disillusioned youth of today whose ideals have been shattered and who cannot cope with the evil of the world with more than apathy and despair. Peter Brook's 1962 production of *King Lear,* with Paul Scofield in the title role, a widely acclaimed production which was brought to the United States, was set against a white background and the actors were costumed in leather so as to emphasize the cold harshness of a chaotic world in which no redeeming factors temper the horror of the tragedy. Yet the Royal Shakespeare Company has not often sacrificed the historical facts of a play for the sake of contemporary meaning. Damnation in Christian terms may not be a matter of great concern to the modern world, but Peter Hall's production of *Macbeth* in 1967, with Paul Scofield in the title role, never let the audience forget that this was a play about the damnation of a human soul.

Shortly before Benson's troupe became established at Stratford, Philip Ben Greet and his company had begun to provide regular performances of Shakespeare's plays at the theatre on the Waterloo Road on the London Bankside which came to be known as the "Old Vic." It had been built originally in 1818 as the Royal Coburg theatre, had had its name changed to The Royal Victoria in 1833, and had been used for a variety of purposes, most notably as a music hall. In 1914 its manager, Lilian Baylis, invited Greet to use it as a theatre for Shakespeare. Among the very first persons whom Greet summoned to London was Sybil Thorndike, who played Adriana in *The Comedy of Errors*, the first production of a Shakespeare repertory company which was to win wide acclaim both in England and in America, which it visited frequently for half a century. The Old Vic troupe, more than any other, was to bring Shakespeare's plays to the ordinary people of London.

Greet continued to direct Shakespeare at the Old Vic until 1918. Among the distinguished directors who succeeded him were Tyrone Guthrie, Glen Byam Shaw, and Michael Benthall. The company survived until 1963 when the theatre was taken over by the newly established British National theatre. The Old Vic gave its last performance on June 14 of that year, a production of *Measure for Measure*. The National Theatre Company, including many actors, such as Laurence Olivier, who had starred in the Old Vic company, has continued to perform Shakespeare regularly at the same theatre on Waterloo Road.

The notables who have acted Shakespeare at the Old Vic include the most distinguished names of the British theatre. Among the more important are Russell Thorndike, Lewis Casson, Eric Portman, John Gielgud, Donald Wolfit, Ralph Richardson, Robert Speaight, Charles Laughton, Maurice Evans, Laurence Olivier, Michael Redgrave, Emlyn Williams, Alec Guinness, Roger Livesay, Robert Helpmann, Jack Hawkins, Trevor Howard, Cedric Hardwick, Richard Burton, Alastair Sim, and Leo McKern. Among the actresses who followed Sybil Thorndike on its stage are Edith Evans, Esmé Church, Peggy Ashcroft, Margaret Webster, Flora

Robson, Elsa Lanchester, Judith Anderson, Vivian Leigh, Jessica Tandy, Joyce Redman, Diana Churchill, Claire Bloom, Wendy Hiller, and Barbara Jefford. Productions at the theatre have exhibited a variety of styles. Ben Greet's interest in Elizabethan simplicity had a profound effect in giving direction to the company. In recent years the company has not differed much from the traditions of the Royal Shakespeare Company at Stratford, the same directors and actors working often at both places.

The American Shakespeare Festival Theatre and Academy since July of 1955 has conducted an annual festival at its Memorial theatre on the banks of the Housatonic River at Stratford, Connecticut. The theatre is a lavish structure which cost $1,000,000 to construct and seats about fifteen hundred persons. It is hexagonal in shape, and it makes some attempt to resemble an Elizabethan theatre on the outside, but it uses a proscenium stage with an extending fourteen-foot forestage. Unlike the productions at Stratford-on-Avon and at the Old Vic, those at Stratford, Connecticut, have tended to look back to the romantic era of Henry Irving and Beerbohm Tree. Settings and costuming have generally been lavish and spectacular, and the company has usually been led by a star, often from Hollywood. Casts have been headed by such dignitaries as Raymond Massey, Nina Foch, Katherine Hepburn, Alfred Drake, Robert Ryan, and Kim Hunter, and the individual performance rather than the unified play has sometimes seemed of most concern. In 1960 Bert Lahr gave a memorable performance as Bottom in *A Midsummer Night's Dream,* a role which Cyril Ritchard took in 1967, doubling in the part of Oberon. In such performances all else is sacrificed to the virtuosity of a supreme comedian, and a relatively minor character comes to dominate the play. A regular performer at Stratford, Connecticut, has been Morris Carnovsky, who has been particularly notable for his appearances as Shylock and King Lear. The company has been somewhat inclined towards imaginative experimentation, such as staging *Much Ado About Nothing* on a Texas ranch and costuming *Troilus and Cressida* so as to make it a play about the American Civil War. A 1968 production of *Love's Labour's Lost* in which the King of Navarre was an Indian guru and Costard a hippie, and in which the songs were sung with a microphone to rock music, was fairly successful in translating

Shakespeare's comedy into a modern idiom. In recent years the company has been using younger actors to an ever greater extent, and it has been moving away somewhat from the spectacular star-dominated performance. It has not, as yet, developed any style of production which may be called its own.

The oldest American Shakespeare festival is that at Ashland, Oregon, which has been giving plays every summer since 1935, except for the war years. Other festivals have sprung up with great frequency. There is one at San Diego, California, and another at Boulder, Colorado. Another began at Antioch College at Yellow Springs, Ohio, under the direction of Arthur Lithgow. In 1962 it became the nucleus of a Great Lakes Shakespeare festival which now performs in a civic auditorium, capable of holding two thousand people, at Lakewood, Ohio, a suburb of Cleveland. The Champlain Shakespeare festival at Burlington, Vermont, under the direction of Edward Feidner, has attained a high degree of excellence. In a very small theatre with an extending platform stage, surrounded by the audience on three sides, its productions have managed to attain an intimacy and simplicity much like that of the Elizabethan stage.

Equally excellent have been the free outdoor performances of Shakespeare's plays given since 1957 in New York's Central Park by the New York Shakespeare Festival company under the direction of Joseph Papp. So successful has this unusual enterprise proved to be that in 1962 New York City constructed the Delacorte theatre in the park for the company's use, and since 1964 a second company has given free performances in the various parks throughout the city, with the help of a specially constructed portable stage. Since 1960 free performances have been given in the nation's capital by the Washington Shakespeare Summer Festival company at the Sylvan Theatre on the grounds of the Washington Monument.

At Stratford, Ontario, a Canadian Shakespeare Festival company has performed regularly since 1953. Under the management of Tyrone Guthrie it opened with Alec Guinness in *Richard III,* and a production of *All's Well That Ends Well,* featuring Irene Worth as the Countess and Guinness as the King of France. A special stage, designed by Tanya Moiseiwitsch, captured the essential features of the Elizabethan stage — probably more closely than ever before in a modern theatre. It consisted of a large platform surrounded by the audience on three sides; a columned inner alcove at the rear; and an acting area above, which could be reached by visible stairs at either side of the stage. Until 1957, when a new theatre was built, this stage was housed within a blue circus tent — which helped to give the entire festival a carnival atmosphere.

The Canadian festival has been an outstanding success since the day of its opening. Under Guthrie's direction a company of excellent young Canadian actors was developed, to be supplemented by actors from the Royal Shakespeare Company and the Old Vic, with occasional Americans, such as Jason Robards, brought up from Broadway. The plays have been directed by Guthrie and by visiting British directors, including Peter Hall, who have maintained at Stratford, Ontario, the major traditions of play production developed at Stratford-on-Avon from the time of Frank Benson. Even more than the Royal Shakespeare Company, that of Stratford, Ontario, because of its special kind of stage, has been able to carry on in our time the kind of simple Elizabethan staging advocated by William Poel and to demonstrate that such a production can make Shakespeare more meaningful to a modern audience than any other kind. In 1956 Guthrie was succeeded as manager by Michael Langham, although Guthrie has continued to direct plays at the festival from time to time.

Some Modern Adaptations

Productions at the various festivals throughout the English-speaking world provide the best insight possible into the various ways by which Shakespeare is being brought to theatre audiences in our own time. There are spectacular productions on Broadway from time to time, less spectacular ones at off-Broadway theatres, productions at schools and universities, and productions by amateur and semi-professional groups of various kinds. The urge to make Shakespeare more meaningful to our own age has sometimes been carried to strange extremes. For instance, in a 1967 San Francisco production, later brought to New York, of *A Midsummer Night's Dream,* the actors coughed throughout the performance so as to indicate that the setting was in plague time; a leopard-skin clad Hyppolita was kept in a cage by Theseus; Helena was played by a male transvestite; and generally one of Shakespeare's most carefree comedies was deliberately distorted so as to display a world utterly corrupt and diseased. This has been one manifestation of a movement in the contemporary theatre which regards the text of a play as ultimately insignificant and gives complete freedom of improvisation to director and actors. There have been other recent attempts to improvise upon the text of Shakespeare, notably a production of *Hamlet* in New York by Joseph Papp in 1968 in which characters and speeches were so rearranged as to bear little resemblance to anything Shakespeare might have written. One of the most unusual and succesful experiments has been Tom Stoppard's play, *Rosencrantz and Guildenstern Are Dead,* first performed in Edinburgh in August of 1966 and later brought to New York where it has played to large audiences on Broadway. In this play the story of *Hamlet* is told from the point of view of Rosencrantz and Guildenstern and becomes a mere background for their tragedy which is the tragedy of helpless and ineffectual human beings caught in an inhuman system of powerful forces beyond their control. This ingenious work, whose success has begun to inspire other such attempts, shared the 1968 New York Drama Critics award with a "rock beat" musical adaptation of *Twelfth Night,* called *Your Own Thing.*

This is one of several musical comedies which have been made from the plays. *The Boys from Syracuse* was adapted in 1938 from *The Comedy of Errors,* and in 1939 a production called *Swingin' the Dream* set *A Midsummer Night's Dream* in nineteenth-century New Orleans to the accompaniment of popular music of the thirties. One of the most popular of such transformations has been Cole Porter's 1948 adaptation of *The Taming of the Shrew* as *Kiss Me Kate,* from which a motion picture was made. In 1957 Leonard Bernstein transformed *Romeo and Juliet* into a musical play called *West Side Story* about feuding Puerto Rican gangs in New York's Harlem.

At the very birth of motion pictures Sarah Bernhardt acted in one-reel movies based upon scenes from Shakespeare. Theda Bara appeared in a silent-film *Romeo and Juliet* in 1916, and among the very first talking pictures was *The Taming of the Shrew* in 1919 which featured Doublas Fairbanks, Sr., and Mary Pickford. Probably the most extravagant production of Shakespeare for motion pictures was Max Reinhardt's *A Midsummer Night's Dream* in 1935, with young Mickey Rooney as Robin Goodfellow and James Cagney as Bottom. Norma Shearer and Leslie Howard appeared in a movie version of *Romeo and Juliet* in the following year, with John Barrymore as Mercutio, Edna May Oliver as the Nurse, and Andy Devine as Peter, her servant. More recently *Romeo and Juliet* has been filmed by Franco Zeffirelli with Italian scenic backgrounds so exotic as almost to submerge the play. Zeffirelli also supplied the scenic background for a recent *The Taming of the Shrew*, with Richard Burton and Elizabeth Taylor as Petruchio and Katherine. One of the most ambitious and relatively successful Hollywood productions has been a *Julius Cæsar* of 1952, with Louis Calhern in the title role, John Gielgud as Cassius, James Mason as Brutus, and Marlon Brando as Marc Antony.

In England the most important actor in Shakespeare films has been Laurence Olivier. He began in 1937 with an *As You Like It* in which he played Orlando to the Rosalind of Elizabeth Bergner. In 1943 he produced his intensely patriotic *Henry V*, which may still be the finest motion picture ever made from a Shakespeare play. He followed this in 1948 with a *Hamlet* which suffered from a forced Freudian interpretation and from very infelicitous cutting; it may well have been the first performance in history in which Hamlet appeared as a blond. In more recent years he has done *Richard III* (1955) and an *Othello* (1965) based upon his own production of that play for the National Theatre company and using the same actors who had appeared upon the stage.

The American actor and producer, Orson Welles, has also been for many years an ambitious experimenter with Shakespeare on film. He has done an *Othello* and a *Macbeth* in Scottish dialect, whose soundtrack had to be replaced because of its unintelligibility to most audiences. His most ambitious undertaking, filmed over a period of many years and with many financial and other difficulties, has been his *Chimes at Midnight*, as it is known in England, or *Falstaff*, as it is called in the United States. To portray Falstaff, Welles rearranged and redistributed lines and whole scenes from

Richard II, the two parts of *Henry IV,* and *Henry V.* Shakespeare's story line is somewhat confused, but the cinematographic technique of the film is superb, and Welles's portrayal of Falstaff in his many moods and aspects is a masterpiece of characterization, as is also the King Henry IV played by John Gielgud.

On television in America several Shakespeare plays have been presented on the Hallmark Hall of Fame, including a *Macbeth* starring Maurice Evans and Judith Anderson, who had performed in Margaret Webster's Broadway production of the play. The British have been somewhat more ambitious, for the BBC has presented more of the plays to television audiences. Its most remarkable achievement probably has been the chronological sequence of Shakespeare's history plays from *Richard II* through *Richard III* called *The Age of Kings* which has been shown regularly to television audiences both in England and America.

Genealogical Tables for the English History Plays

I. THE HOUSE OF PLANTAGENET

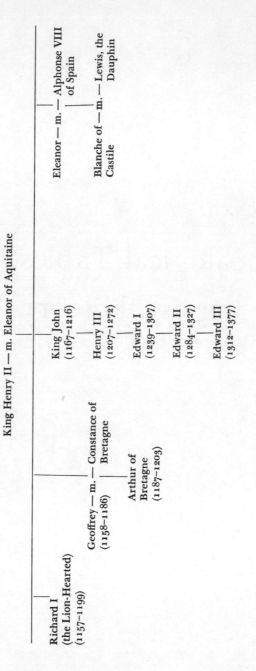

King Henry II — m. Eleanor of Aquitaine

Richard I
(the Lion-Hearted)
(1157–1199)

Geoffrey — m. — Constance of
(1158–1186)   Bretagne

Arthur of
Bretagne
(1187–1203)

King John
(1167–1216)

Henry III
(1207–1272)

Edward I
(1239–1307)

Edward II
(1284–1327)

Edward III
(1312–1377)

Eleanor — m. — Alphonse VIII
of Spain

Blanche of — m. — Lewis, the
Castile   Dauphin

RICHARD II AND THE HOUSE
OF LANCASTER

Edward III — m. Phillipa of Hainault
(1312–1377)

- William of Hatfield (died young)
- Edward, the Black Prince (1330–1376) — m. — Joan of Kent
  - Richard II (1367–1400) — m. — Anne of Bohemia / Isabelle of France
- Lionel of Clarence (1338–1368)
- Edmund Langley Duke of York (1341–1402)
- John of Gaunt Duke of Lancaster (1340–1399) — m. — Blanche of Lancaster
  - Henry Bolingbroke Duke of Hereford King Henry IV (1367–1413) — m. — Margaret of Bohun
    - Henry of Monmouth King Henry V (1387–1422) — m. — Katherine of France
      - Henry VI (1421–1471) — m. — Margaret of Anjou
        - Edward, Prince of Wales (1453–1471) — m. — Anne Neville
    - Thomas, Duke of Clarence (1388–1421)
    - John of Lancaster Duke of Bedford (1389–1445)
    - Humphrey, Duke of Gloucester (1390–1477)
- Thomas of Woodstock Duke of Gloucester (1355–1397)
- William of Windsor (died young)

III. THE MORTIMERS AND
THE HOUSE OF YORK

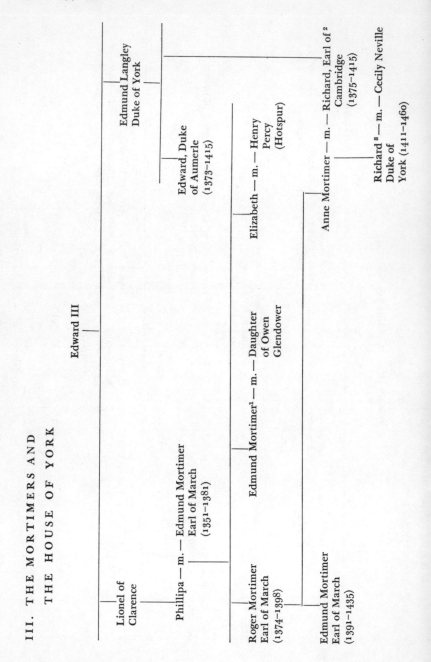

Elizabeth — m. — Edward, Earl of March, King Edward IV (1442–1483)
Woodville, Lady Grey

Edmund, Earl of Rutland (1443–1460)

George — m. — Isabelle Neville, Duke of Clarence (1449–1478)

Richard, Duke of Gloucester — m. — Anne Neville, King Richard III (1452–1485)

Edward V⁴ (1470–1483)

Richard, Duke of York

Elizabeth — m. — Henry Tudor, Earl of Richmond, King Henry VII

1. Shakespeare in *Henry IV, Part I* confused this historically obscure character with his nephew, Edmund Mortimer, Earl of March, who, as the direct descendant of Lionel of Clarence, had a better claim to the throne than King Henry IV.

2. Executed by King Henry V. By his marriage to Anne Mortimer he acquired for his family the right to the throne of the descendants of Lionel of Clarence.

3. Killed at the Battle of Wakefield.

4. Never actually reigned. Murdered in the Tower, along with his brother.

IV. THE HOUSE OF TUDOR

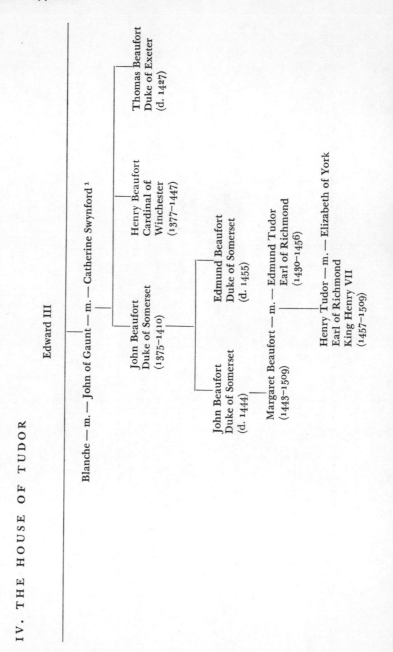

Edward III

Blanche — m. — John of Gaunt — m. — Catherine Swynford [1]

John Beaufort
Duke of Somerset
(1375–1410)

Henry Beaufort
Cardinal of
Winchester
(1377–1447)

Thomas Beaufort
Duke of Exeter
(d. 1427)

John Beaufort
Duke of Somerset
(d. 1444)

Edmund Beaufort
Duke of Somerset
(d. 1455)

Margaret Beaufort — m. — Edmund Tudor
(1443–1509)   Earl of Richmond
                       (1430–1456)

Henry Tudor — m. — Elizabeth of York
Earl of Richmond
King Henry VII
(1457–1509)

Arthur, Prince
of Wales
(d. 1502)

Margaret — m. — James IV
King of Scotland
(1488–1513)

Mary — m. — Charles
Brandon,
Duke of
Suffolk

Katherine of — m. — Henry VIII — m. — Ann Boleyn — m. — Jane Seymour
Aragon   (1491–1547)

King Philip — m. — Mary Tudor
II of Spain   (1516–1558)

Elizabeth I
(1533–1603)

Edward VI
(1537–1553)

James V
(1512–1542)

Henry, Lord — m. — Mary Stuart
Darnley   Queen of Scots
                         (1544–1587)

James I of England
and VI of Scotland
(1566–1625)

1. Catherine Swynford had been the mistress of John of Gaunt before she became his third wife.
Her children were illegitimate, but they were declared legitimate by King Richard II, and this
was confirmed by King Henry IV, although he specifically barred their right to the throne.

A Select Bibliography

◇◇◇◇◇
◇◇◇◇◇ Shakespeare bibliography is so vast and continues to grow
◇◇◇◇◇ each year at so phenomenal a rate that it is possible here
merely to indicate a part of what is available. Since the standard
editions of Shakespeare's works are dealt with in Chapter Six, and
the more important critical studies are discussed in Chapter Seven,
there is no need to repeat this material. Students may find discus-
sion of the more important studies of each of the individual plays
in Ronald Berman, *A Reader's Guide to Shakespeare's Plays: A Dis-
cursive Bibliography* (Chicago: Scott, Foresman, 1965), and they may
find a comprehensive listing of books and articles on every aspect of
Shakespeare's life and art in Gordon Ross Smith, *A Classified
Shakespeare's Bibliography 1936–1958* (College Park: Pennsylvania
State University Press, 1963), which supplements the earlier bibliography by W. Ebisch and L. L. Shücking, *A Shakespeare Bibliography* (Oxford: The Clarendon Press, 1931, with a supplementary
volume covering the years 1930 to 1935). Annual bibliographies appear in *Shakespeare Quarterly* (formerly *The Shakespeare Association Bulletin*), *Studies in Philology,* and *Publications of the Modern
Language Association of America.* There are surveys of each year's
Shakespeare scholarship and criticism in the annual volumes of
The Year's Work in English Studies and *Shakespeare Survey.* The
best collection of Shakespeare's sources, with chapters of critical
commentary for each play, is Geoffrey Bullough, *Narrative and
Dramatic Sources of Shakespeare,* 7v. (New York: Columbia University Press, 1957–69). A useful compendium of information of
every kind is *The Reader's Encyclopedia of Shakespeare,* ed. by
O. J. Campbell and E. G. Quinn (New York: Thomas Y. Crowell,
1966). The following listing includes those works upon which the
author has drawn most fully in the preceding chapters, and to which
he is most indebted. It is largely confined to those aspects of Shakespeare's life, times, and theatre treated in those chapters.

I. THE ENGLISH RENAISSANCE

ALLEN, J. A. *A History of Political Thought in the Sixteenth Century.* London: Methuen, 1928.

ALLEN, J. W. *English Political Thought, 1603–60.* London: Methuen, 1938.

BAKER, HERSCHEL. *The Image of Man: A Study of the Idea of Human Dignity in Classical Antiquity, the Middle Ages and the Renaissance.* Cambridge, Mass.: Harvard Univ. Press, 1947.

BAKER, HERSCHEL. *The Wars of Truth: Studies in the Decay of Christian Humanism in the Earlier Seventeenth Century.* Cambridge, Mass.: Harvard Univ. Press, 1952.

BAUMER, F. L. *The Early Tudor Theory of Kingship.* New Haven: Yale Univ. Press, 1940.

BINDOFF, S. T. *Tudor England.* Baltimore: Penguin Books, 1950.

BLACK, J. B. *The Reign of Elizabeth, 1558–1603.* Oxford: The Clarendon Press, 1936.

BRIGGS, K. M. *The Anatomy of Puck: An Examination of Fairy Beliefs Among Shakespeare's Contemporaries and Successors.* London: Routledge and Kegan Paul, 1959.

BRIGGS, K. M. *Pale Hecate's Team: An Examination of the Beliefs on Witchcraft and Magic Among Shakespeare's Contemporaries and his Immediate Successors.* London: Routledge and Kegan Paul, 1962.

BUCKLEY, G. T. *Atheism in the English Renaissance.* Chicago: Univ. of Chicago Press, 1932.

BUSH, DOUGLAS. *The Renaissance and English Humanism.* Toronto: Univ. of Toronto Press, 1939.

BUSH, DOUGLAS. *Prefaces to Renaissance Literature.* Cambridge, Mass.: Harvard Univ. Press, 1966.

BUTTERFIELD, HERBERT. *The Origins of Modern Science.* Rev. ed. New York: Macmillan, 1959.

CASPARI, FRITZ. *Humanism and the Social Order in Tudor England.* Chicago: Univ. of Chicago Press, 1954.

CASSIRER, ERNST. *The Platonic Renaissance in England.* Austin: Univ. of Texas Press, 1953.

CHEYNEY, E. P. *A History of England from the Defeat of the Armada to the Death of Elizabeth.* 2v. London: Longmans, Green, 1914–26.

CRAIG, HARDIN. *The Enchanted Glass: The Elizabethan Mind in Literature.* New York: Oxford Univ. Press, 1936.

DANBY, J. F. *Shakespeare's Doctrine of Nature.* London: Faber and Faber, 1949.

EINSTEIN, LEWIS. *The Italian Renaissance in England.* New York: Columbia Univ. Press, 1907.

EINSTEIN, LEWIS. *Tudor Ideals.* New York: Harcourt, Brace, 1921.

ELTON, G. R. *The Tudor Revolution in Government.* Cambridge: The University Press, 1953.

ELTON, G. R. *England Under the Tudors.* London: Methuen, 1955.

FIGGIS, J. N. *The Divine Right of Kings.* Cambridge: The University Press, 1922.

GARRET, C. H. *The Marian Exiles: A Study in the Origins of Elizabethan Puritanism.* Cambridge: The University Press, 1938.

HALLER, WILLIAM. *The Rise of Puritanism, 1570–1642.* New York: Columbia Univ. Press, 1938.

HAYDN, HIRAM. *The Counter-Renaissance.* New York: Charles Scribner, 1950.

HELTON, TINSLEY, ed. *The Renaissance: A Reconsideration of the Theories and Interpretations of the Age.* Madison: Univ. of Wisconsin Press, 1961.

HOOPES, ROBERT. *Right Reason in the English Renaissance.* Cambridge, Mass.: Harvard Univ. Press, 1962.

HUGHES, PHILIP. *The Reformation in England.* 3v. London: Hollis and Carter, 1950–4.

HUIZINGA, J. *The Waning of the Middle Ages.* Baltimore: Penguin Books, 1955.

KITTREDGE, G. L. *Witchcraft in Old and New England.* Cambridge, Mass.: Harvard Univ. Press, 1928.

KNAPPEN, M. M. *Tudor Puritanism.* Chicago: Univ. of Chicago Press, 1939.

KNIGHTS, L. C. *Drama and Society in the Age of Jonson.* London: Chatto and Windus, 1937.

KOCHER, P. H. *Science and Religion in Elizabethan England.* San Marino: The Huntington Library, 1953.

LATHAM, M. W. *The Elizabethan Fairies.* New York: Columbia Univ. Press, 1930.

LEWIS, C. S. *The Discarded Image: An Introduction to Medieval and Renaissance Literature.* Cambridge: The University Press, 1964.

LOVEJOY, A. O. *The Great Chain of Being.* Cambridge, Mass.: Harvard Univ. Press, 1936.

MAZZEO, J. A. *Renaissance and Revolution: Backgrounds to Seventeenth-Century Literature.* New York: Pantheon Books, 1965.

MEYER, A. O. *England and the Catholic Church under Queen Elizabeth.* Repr. New York: Barnes and Noble, 1967.

MORRIS C. *Political Thought in England: Tyndale to Hooker.* London: Oxford Univ. Press, 1953.

MURRAY, R. H. *The Political Consequences of the Reformation: Studies in Sixteenth Century Political Thought.* London: Ernest Benn, 1926.

NEALE, J. E. *Queen Elizabeth I: A Biography*. London: Jonathan Cape, 1934.

NEALE, J. E. *The Elizabethan House of Commons*. New Haven: Yale Univ. Press, 1949.

NEALE, J. E. *Elizabeth I and her Parliaments*. 2v. London: Jonathan Cape, 1953-7.

PEARSON, A. F. S. *Church and State: Political Aspects of 16th Century Puritanism*. Cambridge: The University Press, 1928.

PENROSE, BOIES. *Travel and Discovery in the Renaissance, 1420–1620*. Cambridge, Mass.: Harvard Univ. Press, 1955.

POLLEN, J. H. *The English Catholics in the Reign of Elizabeth*. London: Longmans, Green, 1920.

POWICKE, F. M. *The Reformation in England*. London: Oxford Univ. Press, 1941.

RAAB, FELIX. *The English Face of Machiavelli*. London: Routledge and Kegan Paul, 1964.

READ, C. J. *Mr. Secretary Walsingham and the Policy of Queen Elizabeth*. 3v. Oxford: The Clarendon Press, 1925.

READ, C. J. *The Tudors: Personalities and Politics in Sixteenth Century England*. New York: Henry Holt, 1936.

READ, C. J. *Mr. Secretary Cecil and Queen Elizabeth*. New York: Alfred Knopf, 1955.

RICE, E. F., JR. *The Renaissance Idea of Wisdom*. Cambridge, Mass.: Harvard Univ. Press, 1958.

ROWSE, A. L. *The England of Elizabeth: The Structure of Society*. London: Macmillan, 1951.

SELLERY, G. C. *The Renaissance: Its Nature and Origins*. Madison: Univ. of Wisconsin Press, 1950.

SMITH, SIR THOMAS. *De Republica Anglorum*. Eng. tr. ed., L. Alston. Cambridge: The University Press, 1906.

SPENCER, THEODORE. *Shakespeare and the Nature of Man*. New York: Macmillan, 1942.

TAWNEY, R. H. *Religion and the Rise of Capitalism*. New York: Harcourt, Brace, 1926.

TAYLER, E. W. *Nature and Art in Renaissance Literature*. New York: Columbia Univ. Press, 1964.

TAYLOR, H. O. *Thought and Expression in the Sixteenth Century*. 2v. New York: Macmillan, 1920.

TILLYARD, E. M. W. *The Elizabethan World Picture*. London: Chatto and Windus, 1943.

WATSON, C. B. *Shakespeare and the Renaissance Concept of Honor*. Princeton: Princeton Univ. Press, 1960.

WILSON, F. P. *Elizabethan and Jacobean.* Oxford: The Clarendon Press, 1945.

ZEEVELD, W. G. *Foundations of Tudor Policy.* Cambridge, Mass.: Harvard Univ. Press, 1948.

II. THE LIFE OF SHAKESPEARE

ADAMS, J. Q. *A Life of William Shakespeare.* Boston: Houghton Mifflin, 1923.

ALEXANDER, PETER. *Shakespeare's Life and Art.* New York: New York Univ. Press, 1961.

BALDWIN, T. W. *William Shakspere's Small Latine and Lesse Greeke.* 2v. Urbana: Univ. of Illinois Press, 1944.

BROOKE, C. F. T. *Shakespeare of Stratford.* New Haven: Yale Univ. Press, 1926.

CHAMBERS, E. K. *William Shakespeare: A Study of Facts and Problems.* Oxford: The Clarendon Press, 1930.

CHAMBERS, E. K. *Shakespearean Gleanings.* Oxford: The Clarendon Press, 1944.

CHUTE, MARCHETTE. *Shakespeare of London.* New York: E. P. Dutton, 1949.

DE GROOT, J. H. *The Shakespeares and "The Old Faith."* New York: King's Crown Press, 1946.

ECCLES, MARK. *Shakespeare in Warwickshire.* Madison: Univ. of Wisconsin Press, 1961.

FRIPP, E. I. *Shakespeare's Stratford.* London: Oxford Univ. Press, 1928.

FRIPP, E. I. *Shakespeare, Man and Artist.* 2v. London: Oxford Univ. Press, 1938.

HALLIDAY, F. E. *The Life of Shakespeare.* London: Gerald Duckworth, 1961.

HALLIDAY, F. E. *A Shakespeare Companion 1564–1964.* London: Gerald Duckworth, 1964.

HOTSON, LESLIE. *Shakespeare vs. Shallow.* Boston: Little Brown, 1931.

HOTSON, LESLIE. *I, William Shakespeare, do Appoint.* New York: Oxford Univ. Press, 1938.

HOTSON, LESLIE. *Mr. W. H.* London: Rupert Hart-Davis, 1964.

KEEN, A., and R. LUBBOCK. *The Annotator: the Pursuit of an Elizabethan Reader of Halle's "Chronicle" Involving some Surmises About the Early Life of William Shakespeare.* London: Macmillan, 1954.

LEE, SIDNEY. *A Life of William Shakespeare.* Rev. ed. New York: Macmillan, 1909.

McCURDY, H. G. *The Personality of Shakespeare.* New Haven: Yale Univ. Press, 1953.

POLLARD, A. W., *et al. Shakespeare's Hand in the Play of "Sir Thomas More."* Cambridge: The University Press, 1923.

QUENNELL, PETER. *Shakespeare: A Biography.* Cleveland and New York: World Publishing Co., 1963.

REESE, M. M. *Shakespeare: His World and His Work.* New York: St. Martin's Press, 1953.

ROWSE, A. L. *William Shakespeare: A Biography.* New York: Harper and Row, 1963.

SISSON, C. J. *The Mythical Sorrows of Shakespeare.* Oxford: Annual British Academy Lecture, 1934.

SMART, J. S. *Shakespeare: Truth and Tradition.* New ed. with Preface by Peter Alexander. Oxford: The Clarendon Press, 1966.

SPENCER, HAZELTON. *The Art and Life of William Shakespeare.* New York: Harcourt, Brace, 1940.

STOPES, C. C. *Shakespeare's Warwickshire Contemporaries.* Stratford-on-Avon, 1897.

STOPES, C. C. *Shakespeare's Family, being a record of the ancestors and descendants of William Shakespeare, with some account of the Ardens.* Stratford-on-Avon, 1901.

WALLACE, C. W. *Shakespeare and his London Associates.* Lincoln: Univ. of Nebraska Press, 1905.

WILSON, J. D. *The Essential Shakespeare.* Cambridge: The University Press, 1932.

III. LIFE IN SHAKESPEARE'S ENGLAND

BUXTON, JOHN. *Elizabethan Taste.* London: Macmillan, 1963.

BYRNE, M. ST. CLARE. *Elizabethan Life in Town and Country.* Rev. ed. London: Methuen, 1950.

CAMDEN, CARROLL. *The Elizabethan Woman.* New York: Elsevier Press, 1952.

CAMPBELL, MILDRED. *The English Yeoman under Elizabeth and the Early Stuarts.* New Haven: Yale Univ. Press, 1942.

CRUICKSHANK, C. G. *Elizabeth's Army.* Oxford: The Clarendon Press, 1946.

CURTIS, M. H. *Oxford and Cambridge in Transition, 1558–1642.* Oxford: The Clarendon Press, 1959.

FERGUSON, A. B. *The Articulate Citizen and the English Renaissance.* Durham, N.C.: Duke Univ. Press, 1965.

FROUDE, J. A. *English Seamen in the Sixteenth Century.* London: Harrap, 1925.

HARRISON, G. B. *A Second Jacobean Journal . . . 1607–1610.* Ann Arbor: Univ. of Michigan Press, 1958.

HARRISON, G. B. *A Jacobean Journal . . . 1603–1606.* London: Macmillan, 1941.

HARRISON, G. B. *A Second Jacobean Journal . . . 1607–1610.* Ann Arbor: Univ. of Michigan Press, 1958.

JUDGES, A. V., ed. *The Elizabethan Underworld.* New York: E. P. Dutton, 1930.

KELSO, RUTH. *The Doctrine of the English Gentleman in the Sixteenth Century.* Urbana: Univ. of Illinois Press, 1929.

LEE, SIDNEY and C. T. ONIONS, eds. *Shakespeare's England: An Account of the Life and Manners of his Age.* 2v. Oxford: The Clarendon Press, 1916.

MILLER, E. H. *The Professional Writer in Elizabethan England.* Cambridge, Mass.: Harvard Univ. Press, 1959.

MITCHELL, R. J., and M. D. R. LEYS. *A History of London Life.* London: Longmans, Green, 1958.

NICOLL, ALLARDYCE, ed. *Shakespeare in His Own Age (Shakespeare Survey 17).* Cambridge: The University Press, 1964.

POWELL, C. L. *English Domestic Relations, 1487–1653.* New York: Columbia Univ. Press, 1917.

STEVENS, JOHN. *Music and Poetry in the Early Tudor Court.* Lincoln: Univ. of Nebraska Press, 1961.

STOWE, A. R. M. *English Grammar Schools in the Reign of Queen Elizabeth.* New York: Columbia Univ. Press, 1908.

UNWIN, G. *The Gilds and Companies of London.* London: Methuen, 1908.

WILSON, F. P. *The Plague in Shakespeare's London.* Oxford: The Clarendon Press, 1927.

WILSON, J. D., ed. *Life in Shakespeare's England.* Cambridge: The University Press, 1911.

WRIGHT, L. B. *Middle-Class Culture in Elizabethan England.* Chapel Hill: Univ. of No. Carolina Press, 1935.

ZILBOORG, GREGORY. *The Medical Man and the Witch during the Renaissance.* Baltimore: Johns Hopkins Univ. Press, 1935.

IV. THE ENGLISH DRAMA BEFORE SHAKESPEARE

ADAMS, H. H. *English Domestic or Homiletic Tragedy 1575–1642.* New York: Columbia Univ. Press, 1943.

BAKER, HOWARD. *Induction to Tragedy.* Baton Rouge: Louisiana State Univ. Press, 1939.

BASKERVILL, C. R. *The Elizabethan Jig and Related Song Drama.* Chicago: Univ. of Chicago Press, 1929.

BEVINGTON, D. M. *From Mankind to Marlowe: Growth of Structure in the Popular Drama of Tudor England*. Cambridge, Mass.: Harvard Univ. Press, 1962.

BOAS, F. S. *University Drama in the Tudor Age*. Oxford: The Clarendon Press, 1914.

BOAS, F. S. *An Introduction to Tudor Drama*. Oxford: The Clarendon Press, 1933.

BOWERS, FREDSON. *Elizabethan Revenge Tragedy: 1587–1642*. Princeton: Princeton Univ. Press, 1940.

BRADBROOK, M. C. *Themes and Conventions of Elizabethan Tragedy*. Cambridge: The University Press, 1935.

BRADBROOK, M. C. *The Growth and Structure of Elizabethan Comedy*. London: Chatto and Windus, 1955.

BROOKE, C. F. T. *The Tudor Drama*. Boston: Houghton Mifflin, 1911.

CAMPBELL, L. B. *Divine Poetry and Drama in Sixteenth Century England*. Cambridge: The University Press, 1959.

CHAMBERS, E. K. *The Medieval Stage*. 2v. Oxford: The Clarendon Press, 1903.

CHAMBERS, E. K. *The Elizabethan Stage*. 4v. Oxford: The Clarendon Press, 1923.

CHAMBERS, E. K. *The English Folk-Play*. Oxford: The Clarendon Press, 1933.

CHARLTON, H. B. *The Senecan Tradition in Renaissance Tragedy*. Manchester: Univ. of Manchester Press, 1946.

CLEMEN, WOLFGANG. *English Tragedy Before Shakespeare: The Development of Dramatic Speech*. Tr. by T. S. Dorsch. London: Methuen, 1961.

CRAIG, HARDIN. *English Religious Drama of the Middle Ages*. Oxford: The Clarendon Press, 1955.

CUNLIFFE, J. W. *The Influence of Seneca on Elizabethan Tragedy*. London: Macmillan, 1893.

CUNLIFFE, J. W., ed. *Early English Classical Tragedies*. Oxford: The Clarendon Press, 1912.

DIXON, W. M. *Tragedy*. London: Edward Arnold, 1924.

DORAN, MADELEINE. *Endeavors of Art: A Study of Form in Elizabethan Drama*. Madison: Univ. of Wisconsin Press, 1954.

FARNHAM, WILLARD. *The Medieval Heritage of Elizabethan Tragedy*. Berkeley: Univ. of California Press, 1936.

FOAKES, R. A. and RICKERT, R. T., eds. *Henslowe's Diary*. Cambridge: The University Press, 1961.

GARDINER, H. C. *Mysteries End: The Last Days of the Medieval Stage*. New Haven: Yale Univ. Press, 1946.

GREEN, A. W. *The Inns of Court and Early English Drama.* New Haven: Yale Univ. Press, 1931.

GREG, W. W. *Pastoral Poetry and Pastoral Drama.* Repr. New York: Russell and Russell, 1959.

GREG, W. W. *A Bibliography of the English Printed Drama to the Restoration.* 4v. London: The Bibliographical Society, 1939–59.

HARBAGE, ALFRED. *Annals of English Drama, 975–1700.* Rev. by S. Schoenbaum. London: Methuen, 1964.

HARDISON, O. B., JR. *Christian Rite and Christian Drama in the Middle Ages: Essays in the Origin and Early History of Modern Drama.* Baltimore: Johns Hopkins Univ. Press, 1965.

HOGREFE, PEARL. *The Sir Thomas More Circle: A Program of Ideas and their Impact on Secular Drama.* Urbana: Univ. of Illinois Press, 1959.

KOLVE, V. A. *The Play Called Corpus Christi.* Palo Alto: Stanford Univ. Press, 1966.

LEA, K. M. *Italian Popular Comedy.* 2v. Oxford: The Clarendon Press, 1934.

LUCAS, F. L. *Seneca and Elizabethan Tragedy.* Cambridge: The University Press, 1922.

MACKENZIE, W. R. *The English Moralities from the Point of View of Allegory.* Boston: Houghton Mifflin, 1914.

MARGESON, J. M. R. *The Origins of English Tragedy.* Oxford: The Clarendon Press, 1968.

MOTTER, T. H. V. *The School Drama in England.* London: Longmans, Green, 1929.

OWST, G. R. *Literature and Pulpit in Medieval England.* Rev. ed. New York: Barnes and Noble, 1961.

PETTET, E. C. *Shakespeare and the Romance Tradition.* London: The Staples Press, 1949.

PROSSER, ELEANOR. *Drama and Religion in the English Mystery Plays: A Re-evaluation.* Palo Alto: Stanford Univ. Press, 1961.

REED, A. W. *Early Tudor Drama.* London: Methuen, 1926.

RIBNER, IRVING. *The English History Play in the Age of Shakespeare.* Rev. ed. London: Methuen, 1965.

ROSSITER, A. P. *English Drama from Early Times to the Elizabethans: Its Background, Origins, and Developments.* London: Hutchinson's University Library, 1950.

SALTER, F. M. *Medieval Drama in Chester.* Toronto: Univ. of Toronto Press, 1955.

SPIVACK, BERNARD. *Shakespeare and the Allegory of Evil.* New York: Columbia Univ. Press, 1958.

TALBERT, E. W. *Elizabethan Drama and Shakespeare's Early Plays.* Chapel Hill: Univ. of No. Carolina Press, 1963.

THOMPSON, E. N. S. *The English Moral Play.* New Haven: Connecticut Academy of Arts and Letters, 1910.

THORNDIKE, A. H. *English Comedy.* New York: Macmillan, 1929.

TIDDY, R. J. E. *The Mummer's Play.* Oxford: The Clarendon Press, 1923.

WELSFORD, ENID. *The Court Masque.* Cambridge: The University Press, 1927.

YOUNG, KARL. *The Drama of the Medieval Church.* 2v. Oxford: The Clarendon Press, 1933.

V. ELIZABETHAN THEATRES AND THEATRE COMPANIES

ADAMS, J. C. *The Globe Playhouse.* Rev. ed. New York: Barnes and Noble, 1961.

ADAMS, J. Q. *Shakespearean Playhouses.* Boston: Houghton Mifflin, 1917.

ARMSTRONG, W. A. "Actors and Theatres," *Shakespeare Survey 17.* Cambridge: The University Press, 1964. Pp. 191–204.

BALDWIN, T. W. *The Organization and Personnel of the Shakespearean Company.* Princeton: Princeton Univ. Press, 1927.

BECKERMAN, BERNARD. *Shakespeare at the Globe 1599–1609.* New York: Macmillan, 1962.

BENTLEY, G. E. "Shakespeare and the Blackfriars Theatre," *Shakespeare Survey 1.* Cambridge: The University Press, 1948. Pp. 38–50.

BENTLEY, G. E. *Shakespeare and His Theatre.* Lincoln: Univ. of Nebraska Press, 1964.

BRADBROOK, M. C. *The Rise of the Common Player: A Study of Actor and Society in Shakespeare's England.* London: Chatto and Windus, 1964.

CAMPBELL, L. B. *Scenes and Machines on the English Stage during the Renaissance.* Cambridge: The University Press, 1923.

COWLING, G. H. *Music on the Shakespearian Stage.* Cambridge: The University Press, 1913.

CRAIK, T. W. *The Tudor Interlude.* Leicester: Univ. of Leicester Press, 1958.

DE BANKE, CECILE. *Shakespearean Stage Production: Then and Now.* New York: McGraw-Hill, 1953.

FOAKES, R. A. "The Player's Passion: Some Notes on Elizabethan Psychology and Acting," *Essays and Studies Collected for the English Association,* 7 (1954), 62–77.

GILDERSLEEVE, V. C. *Government Regulation of the Elizabethan Drama.* New York: Columbia Univ. Press, 1908.

HARBAGE, ALFRED. "Elizabethan Acting," *PMLA*, 54 (1939), 685–708.

HARBAGE, ALFRED. *Shakespeare's Audience*. New York: Columbia Univ. Press, 1941.

HARRISON, G. B. *Elizabethan Plays and Players*. Ann Arbor: Univ. of Michigan Press, 1956.

HILLEBRAND, H. N. *The Child Actors*. Urbana: Univ. of Illinois Press, 1926.

HODGES, C. W. *The Globe Restored: A Study of the Elizabethan Theatre*. New York: Coward-McCann, 1954.

HOSLEY, RICHARD. "An Approach to the Elizabethan Stage," *Renaissance Drama*, 6 (1963), 71–8.

HOSLEY, RICHARD. "The Origins of the Shakespearian Playhouse," *Shakespeare Quarterly*, 15 (1964), 29–39.

HOSLEY, RICHARD. "The Origins of the So-called Elizabethan Multiple Stage," *Theatre and Drama Review*, 12 (1968), 28–50.

HOTSON, LESLIE. *Shakespeare's Wooden O*. London: Rupert Hart-Davis, 1959.

JOSEPH, B. L. *Elizabethan Acting*. Rev. ed. Oxford: The Clarendon Press, 1964.

JOSEPH, B. L. *The Tragic Actor*. London: Routledge and Kegan Paul, 1959.

KERNODLE, G. R. *From Art to Theatre: Form and Convention in the Renaissance*. Chicago: Univ. of Chicago Press, 1944.

LAWRENCE, W. J. *Pre-Restoration Stage Studies*. Cambridge, Mass.: Harvard Univ. Press, 1927.

LAWRENCE, W. J. *The Physical Conditions of the Elizabethan Public Playhouse*. Cambridge, Mass.: Harvard Univ. Press, 1927.

LAWRENCE, W. J. *Those Nut-Cracking Elizabethans*. London: Argonaut Press, 1935.

LAWRENCE, W. J. *The Elizabethan Playhouse and Other Studies*. 1st and 2nd series. Repr. New York: Russell and Russell, 1963.

LINTHICUM, M. C. *Costume in the Drama of Shakespeare and his Contemporaries*. Oxford: The Clarendon Press, 1936.

MURRAY, J. T. *English Dramatic Companies, 1558–1642*. Boston: Houghton Mifflin, 1910.

NAGLER, A. M. *Shakespeare's Stage*. New Haven: Yale Univ. Press, 1958.

NICOLL, A. *Masques, Mimes and Miracles*. London: Harrap, 1931.

NICOLL, A. *Stuart Masques and the Renaissance Stage*. London: Harrap, 1937.

NICOLL, A. "Studies in the Elizabethan Stage Since 1900," *Shakespeare Survey 1*. Cambridge: The University Press, 1948. Pp. 1–17.

NICOLL, A. *The World of Harlequin.* Cambridge: The University Press, 1963.

NUNGEZER, EDWIN. *A Dictionary of Actors and Other Persons Associated with the Public Representation of Plays in England Before 1642.* New Haven: Yale Univ. Press, 1929.

REYNOLDS, G. F. *The Staging of Elizabethan Plays at the Red Bull Theater, 1605–1625.* New York: Modern Language Assoc. of America, 1940.

ROSENBERG, MARVIN. "Elizabethan Actors: Men or Marionettes," *PMLA*, 69 (1954), 915–27.

SAUNDERS, J. W. "Staging at the Globe, 1599–1613," *Shakespeare Quarterly*, 11 (1960), 401–25.

SELTZER, DANIEL. "The Staging of the Last Plays," *The Later Shakespeare* (Stratford-on-Avon Studies No. 8). London: Edward Arnold, 1966. Pp. 127–66.

SHARPE, R. B. *The Real War of the Theatres.* Boston: D. C. Heath, 1935.

SHIRLEY, F. A. *Shakespeare's Use of Off-Stage Sounds.* Lincoln: Univ. of Nebraska Press, 1963.

SMITH, IRWIN. *Shakespeare's Blackfriars Playhouse.* New York: New York Univ. Press, 1965.

SOUTHERN, RICHARD. *The Medieval Theatre in the Round.* London: Faber and Faber, 1957.

SOUTHERN, RICHARD. *The Open Stage.* New York: Theatre Arts Books, 1959.

SPRAGUE, A. C. *The Doubling of Parts in Shakespeare's Plays.* London: Society for Theatre Research, 1966.

STEELE, MARY S. *Plays and Masques at Court During the Reigns of Elizabeth, James, and Charles.* New Haven: Yale Univ. Press, 1926.

THOMPSON, E. N. S. *The Controversy Between the Puritans and the Stage.* New Haven: Yale Univ. Press, 1903.

THORNDIKE, A. H. *Shakespeare's Theatre.* New York: Macmillan, 1916.

VENEZKY, ALICE. *Pageantry on the Shakespearean Stage.* New York: Twayne Publishers, 1951.

WALLACE, C. W. *The Children of the Chapel at Blackfriars, 1597–1603.* Lincoln: Univ. of Nebraska Press, 1908.

WICKHAM, GLYNNE. *Early English Stages, 1300 to 1660.* 2v. New York: Columbia Univ. Press, 1959–63.

WITHINGTON, ROBERT. *English Pageantry: An Historical Outline* 2v. Cambridge, Mass.: Harvard Univ. Press, 1918–20.

YATES, FRANCES A. *The Art of Memory.* London: Routledge and Kegan Paul, 1966.

VI. THE PUBLICATION OF
SHAKESPEARE'S PLAYS

ALEXANDER, PETER. *Shakespeare's "Henry VI" and "Richard III."* Cambridge: The University Press, 1929.

BALDWIN, T. W. *On Act and Scene Division in the Shakespeare First Folio.* Carbondale: Southern Illinois Univ. Press, 1965.

BENNETT, H. S. *English Books and Readers, 1558 to 1603, Being a Study in the History of the Book Trade in the Reign of Elizabeth I.* Cambridge: The University Press, 1965.

BOWERS, FREDSON. *On Editing Shakespeare and the Elizabethan Dramatists.* Philadelphia: University of Pennsylvania Library, 1955.

BOWERS, FREDSON. *Textual Study and Literary Criticism.* Cambridge: The University Press, 1959.

BOWERS, FREDSON. *Bibliography and Textual Criticism.* Oxford: The Clarendon Press, 1964.

BOWERS, FREDSON. *On Editing Shakespeare.* Charlottesville: Univ. of Virginia Press, 1966.

DUTHIE, G. I. *Elizabethan Shorthand and the First Quarto of "King Lear."* Oxford: The Clarendon Press, 1949.

GREG, W. W. "The Rationale of Copy-Text," *Studies in Bibliography,* 3 (1950), 19–36.

GREG, W. W. *The Editorial Problem in Shakespeare: A Survey of the Foundations of the Text.* 3rd ed. Oxford: The Clarendon Press, 1954.

GREG, W. W. *The Shakespeare First Folio: Its Bibliographical and Textual History.* Oxford: The Clarendon Press, 1955.

GREG, W. W. *Some Aspects and Problems of London Publishing Between 1550 and 1650.* Oxford: The Clarendon Press, 1956.

HART, ALFRED. *Stolne and Surreptitious Copies: A Comparative Study of Shakespeare's Bad Quartos.* Oxford: The Clarendon Press, 1942.

HINMAN, CHARLTON. *The Printing and Proof-Reading of the First Folio of Shakespeare.* 2v. Oxford: The Clarendon Press, 1963.

HINMAN, CHARLTON. "Shakespeare's Text — Then, Now and Tomorrow," *Shakespeare Survey 18.* Cambridge: The University Press, 1965. Pp. 23–33.

HONIGMANN, E. A. J. *The Stability of Shakespeare's Text.* London: Edward Arnold, 1965.

JEWKES, W. T. *Act Division in Elizabethan and Jacobean Plays, 1583–1616.* Hamden, Conn.: The Shoestring Press, 1958.

Kirchbaum, Leo. *Shakespeare and the Stationers.* Columbus: Ohio State Univ. Press, 1955.

McKERROW, R. B. *An Introduction to Bibliography for Literary Students.* Oxford: The Clarendon Press, 1927.

McKerrow, R. B. *Prolegomena for the Oxford Shakespeare.* Oxford: The Clarendon Press, 1939.

Nosworthy, J. M. *Shakespeare's Occasional Plays: Their Origin and Transmission.* New York: Barnes and Noble, 1965.

Partridge, A. C. *Orthography in Shakespeare and Elizabethan Drama.* Lincoln: Univ. of Nebraska Press, 1964.

Pollard, A. W. *Shakespeare Folios and Quartos: A Study in the Bibliography of Shakespeare's Plays, 1594–1685.* London: Methuen, 1909.

Pollard, A. W. *Shakespeare's Fight with the Pirates and the Problems of Transmission of his Text.* Cambridge: The University Press, 1920.

Shroeder, J. W. *The Great Folio of 1623: Shakespeare's Plays in the Printing House.* Hamden, Conn.: The Shoestring Press, 1956.

Sisson, C. J. *New Readings in Shakespeare.* 2v. Cambridge: The University Press, 1956.

Walker, Alice. *Textual Problems in the First Folio.* Cambridge: The University Press, 1953.

Walker, Alice. "Edward Capell and his Edition of Shakespeare." *Proceedings of the British Academy,* 46 (1962), 131–45.

Willoughby, E. E. *The Printing of the First Folio of Shakespeare.* Oxford: The Clarendon Press, 1932.

Wilson, J. D. "The New Way with Shakespeare's Texts: An Introduction for Lay Readers. I. The Foundations," *Shakespeare Survey* 7. Cambridge: The University Press, 1954. Pp. 48–56.

Wilson, J. D. "The New Way with Shakespeare's Texts: II. Recent Work on the Text of *Romeo and Juliet,*" *Shakespeare Survey* 8. Cambridge: The University Press, 1955. Pp. 81–99.

VII. SHAKESPEARE CRITICISM

Babcock, R. W. *The Genesis of Shakespeare Idolatry, 1766–1799.* Chapel Hill: Univ. of No. Carolina Press, 1931.

Bentley, G. E. *Shakespeare and Jonson: Their Reputations in the Seventeenth Century Compared.* 2v. Chicago: Univ. of Chicago Press, 1945.

Eastman, A. M. and Harrison, G. B., eds. *Shakespeare Critics from Johnson to Auden: A Medley of Judgments.* Ann Arbor: Univ. of Michigan Press, 1964.

Halliday, F. E. *Shakespeare and his Critics.* London: Gerald Duckworth, 1949.

Herford, C. H. *A Sketch of Recent Shakespearean Investigation, 1893–1923.* London: Blackie and Son, 1923.

Johnson, C. F. *Shakespeare and his Critics.* Boston: Houghton Mifflin, 1909.

KERMODE, FRANK, ed. *Four Centuries of Shakespearean Criticism*. New York: Avon Books, 1965.

LOVETT, DAVID. *Shakespeare's Characters in Eighteenth Century Criticism*. Baltimore: Johns Hopkins Univ. Press, 1935.

MONRO, JOHN, ed. *The Shakespeare Allusion Book: A Collection of Allusions to Shakespeare from 1591 to 1700*. London: Chatto and Windus, 1909.

MUIR, KENNETH. "Fifty Years of Shakespearian Criticism, 1900–1950." *Shakespeare Survey 4*. Cambridge: The University Press, 1951. Pp. 1–25.

PILLAI, V. K. A. *Shakespeare Criticism from the Beginnings to 1765*. London: Blackie and Son, 1932.

RALLI, A. A. *A History of Shakespearean Criticism*. 2v. London: Oxford Univ. Press, 1932.

RAYSOR, T. M. ed. *Coleridge's Shakespeare Criticism*. 2v. Cambridge, Mass.: Harvard Univ. Press, 1930.

ROBINSON, H. S. *English Shakespearean Criticism in the Eighteenth Century*. New York: H. W. Wilson, 1932.

SHERBO, ARTHUR. "Johnson as Editor of Shakespeare: The Notes," in *Samuel Johnson: A Collection of Critical Essays*, ed. D. J. Greene. Englewood Cliffs, N.J.: Prentice-Hall, 1965.

SIEGEL, P. N., ed. *His Infinite Variety: Major Shakespearean Criticism Since Johnson*. Philadelphia: J. B. Lippincott, 1964.

SMITH, D. N. *Shakespeare in the Eighteenth Century*. Oxford: The Clarendon Press, 1928.

WESTFALL, A. V. *American Shakespearean Criticism, 1607–1865*. New York: H. W. Wilson, 1939.

VIII. SHAKESPEARE IN THE THEATRE, 1642–1968

ARMSTRONG, W. A. "The Art of Shakespearean Production in the Twentieth Century," *Essays and Studies*, 15 (1962), 74–87.

BROWN, J. R. "On the Acting of Shakespeare's Plays," *Quarterly Journal of Speech*, 39 (1953), 474–85.

BROWN, J. R. *Shakespeare's Plays in Performance*. New York: St. Martin's Press, 1967.

DEAN, WINTON. "Shakespeare in the Opera House," *Shakespeare Survey 18*. Cambridge: The University Press, 1965. Pp. 75–93.

DEELMAN, CHRISTIAN. *The Great Shakespeare Jubilee*. New York: The Viking Press, 1964.

DOWNER, A. S. *The Eminent Tragedian, William Charles Macready*. Cambridge, Mass.: Harvard Univ. Press, 1966.

ENGLAND, M. W. *Garrick's Jubilee.* Columbus: Ohio State Univ. Press, 1964.

GLICK, CLARIS. "William Poel: His Theories and Influence," *Shakespeare Quarterly,* 15 (1964), 15–25.

HARBAGE, ALFRED. *A Theatre for Shakespeare.* Toronto: Univ. of Toronto Press, 1955.

HOGAN, C. B. *Shakespeare in the Theatre, 1701–1800.* 2v. Oxford: The Clarendon Press, 1952–57.

JOSEPH, B. L. *Acting Shakespeare.* New York: Theatre Arts Books, 1960.

KITCHIN, LAURENCE. *Drama in the Sixties: Form and Interpretation.* London: Faber and Faber, 1966.

KITCHIN, LAURENCE. "Shakespeare on the Screen," *Shakespeare Survey 18.* Cambridge: The University Press, 1965. Pp. 70–74.

KNIGHT, G. W. *Shakespearian Production, with Especial Reference to the Tragedies.* London: Methuen, 1964.

LAWRENCE, W. J. *Speeding Up Shakespeare.* London: Argonaut Press, 1937.

MARDER, LOUIS. *His Exits and his Entrances: The Story of Shakespeare's Reputation.* Philadelphia: J. B. Lippincott, 1963.

ODELL, G. C. D. *Shakespeare From Betterton to Irving.* 2v. Repr. New York: Dover Publications, 1966.

POEL, WILLIAM. *Shakespeare in the Theatre.* London: Sidgwick and Jackson, 1913.

SHATTUCK, C. H. *The Shakespeare Promptbooks.* Urbana: Univ. of Illinois Press, 1965.

SPEAIGHT, WILLIAM. *William Poel and the Elizabethan Revival.* Cambridge: The University Press, 1954.

SPENCER, HAZELTON. *Shakespeare Improved: The Restoration Versions in Quarto and on the Stage.* Cambridge, Mass.: Harvard Univ. Press, 1927.

SPRAGUE, A. C. *Shakespeare and the Actors: The Stage Business in His Plays (1660–1905).* Cambridge, Mass.: Harvard Univ. Press, 1944.

SPRAGUE, A. C. *Shakespearian Players and Performances.* Cambridge, Mass.: Harvard Univ. Press, 1953.

STOCHHOLM, J. M. *Garrick's Folly.* London: Methuen, 1964.

TREWIN, J. C. *Shakespeare on the English Stage, 1900–1964.* London: Barrie and Rockliff, 1964.

WATKINS, RONALD. *On Producing Shakespeare.* New York: W. W. Norton, 1950.

WEBSTER, MARGARET. *Shakespeare Without Tears.* New York: McGraw-Hill, 1942.

WEBSTER, MARGARET. *Shakespeare Today.* London: J. M. Dent, 1957.

Index